BARRY ISLAND

BARRY ISLAND

THE MAKING OF
A SEASIDE PLAYGROUND,
c.1790–c.1965

Andy Croll

UNIVERSITY OF WALES PRESS
2020

www.uwp.co.uk

British Library Cataloguing-in-Publication Data
A catalogue record for this book is available from the British Library.

ISBN   978-1-78683-586-4
e-ISBN   978-1-78683-587-1

Typeset by Chris Bell, cbdesign
Printed and bound by CPI Group (UK) Ltd, Croydon, CR0 4YY

To Rachel, Tabbi and Oscar

CONTENTS

Acknowledgements

I HAVE ACCUMULATED innumerable debts during the writing of this book. Various colleagues (former and current) in the School of Humanities at the University of South Wales have helped in myriad ways over the years. A full list would take me even further beyond my agreed word count, but a severely abridged version must include Jonathan Durrant, Bev Farr, Jane Finucane, Tim John, Tim Jones, Rachel Lock-Lewis, Darren Macey, Clive Mulholland, Naomi Preston, Andy Thompson, Diana Wallace and Chris Williams.

I would particularly like to thank Alan Jones, Gareth Williams and Alun Withey for several fruitful conversations about Barry's resort history. Dai Smith got me interested in the history of leisure in the first place and his interest in this project convinced me that studying Barry Island's past was a worthwhile pursuit. Special thanks are due to Rob Eva, Scot McNaughton and Steve McCarthy for their encouragement over the years. Steve made sure that I never ran out of pens.

I am grateful to the staff of Barry library, the Glamorgan Archives, the National Archives, the British Library and the library of the University of South Wales for all their help in tracking down a wealth of reading material. Julia Skinner at Francis Frith helped locate maps. Paul Johnson, image library manager at the National Archives, provided invaluable assistance, as did James Franklin at the Ordnance Survey and Penny Icke at the Royal Commission on the Ancient and Historical Monuments of Wales. Tony Woolway at Media Wales and Chris Adams at the *Manchester Evening News* helped with photos of Whitmore Bay in the 1960s. Thanks to Gerwyn Davies at University of South Wales's Print and Design Department for his map-making skills. I am indebted to the team at the National Library of Wales responsible for the 'Welsh Newspapers Online' resource. I began researching the newspapers in the analogue era. Just when I thought I had completed the newspaper research, 15 million digitized articles from 120 Welsh newspapers suddenly appeared online. It proved to be a game-changer. Without that rich, fully searchable data set, the argument in chapter 1 could never have materialized, Lord Windsor's shutdown of the island in the later 1870s – an event of the greatest significance – would have passed me by, and a whole sand-dune's worth of extra data would have gone unread. The digitization of newspaper sources promises to change our view of resort development in the nineteenth century quite fundamentally. It allows us to find scattered references to the smaller 'bathing villages' that have, to date, largely been missed by historians. As a result, the true significance of the smaller resort – in Wales, but elsewhere, too – may become clearer over the coming years.

Laura Williams introduced me to her grandfather, Edward Evans. I am enormously grateful to them both for their time and for Mr Evans's recollections of happy days spent at Whitmore Bay as a child in the late 1930s.

Staff at the University of Wales Press have been unfailingly helpful. The comments of the anonymous reader have been extremely helpful. I am grateful to them for their insightful suggestions. Thanks to Dafydd Jones, Elin Lewis, Siân Chapman and the design team for producing such an attractive looking volume, and to Nic Nicholas for compiling the index. Sarah Lewis must be singled out for especial praise. I missed more deadlines than I care to remember, but she remained calm, patient and supportive throughout. Without her willingness to tolerate my many re-writes, this book would never have made it from my computer hard drive to the bookshelf.

Bill Jones's contribution to this book has been immense. He has read various drafts, provided sage advice, made critical editorial interventions, furnished me with references and happily taken on the role of the Great Encourager throughout. For all that, plus the musical interludes, the friendship and many a pleasant afternoon spent at the former bathing village of Aberthaw mulling over the finer points of resort history, I am deeply grateful. Likewise, Chris Evans deserves a special mention for his support and friendship over the long years of this project. He, too, has read an earlier version of the manuscript. The final product is immeasurably better for the contributions of both Bill and Chris. Sadly, neither of them can be held responsible for any of the shortcomings that remain.

Finally, my greatest thanks go to my family. In Cornwall, the Bindings – Anne, James, Jake and Tom – are all beach aficionados. I thank them for their warm support and hope they might enjoy reading about a beach they visited once on a bitterly cold winter's day. Denis and Maureen McCarthy have been keen supporters of the project from the outset. They have also shared their remembrances of post-war Barry Island. An historian of Whitmore Bay could hope for no better parents-in-law.

Having been brought up in Cornwall, there is no shortage of photographs of a younger version of me on various beaches, from Gyllyngvase to Godrevy. Only one photo shows me on a non-Cornish beach. It was snapped when I was two years old by my late dad, Harry. I am pictured sitting on the sands of Barry Island with my mum, Mary. I am eternally grateful to them both for introducing me to Whitmore Bay, for a childhood full of happy memories (lots of them beach-related) and for so much else besides.

I have been researching Barry Island's history for more than a decade. I have spent countless hours strolling across its sand dunes, reclining on its headlands and paddling at its water's edge. I've spent even longer exploring it in my imagination, in the company of sea-bathing Georgians, day-tripping mid-Victorians and all the other visitors who headed for Whitmore Bay over the years. Life has been a beach – perhaps for a little too long. But I've been fortunate beyond words to have had Rachel, Tabbi and Oscar McNaughton alongside me throughout. Without their forbearance and love, this book would never have seen the light of day. That is why it is dedicated to them.

ILLUSTRATIONS

AUTHOR'S NOTE

B ARRY ISLAND really was an island until the later 1880s when an army of navvies fashioned a great dock out of Barry Sound. When referring to 'the island' in the days before their herculean earth-shifting labours, I have done so in the lower case to underline the point. After its loss of island status, it becomes 'the Island'. At all times, of course, it is 'Barry Island'. When quoting contemporaries, I follow their usage.

Lord Windsor became the earl of Plymouth in 1905. He fades from the Island's story at precisely that moment. For the sake of clarity, on the odd occasion when I have reason to mention him after his elevation, I still refer to him as 'Lord Windsor'. Many Barrians, it should be noted, did so too.

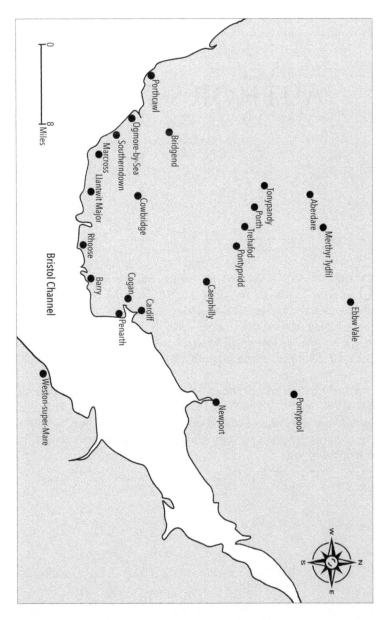

Illus. 2. *Map showing principal places in south Wales named in the text.*

Illus. 3. *Map of Welsh coastal resorts mentioned in the text.*

INTRODUCTION

THE SUMMER OF 1955 was a golden one at Barry Island. The little knuckle of rock, greensward and sand jutting out into the Bristol Channel enjoyed weeks of unbroken sunshine. August was one of the driest months on record. And the holidaymakers came in their hundreds of thousands. Record crowds frolicked on the beach at Whitmore Bay, traders raked in handsome profits, council-run tourist amenities flourished and journalists labelled the town the 'most popular resort' in south Wales.[1] Even Barry's mayor got caught up in the excitement: Barry, he explained to a team of visiting French rugby players, would soon be crowned the 'Blackpool of Wales'.[2] In that sun-kissed year, no one doubted Barry Island's role in the world: it was the seaside playground for the working classes of industrial south Wales.

Even during an *annus mirabilis* such as 1955 one might expect some temporary setbacks. Barry Island's popularity as a tourist resort was never in doubt, but a spell of poor weather could instantly depress visitor numbers. The season got off to an uncertain start. April had been gloomier than usual, and the Easter weekend was nearly a complete washout. Low clouds hung ominously over Barry on Good Friday. The following day saw the Island buffeted by strong winds whilst Easter Sunday was dull and chilly. The pleasure seekers stayed away. Only a handful of coaches made their way across the causeway and half-empty trains steamed into a forlorn station. Cafes and restaurants were largely unvisited. A paltry five deckchairs were hired out on Good Friday, and dispirited attendants dished out just sixty more over the following two days. The fairground was visited by a mere 'trickle of trippers' whilst a much-anticipated Easter parade had to be cancelled because of the lack of sufficient spectators. All the while, Island traders – never slow to remind their fellow townsfolk of the precarious nature of their businesses – grumbled about their bad luck to anyone who would listen.

Yet, at the very moment when all seemed hopeless, 'as if by the wave of a magic wand, the scene transformed on Easter Monday'.[3] And what a transformation. Glorious sunshine from an early hour brought the trippers back to Barry's beach in their droves. Tens of thousands arrived by trains, motor coaches, cars and bicycles. Locals turned up on foot. More than four hundred cars an hour streamed onto the Island in the afternoon. Coach parties and special excursion trains from Birmingham, Coventry and other English towns and cities appeared. And, as usual, most numerous of all were the trippers from the mining valleys to the north – 'the Shonies from the hills', as some Barrians referred to them.[4]

The sudden surge in demand kept cafe owners, traders (now reportedly 'smiling') and municipal employees busy all day. A refreshment bar at Whitmore Bay sold its entire stock of drinks and snacks in just a few hours. More than 3,200 deckchairs had been hired out by lunchtime. Collins's Pleasure Park was packed all day with many keen to view a novel spin on the 'Wall of Death'. Hundreds of spectators 'held their breath' as local man Frank Todd raced around in an Austin Seven car rather than on his usual motorbike. And the promenades and walkways that laced the Island were filled with holidaymakers enjoying the panoramic views of the bay and the Bristol Channel. Barry Island had plainly awoken from its long winter slumber and was humming with life again.[5]

The rest of the 1955 season was blessed with almost uninterrupted clear skies and strong sunshine. Demand for Barry's 'seaside product' soared in line with the rising levels of mercury in the district's thermometers. Whitsuntide was nearly de-railed (literally) by a strike of railway employees. Less than a quarter of the sixty trains expected on Whit Monday arrived. But, undaunted, trippers simply took to the roads instead. Mammoth traffic jams were generated in the process. The customary 2-mile queues on high days and holidays were replaced by 8-mile tailbacks as thousands of cars descended upon the Island. It was nothing less than an 'Unprecedented Car Invasion', proclaimed the *Barry Herald*. At one point, 14,500 vehicles were counted in the Island's car parks.[6] Fortes, an ice-cream parlour at Whitmore Bay, had to take on extra staff to cater for their unexpectedly large numbers of parched patrons. Purveyors of buckets and spades, beach hats and sunglasses watched gleefully as their products flew off the shelves. 'We've never had such a Whitsun in our lives', crowed the management of Rowe's cafe. The council's beach inspector concurred: he had never seen so many visitors on the Island on a Whit Monday in the eighteen years that he had been patrolling the sands.[7]

In July and August, temperatures broke through into the eighties. The hot weather was not without its drawbacks. On one blistering day, more than eighty trippers were treated for heatstroke. And the visitors' unquenchable thirst led to an increased hazard in the shape of unusually large amounts of broken glass on the beach. Council workmen collected fifteen sacks of empty bottles from the sands at the end of a single day in July. But many dangerous shards remained half-buried. In addition to the hundreds who suffered minor cuts that summer, one unfortunate woman had her arm 'severely lacerated'. Such incidents prompted staff of the St John's Ambulance to parade a cadet around

Illus. 5. *'The Kingdom of the Chip': Whitmore Bay, Whitsun 1963. A typically busy bank holiday during the Island's 'golden age'.*

the beach with a large piece of broken glass 'doctored' into his foot in an attempt to shock trippers into realizing the risks of their careless littering.[8]

Cut hands and feet were regrettable but they were widely accepted as an inevitable part of the seaside experience in the 1950s. And in that charmed summer of 1955 most Barrians agreed that the positives of a sun-drenched Island greatly outweighed the negatives. 'Sunshine Means Money', reasoned the *Barry and District News* in August.[9] Throughout the summer months, all of the Island's commercialized leisure spaces – its cafes, restaurants and pleasure gardens, its fairground, the shops in the Western Shelter – were daily thronged with 'pleasure-bent trip-pers . . . intent on taking full advantage of the scorching sun'.[10] And a busy Island meant a windfall for all those who catered for the holiday-ing masses. The council-owned swimming pool at nearby Cold Knap attracted record numbers of bathers in 1955. More than 7,500 surged through the turnstiles on the busiest days. The demand for municipal deckchairs significantly outstripped the supply. Council-run car parks proved such an attraction that vehicles often had to be turned away. (At Porthkerry Park, a stone's throw from the Island, so many cars were parked in the fields on the busiest days that children struggled to find space to play their holiday games.) The corporation's income from its seaside interests rocketed accordingly. Takings in July 1955 were a whopping 81 per cent higher than for the same month the previous year – a piece of news which prompted speculation that, for the first time, rates might be reduced as a consequence of Barry Island's pop-ularity.[11] And all the while the beach traders, kiosk owners and restau-ranteurs made hay while the sun shone. Everything was as it should be at Whitmore Bay.

THE ISLAND'S GOLDEN AGE

Commentators agreed that 1955 was a very good year. But it was not exceptional. The late 1940s through to the mid-1960s could reasonably be thought of as constituting a golden age in the Island's history as a seaside playground. Using the rather more prosaic language of the social scientist, we might say that it was in the middle of its 'consolida-tion stage' – a happy period when a holiday resort is at the peak of its popularity. Visitor numbers at Barry Island were gratifyingly strong and frequently record-breaking.[12] So popular had Whitmore Bay become that there was serious discussion about whether tourism might soon replace the shipment of coal as Barry's primary economic activity. Even as the great crowds gathered at the Island during the August bank holiday of 1955, town leaders and journalists openly speculated about the prospect of the port closing.[13] Years of the south Wales coal industry contracting had led the town's docks into deep trouble. The days when Barry could claim to be the world's leading exporter of coal were long gone. In 1913, more than 11 million tons were shipped out of Barry. This had fallen to 2.8 million tons by 1950 and was to plummet even further over the next two decades to less than 1.3 mil-lion tons.[14] By the early 1960s, the associated trade of ship-repairing

Illus. 6. *Uncertain times for Barry dock:* Barry and District News,
*10 May 1946. Barry's inhabitants, from the 1890s, were acutely aware
that their fortunes depended on the dock's success. Demand for Welsh
coal slumped throughout the interwar and post-war periods. The sight
of an empty dock invariably prompted residents to wonder whether they
could turn the Island's popularity to their economic advantage.*

had also faltered, unleashing a vicious negative multiplier effect which
dragged a range of ancillary businesses into difficulty. Underemploy-
ment amongst Barry's skilled and unskilled dockworkers was already
a problem, leading local business leaders to express fears about the
town's prospects. As the Chamber of Trade put it in a letter to the
town's MP in February 1960, Barry's prosperity had been built on the
docks and its demise 'in a short space of time, will produce great difficulties in the almost immediate future'.[15]

Set against the dock's difficulties, the Island's popularity was a
particularly welcome bright spot. 'Bright Easter for [Island's] Trades-
people – 'We've never had it so good', proclaimed the *Barry Herald*
in its coverage of the start of the 1960 holiday season.[16] Councillors
looked to Barry Island as a potential saviour. They employed Geoffrey
Jellicoe, one of the leading landscape architects of the day, to draw up
plans for a redeveloped seafront. He presented them with a £3 million

scheme that, if it had been acted upon, would have seen Barry become a residential resort complete with new all-weather tourist facilities and an eye-catching hotel built 'dramatically' across Friars Road. The highlight was a miniature railway that was to run from Whitmore Bay over to the Cold Knap via a series of tunnels and bridges. It was to have passed over a new yachting lake filled with houseboats and floating restaurants. The plans also included a state-of-the-art conference centre as a means of ensuring that revenue from tourism poured in throughout the year. Jellicoe was explicit in his report that he saw Barry's future as being firmly based on tourism. 'Today', he wrote, 'the value of the docks for coal export has materially declined, but that of the foreshore [i.e. Barry's tourist sites], owing to the rise in the standard of living, has increased to such an extent that its present amenities are insufficient in the modern world'. Barry's industrial days were behind her, the architect averred, and it was time to say goodbye to the coal-dust and the stevedores. 'Barry is a natural seaside resort. The landscape of the headlands and bays is romantic, the climate is that of a south coast resort, and it is easily accessible not only to South Wales, but to the thickly populated Midlands.'[17]

Jellicoe's plans for the Island were never realized. Not for the first time, as we shall see, an ambitious scheme for Barry Island proved beyond the means of a cash-strapped council. But the early 1960s did see a major investment in the Island's facilities from the private sector. In 1962, after some years of discussion, the holiday-camp provider Butlin's announced that it was to spend £2 million on Nell's Point. With its 800 chalets, its new camp would accommodate 4,000 holidaymakers.[18] Not everyone was thrilled by the news. As at other resorts, the interests of the holiday industry could conflict with those of local inhabitants. A few raised concerns about the impact the construction work would have on anglers who fished off the Point; others took umbrage at the loss of paths around the headland and the redevelopment of Forrest Drive.[19] Major S. A. Luen, a long-time resident of the town, complained at the 'filching away of the coastline for commercial exploitation'.[20] But, notwithstanding such critics, the scheme had some powerful backers including Raymond Gower (the town's MP), the local authority and the Wales Tourist and Holiday Board. They all emphasized the camp's potential as a money-spinner for the town.[21]

Butlin's, no doubt aware that their proposals might lead to some local opposition, had been eager to point out the economic and social benefits that a new holiday camp would bring to Barry. The company explained how the local economy would be boosted by the creation of

200 permanent jobs and 1,000 temporary positions during the holiday season. The town's rateable value would be swollen by tens of thousands of pounds and local traders would gain from the extra business brought to Barry by the large numbers of extra residential visitors in the town. A Butlin's camp at Bognor Regis had reportedly increased some local retailers' turnover by 25 per cent. According to the firm's own estimates, every camper would spend an average of £2 10s. per week in the town. As an added inducement, Butlin's promised that residents would be able to access some of its facilities – including the indoor swimming pool – during the winter months. And if inhabitants were alarmed at the prospect of campers misbehaving, the company sought to reassure them on the point: a church on the premises would cater for various denominations and, in any case, there would be no problems for they were 'proud of the standard of behaviour maintained in the camps'.[22]

The Barry Island camp opened in June 1966. It proved to be an instant success. By the start of the summer season in 1969, 58,000 had already booked their holidays there.[23] To be sure, some inhabitants refused to be won over. One self-styled 'Indignant Old Resident' complained about the noise and extra traffic that the camp brought to the town. Barry, he thundered:

> has always catered for its own people, even if they are mostly trippers from up the valleys. We have managed quite well, thank you, without any help from well-heeled enthusiasts from across the border . . . Why don't all these visitors go to France or Italy or Spain . . . and leave us in peace?'[24]

But most inhabitants took a more relaxed view. Indeed, Barrians' acceptance of holidaymakers was often commented upon by visitors as a reason for their love of the town. Writer Gwyn Thomas was born in the Rhondda in 1913 but moved to Barry in later life. Recalling his interwar trips to the coast, he remembered detecting a 'coldness' at Porthcawl whereas he always 'felt more at home in the loose, lusty jacket of Whitmore Bay'.[25] Similarly, in 1957, septuagenarian Mr Ben Hanson from Staffordshire explained to a local reporter that he had been holidaying in Barry every year for half a century. 'Oh, I know many other places', he said, 'but I've always found the people of Barry very free and easy and comfortable to get along with'.[26]

The idea of exhorting visitors, as the 'Indignant Old Resident' had done, to take their custom abroad and leave Barrians alone would have horrified those who had an interest in the Island's fortunes. The sight of holidaymakers flying out of nearby Rhoose airport for destinations such as the Channel Islands and assorted Mediterranean resorts already gave some of Whitmore Bay's traders pause for thought.[27] By the mid-1960s, planes from Rhoose were routinely flying to exotic destinations such as Majorca, Rimini and Barcelona.[28] Soon, even Barry's own newspapers carried articles extolling the virtues of cheap package holidays to the Mediterranean. 'For little more than the cost of scheduled air fare, [the package tourist] can fly to a sun-drenched resort perhaps 1,000 miles from the United Kingdom and spend 15 days in a large comfortable hotel with full amenities and entertainment', the *Barry and District News* explained in 1969.[29]

Meanwhile, competitors closer to home always threatened to usurp Barry's position as a favourite holiday destination of the working classes. In the early 1960s, Aberavon emerged as a strong challenger. Port Talbot local authority spent £1 million on Aberavon's resort infrastructure, throwing up a seaside pavilion, boating and paddling pools and refreshment kiosks. It let it be known that it intended to spend another £250,000 in the near future in its efforts to create a 'dream beach'. The news ruffled feathers at Whitmore Bay. 'Will Barry take second place to Aberavon as the top Welsh seaside resort?', mused the *Barry Herald*. If it was to head off its rival, the Island had to 'meet the challenge of modern thinking in other towns' by constantly innovating, the paper opined.[30]

But in the enchanted summers of the 1950s and early 1960s, worries about Barry's trippers being lured away to Aberavon or Málaga were only rarely considered. For this was the Island's golden age, a time when the town's residents could be satisfied that their seaside resort was performing a useful social function. As the editor of the *Barry and District News* remarked in August 1955:

> [W]e are happy to think that Barry's beaches have afforded so much relaxation and joy to hundreds of thousands of holiday-makers and local people. Only the most churlish could fail to find some pleasure in watching the delight of the youngsters – and the not-so-young – as they dash into the sea or take a header into the Knap's famous open-air pool.[31]

Everyone, it seemed, agreed that the Island was flourishing. More than that, it was fulfilling its manifest destiny as the seaside playground of south Wales.

BARRY ISLAND AND ITS HISTORIANS

It is worth emphasizing the extent to which Barry Island's rise to pre-eminence was taken for granted by contemporaries. We have already noted Jellicoe's observation that Barry was a 'natural seaside resort'. Likewise, Gwyn Thomas, writing in the mid-1960s, saw nothing puzzling in Whitmore Bay's great success. As he explained it, the Island 'is what it is because it is the biggest and nearest centre of colourful recreation for a huge industrial hinterland'.[32] In other words, it was a simple matter of geography. A fine beach was positioned on the doorstep of the populous south Wales coalfield: it was bound to be packed with working-class trippers during the holiday season.

So much for the views of one of Wales's leading creative writers. But what of the historians? How have they understood Barry Island's history as a seaside resort? In truth, surprisingly few historians have turned their attention to Whitmore Bay. Specialists in the history of coastal tourism have tended to focus on the English experience. As such, they have ignored all manner of Welsh seaside resorts, not just Barry.[33] For their part, Welsh social historians have long since recognized the Island's importance as a popular leisure space in the twentieth century, but this knowledge has not encouraged them to ponder the resort's history. It has been left to scholars with a particular interest in the history of Barry to consider Whitmore Bay's phenomenal rise.[34] It is worth spending a little time thinking about their work, in part because they have identified some key themes in its resort history, in part because the rest of this book will take issue with many of their findings.

Barry's historians have seen little that is problematic in the Island's history. The story they have told has a pleasingly uncontroversial starting point and a clear narrative arc. It is a tale of progress. In their view, the Island's history as a tourist resort began in the early 1890s. This makes a great deal of sense. After all, so much of modern Barry's history started at that pivotal moment. Before the 1880s, Barry was a quiet, rural district, sparsely populated and dominated entirely by agriculture. Even as late as 1881, Barry was a settlement of just seventeen inhabited houses. The nearby village of Cadoxton had 76 inhabited houses. Their combined population stood at just 388. All around them, industrial capitalism had been wreaking havoc, turning empty valleys into outposts of modernity and taking sleepy little port towns and transforming them into bustling metropolises. But the Barry district had managed to avoid such a fate. Cardiff castle was a mere 7 miles from the island as the crow flies, yet anyone travelling by road to Whitmore Bay from Cardiff in, say, 1883, still faced a bone-shaking journey of a couple of hours on pot-holed, winding, country lanes. Isolated, peaceful and undisturbed by the modernizing forces of capitalism, Barry looked like a relic from a bygone age.

However, all this changed with lightning speed after a consortium of Rhondda coal owners joined forces with Lord Windsor, Barry Island's owner, and set about building a coal port at Barry Sound. The decision to proceed with the project was taken in 1882. By the summer of 1889, a massive dock was opened. The project was truly transformative. It joined the island to the mainland, brought a railway into the district for the first time and triggered the construction of a brand-new urban settlement. The scale of the upheaval cannot be overstated. Overnight, a landscape of sheep runs, wheat fields, moors and copses had been turned into a colossal building site. A network of streets was laid out, houses were thrown up and civic buildings were built. Barry had become a cartographer's nightmare. Old maps that had done sterling service for decades were rendered obsolete as lanes, streams, hedgerows and hamlets were obliterated. But the new maps produced in the 1890s were no better, for they were instantly made out of date by the precocious young town that was constantly overgrowing its boundaries.

To witness such turmoil at close quarters was a dizzying experience. As a journalist remarked, the emergence of Barry was 'one of the industrial romances of this generation'.[35] Contemplating it from the safe vantage point of today is still a sobering act. It demands that we think imaginatively about how to describe the cataclysm. Dai Smith has captured it best. In his words, Barry was nothing less than a 'meteor fragment hurled into the space of Welsh life'.[36] Viewed from the position of the rural folk who stood and watched the navvy teams blast their way across the landscape, the splashdown of a meteorite in the waters of Barry Sound might have been marginally less bewildering.

The new railway was an integral part of the dock project. For Barry's historians, this was the critical factor that turned Whitmore Bay into a tourist hotspot. Within months of the first passenger services running into Barry in December 1888, railway excursionists began exploring the Island. Their numbers grew with each passing year as Whitmore Bay was 'discovered' by more and more tourists. By 1892, enough were heading for Barry's seafront for Brian C. Luxton to declare that this was the year that the Island enjoyed 'its first full season as a holiday resort'.[37] Once that milestone had been passed it was full steam ahead. Visitor numbers mushroomed throughout the 1890s. By the middle of the decade, Barry was already rivalling Penarth, its neighbour, as a seaside playground. By the early 1900s, it was routinely referred to as one of the most popular seaside resorts in south Wales. Little wonder, then, that Barry has been characterized as a striking example of a 'railway resort'.[38]

As chronicled by its historians, the Island's journey from its discovery in the later Victorian years to its golden age in the 1950s and 1960s was straightforward. They tell how Whitmore Bay went from strength to strength, its development encouraged by various supportive figures in the district. Lord Windsor, the Island's owner was, according to Luxton, determined 'to make Barry Island an attractive seaside resort'. Likewise, Barry councillors were happy to engage with various resort development initiatives.[39] Some limited improvements were made in the 1900s and 1910s, but just as momentum was building, the Great War intervened and paused proceedings. Nevertheless, the setback was only temporary and in the early 1920s the local authority invested heavily in resort facilities: shelters, a permanent seawall, a promenade and, at the nearby Cold Knap, a lido and Marine Lake all soon appeared. A fairground, run by private entrepreneurs, was opened and added to the resort's appeal. Visitor numbers continued to grow throughout the 1920s and 1930s, peaking in the immediate post-war decades. By the 1950s and 1960s, the Island had effloresced into the wildly successful trippers' playground that we encountered at the start of this introduction.

These are the broad outlines of the story told by Barry Island's historians to date. True, if one looks carefully enough, one can find clues in the historical literature that hint at a more complicated story. For all the general agreement concerning the Island's discovery by tourists in the later 1880s and early 1890s, Iorwerth W. Prothero revealed that at least some visitors were heading for the island in the 1860s and 1870s.[40] Prothero found evidence of trippers from Cardiff picnicking on the island. And he described an interesting attempt on the part of one of the island's owners in the mid-1870s to stimulate tourism to the Barry district. J. D. Treharne, apparently recognizing Whitmore Bay's potential as a watering place, opened a little hotel at Friars Point, just a few hundred feet from the beach. He seemed to have enjoyed some success, for according to Prothero, in the summer of 1876, some 12,000 visitors made it over to the island.[41] This is an arresting fact and, at first sight, should have been grounds enough for rethinking Luxton's assertion that 1892 was Barry's first full season as a seaside resort. However, as Prothero points out, Treharne's scheme was ill-fated. Within just a few months he had abandoned his project and sold the island to the Windsor estate.[42] Thus, Treharne's initiative is presented to us as a lost opportunity – a false start in Barry Island's history as a resort.

What of Prothero's finding that some visitors headed for Whitmore Bay in the 1860s? It has been incorporated into the historical narrative but without being accorded any further significance. Prothero was unable to give any indication of the numbers of visitors who made the journey from Cardiff to the island in these mid-Victorian years. Reasonably enough, one reviewer of the volume in which Prothero's essay appeared came away with the impression that Whitmore Bay in the 1860s might have been visited by a few 'eccentric Victorian seabathers', but it was mostly empty – the 'haunt of rabbits and seabirds'.[43] Certainly, no one who has seriously studied the Barry district in the nineteenth century has found any reason to think that coastal tourism made any appreciable contribution to the local economy.[44] Matthew Griffiths, for example, produced a deeply researched essay on the social and economic life of the district in the Georgian and Victorian years. He uncovered plenty of evidence to show that agriculture dominated the lives of the small population but none to suggest that tourism contributed anything to the economy.[45] To the extent that visitors did make it over to Whitmore Bay in the decades before the dock's construction, they were, it seems, but fleeting presences.

Given the above, we can see why Barry's historians have accepted the suggestion that Barry's resort history only began in the 1890s. It seems that it must be this way, almost by definition. After all, seaside resorts were urban places, not rural backwaters. And they were dynamic settlements characterized by innovation, development and sweeping transformation. Their visitors changed them. At resorts throughout the country, tourists' spending sparked frenetic activity on the supply-side. Investors poured money into seafronts that became increasingly engineered spaces. Promenades were laid out, seawalls were built, ornamental gardens were opened and pleasure piers were constructed.[46] As holidaying by the seaside became an ever more popular pursuit, so the new resorts became nodes of sociability. They were meeting places where great playful crowds gathered to enjoy the seascape. Coastal tourism not only produced distinctive built forms, it also led to urban expansion.[47] Some of the most impressive examples of urban growth in the nineteenth century were to be found at the seaside. Brighton, for instance, was the fastest growing town in the country in the 1820s. At the other end of the century, and the other end of the country, Blackpool underwent a similar experience. Its population trebled between 1871 and 1891 and then doubled between 1891 and 1901.[48]

How very different was Barry's experience. The picnickers who made it across to Whitmore Bay in the 1860s and 1870s did not spark any urban development. How could they? There was nowhere for the trippers to spend their money, no town to cater for their needs, no amusements to keep them entertained. Consequently, the little island remained untouched by the developers. Treharne's failed hotel scheme in the mid-1870s merely confirms the point: Barry Island had to wait until the great cataclysm of the 1880s before its history as a seaside resort could properly begin.

REVISING THE STORY: THE AIMS OF THIS BOOK

Given that scholars are in agreement about the key dates and critical moments in Barry Island's history as a seaside resort, one might suppose that the task of the historian intent on writing a book about Whitmore Bay's development is merely to accumulate more detail, to add a few more pieces to the jigsaw puzzle. After all, we already have the big picture and all the big questions have been answered satisfactorily. We know why the beach suddenly came to the attention of tourists in the 1890s. We know when its seafront took the shape that it retains to this day – with its shelters, its seawall, its gardens and its fairground. Above all, we know why it became the trippers' resort par excellence. Gwyn Thomas, it seems, was right. Once the railway had been opened, it really was a straightforward matter of geography. With the emergence of the south Wales coalfield as a great centre of population, it was only a matter of time before Whitmore Bay was turned into the 'Kingdom of the Chip' – that wonderfully boisterous expression of a vibrant popular culture.[49]

But can we be so certain about the accuracy of the conventional wisdom? It is argued in this book that Barry Island's history as a seaside resort was by no means as straightforward as it has been portrayed. On the contrary, it was altogether a much more extended, complicated, more contested and, frankly, more interesting process than historians have realized. Indeed, on almost all points of interpretation, the ortho-dox account misleads. It does so, in part, because it overlooks a full cen-tury of the Island's resort history. Starting the story in the 1790s, when it should properly begin, instead of the 1890s, changes the meaning of everything. Old certainties suddenly appear shaky; long-established truths are shown to be no such thing; and the Barry Island of the 1950s and 1960s, far from seeming to be an historical inevitability, takes on an entirely different appearance – one outcome out of a range of possibil-ities. Not only might other Whitmore Bays have developed – a range of different Whitmore Bays had already existed.

In writing this book, I have taken it for granted that the Island has its own intrinsic historical significance as a tourist attraction. It has been a treasured leisure space for generations of visitors. For that reason alone, it is worth getting the story of its development right. But it has a much wider significance, too. Barry Island has much to teach us about the British seaside experience more generally, and the Welsh contribution specifically. As a case study, it casts an illuminating light on the resort development process. It reminds us, for instance, how a resort's destiny could be determined by powerful landowners – even into the early twentieth century. Just as important, it forces us to recognize how tourists themselves could play a decisive role in the making of resort. In the pages that follow, Barry's visitors emerge as full and vigorous participants in the Island's history. They were never just an amorphous mass who, unthinkingly, turned up on the first trains and kept returning, just as unthinkingly, every year thereafter. Furthermore, Barry Island requires us to think carefully about our most basic terms. Barry's experience of coastal tourism problematizes the very concept of a 'seaside resort' in ways that other places, including the likes of Blackpool, Bournemouth and Brighton, simply do not.

Our first task is to revise the accepted understanding of the Island's chronology. In particular, we must overturn the idea that Barry only began its career as a seaside resort in the early 1890s. In chapter 1, it will be shown that Barry was functioning as a 'proper' seaside resort as far back as the 1790s. This might seem like an unlikely proposition. We have seen how the Barry district plainly lacked so many of the accoutrements and characteristics usually deemed to be essential elements of a proper resort: no piers, no promenades and no town – just farmsteads and the odd village and hamlet. However, John K. Walton has usefully reminded us that 'the category "seaside resort" is far from straightforward'.[50] He has argued that the British 'seaside resort system' as it developed during the eighteenth and nineteenth centuries was remarkably diverse. It was a system that included, at one end, large cities that specialized in catering for tourists and, at the other, tiny fishing hamlets and agricultural villages 'which catered for a handful of summer visitors as a supplement to the main business of its inhabitants'.[51]

Thus, scholars have long been aware of the heterogeneity of the seaside resorts.[52] Nevertheless, the extent to which they have focused on the larger, developed resorts shows how easy it has been to overlook the importance of the smallest of seaside places. Barry Island has certainly suffered this fate. Barry's historians have noted that Whitmore Bay attracted visitors before the 1890s but, because the district remained undeveloped, they have severely downplayed the significance of the tourist interest in Whitmore Bay. Contemporaries did not make this mistake. They were perfectly aware of the Island's appeal and of the importance of tourism to the hamlets of the Barry district. Tellingly, when they wrote of Cadoxton, they invariably referred to it as a 'bathing village' – a very particular type of resort. Its inhabitants, for many decades before the 1890s, were well used to dealing with a small, but significant, number of visitors. They had been coming to the island from the late eighteenth century, long before the mid-Victorian trippers from Cardiff noted by Prothero. The Georgian and early Victorian visitors were lured to Whitmore Bay by its fine bathing opportunities. They were, it must be said, a distinct type of tourist. They preferred solitude over sociability, peace and quiet over the busy crowds that gathered at the fashionable resorts. But the little island's visitors were anything but oddballs and eccentrics. They were eminently respectable and well-to-do figures who valued the opportunity that Whitmore Bay offered them to commune with nature.

Significantly, a century of tourism did not transform the Barry district. This is one of the reasons why historians have overlooked it. Tourism undoubtedly boosted the local economy as visitors came to stay, often for weeks at a time, but their presence led to no urban growth. When set against the Brightons and Blackpools of the world, Barry and Cadoxton look like curious exceptions. But if we place them alongside many other little bathing villages situated along the coast of Wales, not to mention Scotland and the south-west of England, they suddenly look quite typical. The Welsh coast was lined with such settlements. Some were small towns, others were barely hamlets, but they appealed to those nineteenth-century tourists who preferred to holiday away from the madding crowds. These were visitors who, precisely because they viewed the coast through Romantic eyes, valued the isolation and seclusion that these Welsh resorts offered them.[53] Contemplation of Barry's pre-1890 resort history thus has the important effect of allowing us to revise our understanding of the Welsh contribution to coastal tourism. This is urgently needed, for as matters stand, Wales has tended be dismissed by resort historians as a place that did not pull its weight. English resorts dominate the historiography: they have been lauded as centres of innovation. Indeed, England has been credited as the place where the seaside holiday was 'invented'.[54] The Welsh seaside experience, in contrast, has often been adjudged to have been just a pale imitation, its resorts apparently few in number, small and unremarkable. As Nigel Yates put it, 'it is perhaps surprising, given the length of its coastline,

that Wales should not have made a greater contribution to the development of British seaside resorts in the nineteenth and twentieth century'.[55]

Here, a different argument is advanced. For the history of Barry
Island alerts us to the dangers of dismissing Wales's role in the development of seaside holidays on the grounds that its coastline was not
littered with pleasure piers and winter gardens. As Peter Borsay has
rightly observed, it is more profitable to think of Wales as specializing
in the smaller, remoter resort.[56] Wales offered a *different* type of seaside
experience – less eye-catching than that of its neighbour, to be sure,
but nonetheless important for that. A handful of its coastal settlements
were transformed by tourism into places that conformed to our precon-
ceptions of what a 'proper' Victorian resort should look like. Tenby was
one such, Aberystwyth another. But many more were small, even tiny,
settlements. They combined an interest in tourism with other economic
functions, agriculture being the dominant one, and they remained
untouched by the developer's hand. They are interesting early examples
of 'sustainable tourism'.[57] Barry and Cadoxton were just such places. The
Barry district in the century before 1890 compels us to pay attention to
Walton's reminder about the rich diversity of the British seaside experience. A successful seaside resort could be a place of solitude just as
much as a site of gregarious sociability, and tourism could contribute to
a settlement's economy without utterly transforming it. Indeed, without
prompting any discernible changes at all.

Armed with this new chronology, the 1880s and early 1890s take
on an altogether different appearance. These years still constitute a
watershed moment in the Island's resort history, but instead of form-
ing a starting point they should properly be seen as a turning point.
As turning points go, it was undeniably a critical one. The explosion
in visitor numbers prompted by the new railway was unprecedented.
But Whitmore Bay had gone through other turning points in its development. One such occurred in the mid-Victorian period. In the years
between *c*.1790 and *c*.1850, Barry Island had been a resort of the very
wealthy. At least one marquess holidayed at Whitmore Bay. However,
as chapter 2 shows, by the 1860s, the Island was still attracting a select
crowd, but it was broadening its appeal. Cardiff's middle-class citizens
were making a beeline for Barry in the summer months. So were some
upper-working-class trippers. Parties of them came by road, but many
more were brought to the Island by pleasure steamers, a reminder that
we should not overstate the significance of the railway. Important as the
steam locomotive was to become in Whitmore Bay's history, it was the
steamboat that first popularized Barry's beach.

If we recognize the Island's long pre-1890 career as a tourist resort, any idea that it was bound to become a working-class resort is shattered. Whitmore Bay did indeed flourish as a 'miners' paradise', but that should be seen as just one more stage through which it passed. It had already been other types of resort. Certainly, when mid-Victorians contemplated the island's future, it did not seem at all obvious to them that it was destined to become a workers' playground. They thought it would become a bourgeois retreat, a marine suburb that would be populated by Cardiff's wealthiest merchants. Factoring that sense of possibility back into the Island's history – the notion that other outcomes were always possible – has the useful effect of reminding us that the 'Kingdom of the Chip' had to be 'made', it did not simply happen. The Whitmore Bay of the 1950s and 1960s was the product of power exercised (and sometimes misused); of alternative development goals pursued (and sometimes realized); and, significantly, of struggle and conflict.

In chapter 3 our attention is directed to one of the most important single actors in the Island's history – its aristocratic owner from the late 1870s, Lord Windsor. Resort historians have long been aware that powerful landowners could determine the social tone of British seaside resorts. In most cases, when they had the opportunity, they tried to build the most select resorts possible. Yet in Barry's case, a great landowner stymied plans to turn Whitmore Bay into a high-class watering place. Windsor, for various commercial reasons, sought to keep the island entirely undeveloped. In a move that has gone entirely unnoticed by historians, he went further and instituted a complete visitor ban. He closed the island to all tourists and, at a stroke, ended at least eighty years of Whitmore Bay functioning as a bathing place. Cardiffians were instantly deprived of their seaside retreat. It was a vivid demonstration of landlordism. Hardly any Victorian landowners shut beaches. They were aware of how much hostility such a move could generate. Windsor stood out from the crowd. He closed Whitmore Bay and turned the island into his own private hunting ground.

From chapter 4 onwards, we see how the visitors reclaimed Barry Island. Windsor never formally revoked the ban but the altered circumstances (all of his own making) of the 1880s meant that it became impossible for the estate to maintain it. Once he gave the go-ahead to the dock project, his shutdown became meaningless. The Barry Railway Company – of which he was chair – was the means of bringing thousands of tourists back to Whitmore Bay. The town that he had helped to create was quickly filled with thousands of citizens who expected to be allowed onto the Island. It was not long before they had their own ideas about how the seafront should be developed for the good of the town. Lord Windsor, in other words, was no longer a potentate at Barry Island.

There was certainly no shortage of Barry inhabitants keen to push the cause of resort development. They have done so throughout the twentieth century. However, they were not to be the key players in shaping the Island's subsequent history. A central argument of this book casts the visitors themselves, and especially those from the great south Wales coalfield, as the decisive actors. By exercising their agency, the trippers claimed Whitmore Bay as their own. They did so notwithstanding the hostility of the Windsor estate and the numerous discomforts that they had to endure along the way. Windsor was later to be remembered by some Barrians as a friend of the excursionists from the valleys. However, in this book, a radically different assessment is offered of the 'good earl'. He emerges as an obstructive figure who, if he had had his way, would have kept the Island to himself and his well-to-do friends. Barry Island became a working-class resort largely in spite of Robert George Windsor-Clive, not because of him.

In summary, the Barry Island that blossomed into being by the mid-twentieth century has much to teach us about the complexity of the resort development process. Far from being a 'natural' or inevitable outcome, it was the product of different social groups clashing. Each group entertained different ideas about how that strip of golden sand at Whitmore Bay might best be used. The trippers cherished it as a place of escape from work and domestic duties. Barry's town leaders and business community looked at it as a place of economic opportunity. Lord Windsor saw it as a private asset, to be shared with the visitors and the townsfolk only grudgingly. Gwyn Thomas was clearly correct to assert that the proximity of the Island to the coalfield was an important factor in its development as a trippers' playground. But there was so much more to Barry Island's history than that.

Even as it developed into what seemed like the classic British working-class seaside resort, the Island did so in its own distinctive way. Whitmore Bay had never been more popular. By the interwar period it attracted more than 1 million visitors every holiday season. Yet, curiously, tourism had never mattered less to the district (at least not since the late eighteenth century). In part, this was because of the dock's continued importance. Industrial capitalism had breathed life into urban Barry and even when the coal trade began to contract alarmingly in the interwar years, the dock remained the mainstay of the town's economy. A 'candyfloss' industry such as tourism was never likely to provide Barry with its *raison d'être*. However, given Whitmore Bay's great popularity, we might have expected tourism to have made at least a sizeable contribution to the town's income. Yet this did not happen for two reasons. First, the more lucrative type of holidaymaker – the middle-class residential tourist – largely stayed away from Barry Island, put off by its working-class surroundings and plebeian amusements. Secondly, the district's geography meant that precious few of the trippers made it into the town. The beach was separated from the town by a long walk around a great coal dock. Trippers, once at Whitmore Bay, tended to stay there. As a consequence, the tourism multiplier effect was woefully weak. Commentators in the 1950s might confidently declare that 'Sunshine means money', yet, in truth, Barry town profited barely at all from the trippers. That 1955 was the first year that councillors could even contemplate a rate reduction thanks to the visitors' shillings makes the point. Tourism at Barry Island was not a great cash generator. If those mammoth crowds that had so graced Barry's seafront in 1955 had stayed away, remarkably few Barrians would have been materially worse off. They lived in a town that had a hugely popular seaside, but whether they were residents of a 'seaside town', in the fullest sense of the term, was extremely doubtful.

At every stage of its history as a tourist attraction, then, Barry confounds expectations and makes us think carefully about the dynamics underpinning resort development. All the while, it illuminates big themes in the history of coastal tourism and popular leisure. And throughout its long history one thing is certain: Whitmore Bay should be thought of not only as a veritable visitors' paradise but also as an historian's delight.

CHAPTER ONE

'[M]UCH FREQUENTED DURING THE BATHING SEASON'

BARRY ISLAND AND WELSH COASTAL TOURISM, c.1790–c.1860

PRECONDITIONS FOR THE RISE OF COASTAL TOURISM IN WALES

TOURISM TO WALES only began in earnest in the final third of the eighteenth century. Before the 1770s, the principality was rarely visited by outsiders. It was widely seen as a primitive and uncivilized corner of the land – an inaccessible place of 'monstrous' mountains and uninteresting, uncultured inhabitants.[1] Henry Wyndham, an early tourist, remarked that he had gone six weeks without encountering a single English tourist during his peregrinations in Wales in the summer of 1774. He thought that the 'general prejudice' against all things Cambrian accounted for the absence of his fellow countrymen. As he put it, genteel metropolitan types took it for granted that 'Welsh roads are impracticable, the inns intolerable, and the people insolent and brutish.'[2]

Given such beliefs, it is remarkable that within a few years Wales had become fashionable. The Romantics did much to bring about this transformation in perception. Almost overnight, the very characteristics that had made the land west of Offa's Dyke deeply unattractive to visitors were now the very features that turned it into a tourist hotspot. Romantics were fascinated by Wales's supposed primitiveness. Their newfound interest in the grandeur of nature meant that the principality's mountainous regions went from being barren spaces to repositories of the sublime. Landscape painters imbued with the spirit of Romanticism had plenty to keep them interested, whether they were looking for dramatic cliff faces or a surfeit of waterfalls.[3] Likewise, poets found much in the Welsh landscape to stir their Romantic imaginations. Meanwhile, antiquarians discovered Wales to be place with a rich and varied history.

One consequence of this profound reconceptualization was that Wales, like other 'remote' and 'untamed' areas of Britain (including the Scottish Highlands and the English Lake District), suddenly found itself on the itineraries of many tourists.[4] A 'nascent tourist industry' developed to support travellers on their 'Celtic Tour'.[5] Hotels sprang up at key locations and a veritable flood of tour guides appeared: between 1770 and 1815, at least eighty titles dedicated to Wales were published.[6] As Hywel M. Davies has put it, 'Accounts of Wales were so numerous during the last two decades of the eighteenth century that "Welsh Tours" constituted a literary type.'[7] Tourists' interest in the principality was only strengthened by the wars with France (which made Continental tourism impracticable) and the fact that new turnpike roads had made travelling a more comfortable experience (in parts of Wales at least).

There was another factor that brought tourists to the principality in the late eighteenth and early nineteenth century: a newfound interest in the beach. This development, too, was based on a rethinking of what had once been an accepted truth. In the medieval period, Christendom had been gripped by something of a 'beach phobia'. It is easy to see why this should have been the case. The Bible, the key source of wisdom for medieval people, depicted the sea as a threatening space of mystery and destruction. In Genesis, the ocean was portrayed as part of the terrifying 'abyss' that had preceded creation. Then there was the story of the Great Flood in which the ever-rising waters came close to wiping out life. And whilst the sea could bring peaceful traders, it could also be the means by which hostile forces – such as Vikings – arrived. Hardly a wonder that the beach became, in the minds of many, a 'sacred threshold', a place that should 'only be approached with the greatest trepidation'.[8]

Nevertheless, a very different understanding of the sea emerged. As the eighteenth century unfolded, so the notion that the beach might in fact be a place of healing gained credence. Medical authorities began celebrating seawater's near-miraculous curative powers.[9] One of the most enthusiastic supporters of hydrotherapy was Dr Richard Russell. His *Dissertation on the Use of Seawater in the Diseases of the Glands* (published in Latin in 1750 and in English two years later) summed up the new orthodoxy. In Russell's view the sea was not an instrument of God's wrath; it was a divine gift that provided mortals with a 'common Defence against the Corruption and Putrefaction of Bodies'.[10] The list of ailments that Russell asserted could be treated with seawater was certainly impressive. It included tumefaction of the glands of the knees, 'cutaneous Eruptions', leprosy (in both its 'moist' and 'dry' forms), gonorrhoea, herpes in the face, obstructions of the rectum, cholic, hardened glands in the neck, 'hectic fever' and swelling of the upper lips and nostrils. Once established, the proposition that seawater and, soon enough, sea air, were powerful remedies went on to enjoy a long life. Throughout the nineteenth century, medics issued advice on how best to get the health benefits of a visit to the beach.[11]

We should note that bathing was not just an elite activity. Labourers had their own ideas about benefits of sea immersion and did not need Dr Russell to be encouraged into the water. We know precious little about such popular bathing habits but there is enough evidence from around the coasts of Britain for us to be certain that members of the working classes were bathing. A travel guide to Wales penned in 1805 contained one such description of a Welsh 'aquatic orgy'. The author reported that the 'natives of both sexes among the mountains on the sea-coast of Cardiganshire, and probably in other places', were 'much addicted to sea-bathing, during the light summer nights'. On Saturday evenings, the participants left their villages in the hills and headed for the beach, noisily blowing horns as they went. Once at the water's edge, they stripped and took 'a promiscuous plunge without any ceremony'. They returned home at daybreak, just as noisily as they had left.[12]

Nevertheless, it was the social elite that had the means to stay at the seaside for extended periods. As they did so, specialist seaside resorts began to emerge. Early examples were the Yorkshire resorts of Whitby and Scarborough in the 1710s and 1730s respectively. In the second half of the eighteenth century, resorts within reach of London, such as Brighton, Worthing, Southend and Weymouth, all flourished.[13] By the mid-nineteenth century, the sea-bathing 'mania' was contributing to the urban economies of coastal towns all around the coast of the United Kingdom, from the south-west of England to the north-east of Scotland.[14]

WALES'S LARGER SPECIALIST WATERING-PLACES

The coast of Wales was fully implicated in the rise of sea-bathing as a cultural practice. Yet we would be forgiven for drawing the opposite conclusion if we only concentrated our attention on the towns that specialized in seaside tourism. After a century of development, Wales had a mere handful of developed resorts: Tenby, Aberystwyth, Llandudno and Rhyl were the largest.[15] It will be argued here that we should not see these 'bigger' resorts (they were still small by English standards) as being representative of the Welsh experience. However, for the moment, it is important that we note their presence as significant centres of coastal tourism in the principality. In all four cases, tourism had clearly invigorated their local economies and led to some significant urban growth.

In south-west Wales, Tenby had long been declining as a port and a centre of fishing. Its faltering economy was only able to support a population of around 850 at the start of the nineteenth century. However, the arrival of bathers from the 1780s soon gave the little town a new lease of life.[16] It was already being described as a 'Bathing place of very fashionable resort' by the late 1790s.[17] It was widely regarded as the leading Welsh seaside resort in the Georgian period. In the early 1800s, a bath-house and hotels had been built. By the 1820s, with its circulating library, theatre, public reading room stuffed with London newspapers and special seats installed in the parish church just for visitors, Tenby was a town that quickly bore the imprint of its willingness to appeal to the tourist market.[18] As the Revd John Evans noted in 1803, its 'aquatic celebrity' had led to 'considerable improvement' and the building of 'many modern houses'.[19] And its success further boosted its fortunes: by 1851, its population had risen to almost 3,000. This was a substantial enough increase to place it thirty-sixth in John K. Walton's table of the fifty largest resorts in England and Wales.[20]

Aberystwyth, on the coast of mid Wales, had a similar experience. Home to about 1,700 inhabitants in 1801, it was an unprepossessing place: according to one early visitor, it had a 'gloomy appearance'. Nevertheless, its 'romantic shore' was attractive enough to draw 'crowds of company' to it for the purposes of therapeutic sea-bathing. The bathers came in large enough numbers to lead to the construction of new houses to accommodate them (nineteen were built over the winter of 1823–4 providing eighty more beds for visitors).[21] And other tourist-inspired improvements followed, including a scheme to build a 'new and elegant' theatre.[22] Work on a promenade began in 1819 and assembly rooms were opened in 1820. By 1831, Aberystwyth was playing host to some 1,500 staying visitors every season.[23] By 1851, its population had reached over 5,100 making it the twenty-first largest seaside resort in England and Wales by population.[24]

In north Wales, the fortunes of Rhyl and Llandudno were also materially improved by seaside tourism. Again, both settlements were small. In 1851, Rhyl only had 1,500 inhabitants, Llandudno just 1,100. But, in both cases, the arrival of sea-bathing visitors soon triggered investment in tourist infrastructure. By the early 1830s, Rhyl possessed a 'commodious' hotel, a bathing house offering warm seawater and vapour baths and piers specially built to accommodate the steam packets that were operating out of Liverpool.[25] By the late 1840s, Rhyl's popularity with the inhabitants of Liverpool and Manchester meant that visitors were obliged to book their lodgings 'long before they are wanted'.[26] By the mid-point of the century, Llandudno had a number of hotels, a reading room and a Turkish bath and was set fair to develop into a fashionable resort. By 1911, its population of 10,469 made it the largest Welsh resort, and the thirty-ninth largest in England and Wales. Rhyl, with its 9,000 inhabitants, was not far behind.[27]

The four largest Welsh seaside resorts were relatively small when compared with English seaside towns. When Nigel Yates observed that Wales had made only a disappointing contribution to the development of the British seaside resort, he certainly had a point.[28] If we are looking for examples of coastal tourism's potential to transform urban economies and bring about explosive urban growth, we will not find much to interest us along the principality's coastline. But the size of a seaside town's resident population is only one indicator of tourism's significance. We are in danger of missing an important element of the story of Welsh seaside tourism if we are only on the lookout for equivalents of Brighton and Bournemouth. For besides those few Welsh towns that edged their way into the lower echelons of the league table of the top-fifty largest resorts, there were many more that played their part in the tourist boom of the nineteenth century. Tourism became woven into their economies, even if it did not always lead to dramatic change. There is a striking diversity to the Welsh seaside experience that can be missed entirely if we take too restrictive a view of what constitutes a 'proper' seaside resort.[29] And, just as importantly, we are in danger of missing a very particular type of tourist: the visitor who shunned the big crowds, who avoided the urbane sophistication of the more fashionable, sector-leading watering places, and who wanted, instead, a more relaxed seaside experience. The bathing villages of Wales catered for just such a tourist.[30]

'[L]ARGELY RESORTED TO BY THOSE WHO . . . SEEK A QUIET SPOT': WALES'S SMALLER RESORTS

The society-loving seaside visitor is a stock figure in our histories. This is the tourist who, when not bathing, frequented the bustling assembly rooms, the coffee houses, the theatres and concert halls that had been built specially to keep them amused. When they were not looking at the sublime seascape, they were 'ogling each other' on the promenades – those purpose-built 'spaces of intensive display and observation'.[31] But such a seaside sojourn was not to everyone's taste. Throughout the century, there were plenty of tourists who wanted to forgo the disadvantages of holidaying in an overly busy, fashionable watering place. When, in 1790s, Henry Skrine visited Caernarfon, a coastal town in north Wales with a population of approximately 3,500, he was struck by how 'several English families' preferred 'to make it their summer residence for the purpose of avoiding the crowded inconvenience of the more polished, but less simple, public places in the south of England'. There were enough of such well-to-do visitors from England to have a material effect on Caernarfon's appearance: the money spent by the 'strangers' had led to 'much improvement and a superior display of elegance'.[32]

By the later nineteenth century, it was widely recognized that there was a distinct and select group of tourists who found the larger resorts unappealing. Most of the 'annual flitters from the bustle and worry of big towns . . . crowd to the popular seaside resorts where they pay exorbitantly for inferior lodgings and spend their days in the noise and confusion of "London by the sea"', one writer observed. He was impressed by those 'few' who preferred 'a quiet spot where trippers [were] an unknown quantity'. For them, a vacation in a small bathing village, 'where one may lead a perfectly free, unconventional life', was 'the only holiday worth having'. He advised such reclusive tourists to head to north Wales, but cautioned against Llandudno – it was an 'over-crammed Welsh Margate'.[33] 'Medicus' agreed. In 1884, in an article in the *Girl's Own Paper*, he expounded the benefits of the smaller resorts. At the developed watering places, one faced the difficulties of securing a lodging-house, the discomforts of staying in such lodgings, 'the same attempts at extortion everywhere' and 'the same "enjoyments" as they are called'. Medicus advised his readers to rethink their approach to sea-side holidays. For a truly healthy vacation, one should 'seek out any of the hundred and one quiet little villages around the shores of say Corn-wall or Wales, where the trees often grow down to the water's edge, where you can gather ferns and seaweed and shells all at one time'.[34]

There were plenty of these smaller Welsh resorts to choose from. Llantwit Major was one such. It was an urban place, to be sure, but a sleepy one. A small town in the Vale of Glamorgan, Llantwit's population hovered around 1,000 throughout the Vic-torian period. It had a rocky beach, with here and there a strip of sand, nearly a mile-and-a-half from the little town's centre. It was nowhere near 'seaside' enough nor developed enough for most Victorian coastal tourists. But to its loyal devotees it was the per-fect marine retreat. It was 'readily and largely resorted to by those who . . . seek a quiet spot', remarked one observer in 1869.[35] Later, in 1893, a writer enthused about Llantwit's simplicity. Its lack of a pier and the absence of even the simplest promenade meant that visitors did not have to worry overly about their appearance for it would be 'a waste to dress much . . . there are so few to see one, and no one to criticise'. To be able to wander around without gloves, 'gives one a sense of freedom from conventionality which, after a rigid town life, is quite refreshing', he declared.[36] Another tourist praised Llant-wit for being the ideal retreat for those who wanted to have 'a quiet holiday and enjoy the simple life'.[37] So many wanted such a holiday experience that sometimes the influx of tourists threatened to shatter

Illus. 7. *Barmouth beach, with Cader Idris in the background.
Barmouth flourished as a seaside resort throughout the nineteenth
century. But, like so many other Welsh resorts, it remained a small
place. The Welsh seaside experience showed that a popular resort did
not necessarily experience explosive urban growth.*

the peace. In the later 1860s, between 400 and 500 'strangers' were
lodging in the town every week during the bathing season, swelling
the town's population by 50 per cent.[38]

Wales proved to be a rich hunting ground for those tourists who
preferred their seaside towns to be on the quieter side. Some ended up in
places such as Abergele, a little market town in north Wales. With fewer
than 1,800 inhabitants in 1801, it did not appear to have much going for
it: one visitor described it as a 'small shabby town'.[39] Another, Richard
Fenton, thought it was a 'small mean town' when he passed through it in
the early years of the nineteenth century. Yet, he noted, sea-bathing tourists frequented it in some numbers. In his opinion, Abergele symbolized
all that was wrong about the 'the general [bathing] Mania prevailing all
over the Kingdom': Fenton thought that bathers were so keen to immerse
themselves in the briny that they took leave of their senses. The fashion

for 'quitting home and every comfort for 3 Months every Summer, to experience all the miseries of contracted Apartments and every species of imposition' was too much for him to comprehend.[40] The tourists were not put off by Fenton's grumblings. By the 1820s, there were so many visitors arriving in Welsh-speaking Abergele from England that extra divine services, conducted in English, had to be held.[41]

Fenton's disinterest in sea-bathing made it hard for him to fathom Abergele's appeal. He was similarly unimpressed with another popular bathing resort, Barmouth, a small port and market town on the coast of Cardigan Bay. He thought it a 'very disagreeable place' because of the way strong winds blew sand all about the streets.[42] But, again, he was out of step with many of his contemporaries. Not only were bathers lured there by its fine beach, but visitors of a Romantic disposition were impressed by its scenery. Whilst standing on the sands, it was possible to see Cader Idris, one of the Romantics' favourite Welsh mountains.[43] The views were 'strikingly magnificent', proclaimed one writer in 1833.[44] As early as 1804, it was noted that Barmouth was 'frequented during the summer season by many genteel families from Wales, and the west of England, as a sea-bathing place'.[45] By the late 1820s and early 1830s, Barmouth was attracting so many visitors from England that, just as at Abergele, a second divine service had to be held in English every day during the summer months.[46]

Barmouth, in fact, was peculiarly successful. It had a hotel 'provided with every accommodation' (including warm and cold seawater baths), a 'capacious' boarding house and 'numerous respectable lodging-houses'. A billiard-room had been erected by the hotel owner.[47] A remarkably fashionable set of tourists were holidaying at Barmouth by this time. In September 1834, for example, its visitors included the archbishop of Dublin and his entourage, Thomas Arnold (the headmaster of Rugby School), a brace of lords and ladies, an earl, a marquess, an assortment of military men, a number of vicars, plus well-heeled visitors from as far afield as Edinburgh, Birmingham, Weymouth, Cheltenham and even Barbados. Invariably, given such elite visitors, the bathing village became quite a cultural enclave during the summer months. Harp performances were common, and concerts and balls 'frequently enliven[ed] the leisure hours of the health[-] and pleasure-seeking invalids and *elegantes*'.[48] By the 1850s, it had assumed a quieter air. As one travel writer commented, it had 'a very secluded and somewhat lonely appearance'. The walks it offered, after a dip in the sea, were 'solitary and romantic'. Yet, far from being off-putting, its remoteness made it 'pleasing to a certain class of visitors who seek for retirement rather than the customary gaiety and amusements of a fashionable watering place'.[49]

Barmouth's popularity showed that the Welsh coastal settlement that offered safe sea-bathing, a quieter, simpler urban setting, and a surfeit of Romantic scenery, was well positioned indeed to profit from tourism. However, such places had to be sold to potential visitors. From an early date, local promoters of tourism became adept at marketing their towns.[50] Take, for example, a promotional notice praising the attractions of the small cathedral city of Bangor in north Wales. It appeared in a newspaper in 1808. With just 1,200 inhabitants in 1801, Bangor was easily passed by. True, most travel writers agreed that it was pretty enough, but it was notably short of artificial amusements. As one observer commented, 'there is very little to attract notice in this place'.[51] It was crucial, therefore, that Bangor's boosters made the most of its natural assets. Above all else, this involved underlining its suitability as a bathing place. The author of the 1808 puff piece explained how the currents that swirled around Bangor's beach had flowed straight across from the nearby isle of Anglesey and, consequently, were of the 'most pure, saline excellence, clear and pellucid'. The seawater's credentials as a health-boosting agent were thus firmly established. But, as the author was at pains to point out, Bangor offered more than just fine bathing. It was also a base from which visitors could see for themselves many of the mountains, lakes, waterfalls and castles that had made Wales such a tourist attraction: 'grand scenery, which forms a subject of delightful contemplation' was all around, the booster insisted.[52] Such promotional material doubtless helped to stimulate tourist interest in Bangor. There was enough demand from sea-bathing visitors to merit nine bathing machines by the late 1800s, and its champions were able to tout the town as a 'fashionable and genteel resort'.[53]

The importance of tourism to these small coastal towns varied from place to place and over time. At Tenby, for instance, it came to matter greatly and, whilst it did not produce the spectacular growth that occurred at some of the leading English resorts, it undoubtedly arrested the little port's economic decline.[54] Swansea, in contrast, was far less reliant upon its sea-bathing visitors. It had other strings to its bow, functioning as a busy port and an important centre of copper smelting. However, tourism was still a significant source of income for the town. In the early 1800s, such was the 'great influx of genteel company' that it was often difficult to find places to stay.[55] Robert Anthony has argued that coastal tourism contributed positively to Swansea's population growth in the late eighteenth century.[56] The same can be said about Barmouth's experience. After it was connected to the railway network in 1867, its visitor numbers swelled appreciably.[57] By the early 1880s, it routinely received hundreds and sometimes thousands of day-trippers every day during the summer months. These were in addition to a large number of resident visitors.[58] The money that they brought into the town helped to fuel a steady rise in Barmouth's population, from 1,500 in 1881 to 2,100 in 1911.[59] And at Abergele, too, the population rose slowly but steadily, from 1,700 in 1801 to 3,300 in the early 1860s – a figure it was to maintain, more or less, throughout the rest of the Victorian period. As Jones and Smith explain, this population rise occurred at a time when the populations of neighbouring villages were in decline: a point that can be made about many of Wales's coastal small towns in these years.[60] If demography is any guide, tourism helped to sustain these seaside places even if it did not necessarily lead to dramatic growth.

Some of the settlements that were affected by the tourists' presence were very small indeed. Mere hamlets, they had no urban infrastructure whatsoever. Inhabitants simply rented out whatever spare space they had in their houses. That there was a demand for such rural retreats is certain. Consider, for example, a notice placed in the *Cambrian* newspaper in February 1816 by a gentleman looking to rent a ready-furnished house, 'on any part of the sea coast of South Wales', for six months over the summer. It had to be within walking distance of the sea but, crucially, 'not in a town'.[61] His request was not an unusual one. Coastal hamlets and villages were inundated annually by elite visitors from nearby towns. St Bride's Bay in Pembrokeshire was one such area. By the early nineteenth century, a number of the local gentry and tradesmen from the market town of Haverfordwest had developed the habit of holidaying in the tiny coastal hamlets of Little and Broad Haven, some six miles away, during the summer months. Bathing machines were certainly on the beach at Broad Haven in the early 1810s, where 'many little villas' had been given over to the tourists.[62] In the summer of 1828, it was reported that there was scarcely a Haverfordwest tradesman who was not in Little Haven: it had become de rigueur for a man of substance to spend 'a week at least at "The Haven", with his family'.[63]

In Wales, tourists could be found on any stretch of coast where there were cottages, no matter how few, near to a bathing beach. Glamorganshire abounded with such places. Within just a few miles of Barry Island, bathers could be found staying at the tiniest of settlements. They were vacationing at Fontygary, at Wick and at Southerndown, for example.[64] They were at Aberthaw, a down-at-heel little harbour that was in terminal decline until bathers started staying in the 1810s and 1820s. Residents let out rooms in their cottages to visitors, summer after summer, for decades.[65] The tourists were also at Marcross, a place that never had more than twenty inhabited houses throughout the nineteenth century, yet was described variously as a 'delightful watering-place' and an 'isolated, but pleasant and beautiful bathing place'.[66] This secluded hamlet was a favourite with sea-bathers from Bridgend. It had been attracting visitors from at least the early Victorian period, and it was still drawing tourists who desired 'rest and quietude in a healthy sea-side locality' in the later Victorian years.[67]

There were two other tiny settlements on the Glamorganshire coast that were frequented by holidaymakers who relished the relaxed seaside holidays on offer there: the little villages near Barry Island – Cadoxton and Barry.

AN 'UNMOLESTED RETREAT': BARRY ISLAND AND ITS RURAL ENVIRONS

If it had not been for Cadoxton and Barry's proximity to the island's sandy bay, it is unlikely that any nineteenth-century tourists would have ever been drawn into the district. Barry was a hamlet of just twenty inhabited houses. Occasionally, its population reached one hundred, but eighty was a more typical figure. Cadoxton was slightly larger: some 200 people lived there at the start of the nineteenth century; by the century's midpoint this had risen, but only to 260. Most travel writers bypassed the Barry district altogether, preferring to take the road between Cardiff and Cowbridge, the nearest urban settlements of note, rather than the 'bad' coastal lanes.[68] For those who had read their copies of Samuel Lewis's *Topographical Dictionary of Wales*, their decision to skirt around the Barry district would have caused them little regret. When Lewis came to write about Cadoxton, he could only muster six sentences. Once he had discussed the village's religious institutions and its distance from Cardiff, he was left scratching his head. The best he could come up with was an obscure fact about the locals' use of limestone as a soil conditioner, and a cursory description of the rather unimpressive ruins of Barry castle.[69]

If he had been feeling generous, Lewis could have pointed out that Cadoxton was a 'pleasant village'.[70] However, in a district that was bursting with 'pleasant' villages, it was hardly a characteristic that would bring tourists flocking to seek it out.[71] Beyond its coastal location, there was nothing to capture the attention of the traveller intent on experiencing 'Romantic Wales'. The district was merely one more agricultural area.[72] Its countryside was attractive enough, no doubt, comprised as it

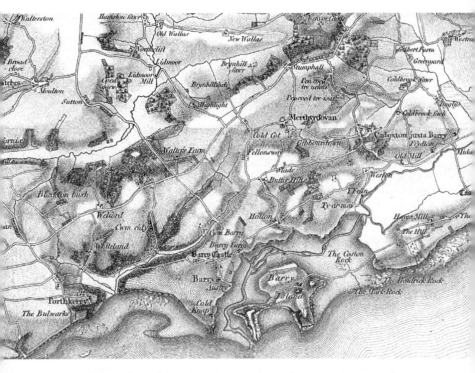

Illus. 8. *Map of the Barry district, 1833. The Barry district in the Georgian period was a place of fields, copses, scattered farmsteads, tiny hamlets and Cadoxton, a small village. Little had changed as late as the summer of 1884.*

was of meadows, pasture land and arable fields interspersed with, here and there, areas of woodland. Its social life would, in the mid- and late Victorian years, come to be thought of as interesting by antiquarians. Driven by a desire to capture the folkways of a fast-vanishing pre-industrial mode of living, they would come to notice how the villagers from Cadoxton held harvest festival parties in fields 'by the sea side', for instance, or comment on the ploughing matches and hare-coursing events that kept the inhabitants amused.[73] But that was for the future. In the early nineteenth century, the inhabitants' celebrations of feast days and festivals and their rural sports were all deemed unremarkable – so they duly went unremarked.

The one notable feature of the Barry district was the island that nestled, close to the shore, in Barry Sound. For tourists of an historical bent,

Barry Island had its appeal. Late eighteenth- and early nineteenth-century travel writers who were familiar with the recently republished work of the renowned Tudor antiquary John Leland, knew of its significance as a holy isle. In its medieval days it had been a site of pilgrimage. Devotees of Baruc, the sixth-century Welsh saint who reputedly drowned in the waters of Whitmore Bay and was buried on the island, had been trekking to Barry to pay their respects for generations. Leland described how, in his day, the isle had 'in the middle of it a fair little Chapel' dedicated to the saint.[74] (Baruc's chapel had been engulfed by the sand dunes long before the start of the nineteenth century and would not be rediscovered until the archaeologist John Storrie uncovered it in the mid-1890s.[75]) The Georgian travel writers also knew, from the writings of the late twelfth-century monk Gerald of Wales, about a curious hollow rock on the island. According to Gerald, as the cavity filled and emptied with each rising and falling tide, all manner of mysterious tapping and hammerings could be heard; it was as if a team of blacksmiths were at work underground.[76]

It was Gerald's description of the subterranean knocking that lured one travel writer, the Revd John Evans, over to the island in 1803.[77] He failed to find the rock in question and soon regretted his decision to visit the isle for he was quickly overwhelmed by its remoteness. After making his way over at low tide – when the sands were all exposed save for a small stream of fresh water – he noticed the large colonies of rabbits, the gently rising hills 'covered with maiden turf' and the farmhouse – the only building standing on the island. But it was the isolation that most struck him: 'truly a more unmolested retreat cannot be imagined'. In his estimation it took a special sort of person to find the island appealing, someone who possessed 'sufficient fortitude to brave the *ennui* of continual quietude'. He was depressed by the 'characteristic dreariness, heightened by the hoarse sounding ocean': it was a place that 'inspired melancholy'. When he climbed one of the island's hills and looked back across the channel to the 'well wooded, but thinly inhabited country', he was chilled by the thought that the next rising tide would leave him marooned there for twelve hours. To anyone 'accustomed to the luxury of society, and other pleasurable amusements, Barry will not furnish a single inducement to visit or reside', he concluded glumly.[78]

The Revd Evans was clearly not going to be holidaying at Barry Island any time soon. Nevertheless, importantly, he did recognize that some tourists might take a different view: 'To a party, who have all their amusements among themselves, it may be tolerable for a time', he conceded. And, whilst he did not recommend it to 'delicate females' because of the lack of bathing machines, he accepted that 'for those desirous of sea-bathing in retirement . . . the water and the sands are reasonable inducements'.[79] It is a crucial observation: notwithstanding Barry's complete absence of any urban centre, its relative remoteness and the secluded nature of the island, Evans could still see why it might be to the taste of some visitors.

'[C]ROWDED WITH COMPANY': THE BATHING VILLAGES OF THE BARRY DISTRICT

Evans was right. Whitmore Bay, with its particularly fine sandy beach, had much to offer the more reclusive bather. Indeed, such visitors had been heading over to the island for some time. Travel writer Henry Skrine was aware of them when he toured through south Wales in the later 1790s. He noted that Whitmore Bay was a bathing place 'crowded with company' notwithstanding the fact that it was 'extremely difficult of access' and there were 'few attractions' beyond the beach itself.[80] Some stayed on the island in its sole building, a farmhouse that doubled as a lodging house 'for those desirous of sea-bathing in retirement'.[81] It had a number of 'commodious' rooms and was next to a 'prolific Leech-pool', an added attraction for invalids and the sickly who wanted to go to Whitmore Bay for the benefit of their health.

Some holidayed on the island itself, then, but others stayed in Cadoxton and Barry. Because commentators had little reason to take notice of the district, and there was no local newspaper until the late 1880s, the archival sources only contain scattered references to such tourists. But the limited evidence we have all leads to the same conclusion: Barry and Cadoxton were yet two more little sea-bathing villages. Newspapers published outside the Barry district are our best source of information. They show conclusively that the island was well visited by long-stay bathers. In 1840, for instance, the *Bristol Mercury* remarked that Cadoxton was 'much frequented in the Bathing Season by respectable people'.[82] A few years later, the *Cardiff and Merthyr Guardian* told of how the neighbourhood was 'every year more frequented during the summer season for sea-bathing, numbers annually resorting there from many miles' distance'.[83] A decade later, the same paper repeated the fact: Cadoxton was 'much frequented during the Bathing Season'.[84] In August 1864, the *Cardiff Times* noted that the 'little village is at present full of visitors, who come here for the sake of sea-bathing, from the hills [i.e. the south Wales coalfield] and other places'.[85] In July 1866, it informed its readers that the bathing season was at its height and, in the Barry district, 'a goodly number of strangers are to be seen daily taking their walks to and fro along the narrow lanes and the sea shore'.[86] A few weeks later, it was reported that the 'little village' of Cadoxton was being 'visited by many strangers from different parts of the country for the purposes of bathing and enjoying and thereby recruiting their health, and regaining their strength'. By now, many of Cadoxton's tourists hailed from the coalfield. Its southern boundary was a mere thirteen or so miles from the Barry district, as the crow flies. As one observer put it, Cadoxton's 'pure atmosphere' was especially appreciated by those visitors who came from the 'smoky towns and mineral districts', for they relished the opportunity to bathe at Barry Island and take health-enhancing walks across Cadoxton Moors.[87] A decade later, Cadoxton was still drawing tourists. In 1875, the *Cardiff Times* commented on how the village's population was routinely augmented by the arrival of 'considerable' numbers of sea-bathing holidaymakers during the summer seasons.[88]

It is clear that the 'social tone' of Barry Island was high throughout the period from the 1790s to the 1870s. The references to the arrival of 'respectable people' are unambiguous enough. We should not underestimate just how respectable they might have been. On at least one occasion, a member of the nobility holidayed at Whitmore Bay. In the summer of 1825, no less a figure than the second marquess of Bute stayed at the island's lodging house. A newspaper was glad to report that 'his Lordship's health was much benefited' as a consequence.[89] By the mid-Victorian years, Cardiff's bourgeoisie were probably the main group of resident visitors along with tradesmen and others from the booming coalfield. Cardiff was just 8 miles from Barry. It was about to embark upon a period of sustained and breakneck urban growth, courtesy of its role as a coal port. Cardiff had grown modestly in the Georgian period. It was home to about 2,000 inhabitants in 1801. By 1841, some 10,000 resided in the town. However, the mid-Victorian years were ones of sustained expansion. In 1861, Cardiff's population stood at 33,000; in 1881, it was 82,000.[90] At least two former mayors of the town, W. B. Watkins and William Alexander, were devotees of Barry Island. Watkins 'often' bathed there, regarding it as 'the most charming and picturesque spot'; Alexander brought his family to Barry for months at a time during the summers. He rented a cottage in Cadoxton for the purpose.[91] Other resident visitors were of more modest means. In 1837, a draper from Caerphilly (some 13 miles away) was recorded as holidaying in the Barry district in order to enjoy the restorative effects of daily dips at Whitmore Bay.[92]

Significantly, the first day-tripping parties made it to Barry Island in the Georgian period. Many came by steamboat. The earliest reference we have to Bristol Channel steamboat excursions is of a trip that ran in May 1817.[93] It was not long before they began heading to Whitmore Bay. In July 1824, the steam packet the *Lady Rodney* sailed out of Bristol with a group of excursionists on board. After visiting Weston-super-Mare, the vessel made for Barry Island. The party, 'attended by a capital harper', was ferried onto the beach in rowing boats. They 'amused themselves for some time on the Island'. The activities included a spell of contra-dancing on the sands. So successful was the event that the ship's proprietors were encouraged to run several more excursions the following month. A further indication of the popularity of such trips is provided by the fact that the pleasure-seeking Bristolians were not the only excursionists at Whitmore Bay that day: they shared the beach with another 'party of pleasure from Cardiff'.[94]

These contra-dancing trippers were clearly well-to-do. However, by the early Victorian period, some working-class excursionists were also enjoying Whitmore Bay's delights. One of the first parties of railway excursionists to make it to Barry Island arrived in August 1845. Ironmaster Robert Crawshay brought 350 of his workers down from Merthyr to Cardiff by means of the recently opened railway. A short journey on a steam packet took them to the island. 'Having arrived safely there, they, after allowing themselves reasonable time to look around them, stuck into the twenty rounds of beef which had been generously provided for them by their liberal employer.' The workers' own band accompanied them as they ate, and then played for the benefit of another pleasure party aboard a steamer that passed close by the island. The Merthyr trippers stayed until the early evening. They returned to Cardiff, walked 'in regular order and with imposing appearance' to the station and then caught the train back home, arriving at 11.00 p.m.[95] Given that south Wales was a stronghold of Chartism, local elites were eager to support any venture that might bring social classes together. On that day in 1845, Whitmore Bay was pressed into service by an ironmaster keen to foster good feeling between the forces of Capital and Labour.

Barry Island received day-trippers from closer to home, too. By the mid-Victorian years, the growing town of Cardiff was regularly sending visitors to the Cadoxton district. It took just a couple of hours, by horse and trap, to get to Barry from Cardiff. One of the earliest references we have of Whitmore Bay being used as the venue for a Sunday school treat appeared in the *Cardiff Times* in August 1862. Cardiff Wesleyans made for Cadoxton, in the first instance, spending the morning playing games, making speeches and awarding themselves prizes. Then they crossed over to the island to consume a hearty al fresco lunch. A number of the young scholars 'enjoyed the luxury of sea-bathing'. They stayed until the early evening and were back home by 9.00 p.m.[96]

Day-trippers such as these had no impact on the local economy: they arrived, stayed a few hours on the island and then departed. (As such, they had much in common with their twentieth-century equivalents, as we shall see later.) The resident holidaymakers, in contrast, certainly did influence the economic life of the district. From an early stage, individuals took advantage of the commercial possibilities of coastal tourism. In the 1810s, one Mr Hamar, a coal merchant from Pontypool, a coalfield community nearly 25 miles away, leased the island's farmhouse specifically with the intention of turning it into a guesthouse. With its eighteen rooms, a coach-house and stabling for sixteen horses, it was an impressive addition to the island's resort facilities.[97]

Meanwhile, residents of the Barry district were able to benefit from the tourists' interest in Whitmore Bay. Many sub-let rooms to visitors during the summer months. Property owners sometimes let out entire houses. A number of Cadoxton's farmers were certainly providing accommodation for visitors throughout the early and mid-Victorian periods.[98] In the 1840s, local and regional newspapers carried advertisements that gave details of houses for let during the bathing season. In 1840, for example, the *Bristol Mercury* informed its readers that there was a 'Neat Cottage' in Cadoxton, with splendid views across the Bristol Channel. It was available for summer hire for a 'small respectable Family'. The healthiness of the district was always underscored in such announcements. The *Mercury*'s readers were reassured that Cadoxton's air was so pure that the village's inhabitants routinely lived to a very great age: 'there is one now living bordering on a Hundred Years of Age, with several above Eighty'.[99]

The effect of the tourism multiplier was felt beyond the ranks of the property owners. Local innkeepers, for instance, benefited from the tourists' presence. One, the proprietor of the Wenvoe Arms, was advertising his establishment to sea-bathers and other visitors in the early 1860s.[100] Doubtless, the owners of the other two inns – the William IV and the Three Bells – saw their takings rise when the bathers were in residence. The village's handful of shopkeepers, too, must have profited from the increase in trade that accompanied the arrival of the visitors every summer season. David and Mary Jenkins, the village's carriers at the century's mid-point, would certainly have boosted their income by ferrying visitors to and from the island.[101] Meanwhile, the local vicar and the two chapel ministers (one Baptist, the other a Methodist), stood to reap a different reward – increased congregations – during the bathing months. The general point needs to be emphasized: Cadoxton was a settlement of just sixty or so households. Its inhabitants were bound to notice, and often profit from, the tourists. And whilst tourism did not lead to any obvious development, one effect may well have been to help maintain the population of the district. As was the case in other little bathing villages we have had reason to notice, Cadoxton did not lose inhabitants during the course of the century. On the contrary, its population rose gently: from 240 in the early 1840s to 300 in 1881.

CONCLUSION

In this chapter, we have seen how Whitmore Bay drew a steady stream of visitors to it from the late eighteenth century. Some were day-trippers. Before the early 1820s, they journeyed to Barry by road. Thereafter, many of them were deposited on the island by steam packets. They stayed for a few hours then headed home. Importantly, there was another set of tourists to be found at Barry: the resident holidaymakers who stayed in the district for weeks at a time during each bathing season. By the 1810s, some stayed on the island itself, taking rooms at Mr Hamar's guesthouse. Others lodged in Cadoxton village and Barry hamlet.

From an early date, tourism was an element of the district's economy. Nevertheless, the arrival of the tourists did not produce any sweeping changes in the Barry district. Their numbers were small, although they were significant enough given the tiny populations of Cadoxton and Barry. Perhaps because they consciously eschewed the commercialized seaside experience on offer at the fashionable resorts, they generated little in the way of demand for specialized amenities. Potential investors had no incentive to develop the tourist infrastructure of these little places. There was none of the large-scale investment in resort technology that was evident at the bigger, more popular, resorts: no pleasure piers, no promenades, no assembly rooms or coffee houses. There was no urban development of any kind, in fact. And the impact of this type of tourism on the natural environment of Whitmore Bay was negligible. For decades, the island's 'natural capital' was entirely unaffected by the visitors' presence.

Far from being anomalies, Barry and Cadoxton were quite typical in this respect. A plethora of bathing villages and small towns around the coast of Wales were able to accommodate goodly numbers of visitors without experiencing any great disruption. In part, this was because there were not enough visitors to stimulate activity on the supply side. At more obviously popular settlements, such as Aberystwyth and Tenby, entrepreneurs rushed to invest in the expensive house-building schemes or 'improvement' projects. Not so at little Barry and Cadoxton. But there was another reason why such investment did not occur: many of these smaller 'resorts' were simply too tiny and too isolated. As the *Monmouth-shire Merlin* put it in July 1836, 'The Welsh shores are now assuming a very animated appearance; every dwelling and cottage contiguous to the sea being in requisition for the numerous parties in search of health and pure air.'[102] The *Merlin* was making the point that even the tiniest hamlet, with just a handful of cottages, could, if they were within walking distance of a bathing beach, play host to small parties of tourists. The fact that many of these villages, Barry and Cadoxton included, were often two or three hours' ride from the nearest market town, worked to keep the numbers of visitors at sustainable levels.

Commentators agreed that the majority of coastal tourists headed for the 'proper' seaside towns. These were the highly developed settlements with their enticing array of artificial amusements and urban comforts. Yet there was another group of tourists: visitors who purposely sought out the smaller bathing villages, cherishing them because of the opportunity they offered for escape from the bustling holiday crowds of the bigger resorts. What the Welsh coast lacked in bigger seaside towns it more than made up for in its surfeit of quiet bathing spots. Few could match Barry Island when it came to peace and solitude. It was a little island, just off the coast of an undeveloped rural district. It was isolated enough to keep visitor numbers down, but not so isolated as to make it completely inaccessible.

In the early decades of the nineteenth century, only the more genteel visitors – including peers of the realm – made it over to Whitmore Bay. Only they had the time and the means to enjoy such seaside sojourns. But improvements in the transport system meant that members of the lower middle and upper working classes were increasingly able to enjoy a day trip to Barry Island. The new railways that connected the industrial valleys with Cardiff, and the pleasure steamers that paddled their way out of Cardiff and up and down the Bristol Channel, brought Whitmore Bay closer than it had ever been to many centres of population in south Wales. The presence of two Cardiff mayors at Cadoxton in the 1860s was especially noteworthy. It spoke of the fact that Cardiff was growing apace, and elite Cardiffians were starting to look around for a marine suburb. As we shall see in the next chapter, Barry Island was, for long, the obvious candidate to become such a place.

CHAPTER TWO

THAT 'FAVOURITE PLACE'

CARDIFF'S BATHING RESORT, c.1860–1877

ON A SATURDAY MORNING in July 1876, Cardiff baked under a cloudless sky. A small group of male friends, finding the roasting temperatures too much to bear, decided to take their leave of the broiling town. A perusal of the local newspaper advertisements confirmed that a steamer was scheduled to start for Barry Island at 3 o'clock. Buoyed by the thought of a cooling cruise down the Bristol Channel to see Whitmore Bay for the first time, the companions caught a cab and 'were driven lazily to the tune of six miles an hour down to the pier-head'. Once there, they joined 300 other excursionists on board the steamer *Marie Joseph*.

The voyage itself did not have quite the recuperative effect that they had hoped. They were perched 'uncomfortably' on the steamer's paddle-box and there was not the slightest hint of a refreshing sea breeze. It was as if they were steaming through 'an ocean of fire'. Nevertheless, most of their fellow passengers appeared to be enjoying themselves: 'Matronly ladies and eligible misses read novels under the awning which covered the after-deck; the crowd on the foredeck – typical working-men, in some cases with their wives or sweethearts – took to drinking beer and porter, or beverages of the teetotal class.' And at least there was the consolation of the ever-changing scenery: the red cliffs of Lavernock Point, the islet at Sully and the numerous 'little bays and pretty homesteads nestling snugly in the coves along the shore'. After some forty-five minutes, Barry Island finally heaved into sight.

The *Marie Joseph* approached a jetty at Friars Point but, because of the low state of the tide, was unable to tie up. Some of the passengers disembarked via a makeshift plank bridge that had been extended across to the little pier; others were ferried over to the beach in small boats. At first sight, on such a sweltering day, the island looked 'uninviting' and 'barren': there was 'scarcely a tree or a shrub to be seen higher than a hawthorn hedge, and the grass look[ed] parched and brown'. But the party's spirits rose when it was realized that there was a hotel, in a 'large and well-built house', at Friars Point. In a spacious smoke-room, 'well-furnished with tables and chairs' and packed with a 'thirsty throng', the visitors imbibed 'a copious draught of the most refreshing beverage which the house could supply'. Constitutions revived, they headed for the rocks at Nell's Point where, because 'society has not imposed the same restraints upon us as upon the gentler sex', they stripped-off and 'plunge[d] exuberantly into the "limpid blue" water'. Then, as the sun set, the group retired to Friars Point to 'contemplate the peaceful beauty of the scene'. A much pleasanter return journey in the twilight, with 'a cool vapour hanging over the water', brought this happy excursion to an end.[1]

The account of this day trip, published in the *Western Mail*, is one of the fullest we have of the island and its visitors in the 1870s. It reveals much that is interesting. For instance, we learn just how easy it was to get to Whitmore Bay from Cardiff at this time. The trippers decided, on a whim, to go to Barry Island because of the hot weather; the pleasure-steamer service made it a simple matter to get there. The *Mail*'s report tells us something about the island's visitors. Some were clearly well-to-do and all were respectable, but there was a degree of social mixing going on here. Working-class men and women were on board the *Marie Joseph* alongside 'matronly ladies' and 'eligible misses'. Meanwhile, we catch a glimpse of the spatial organization of the beach: Nell's Point, it seems, was reserved for bathing (and, therefore, naked) men. And we are reminded why, for decades, visitors had been lured onto the island: 'for those who delight in pure air, in a fine sea view, and in a ramble along the rocky shore, few places are better than Barry on a summer evening'. Finally, we learn about recent efforts to develop the island's resort amenities: the jetty had been constructed at a cost of £1,600 just a couple of years earlier by the island's owner, J. D. Treharne.[2] Treharne had spent a similar amount turning the rather ramshackle residence of a former owner, Francis Crawshay, into a well-appointed hotel.[3] Newspaper advertisements explained that the hotel was open 'for excursionists and parties', that Whitmore Bay had 'every facility for a good bathing place', that there was a croquet ground, a skittle alley, swings and other amusements in the grounds of the hotel and, importantly, that 'The whole of the Island is Free to Visitors'. It was, proclaimed the notices, 'One of the finest Bathing Places in Wales'.[4] This was an island that was clearly in the process of being developed as a tourist resort.

It was a point well understood by the visitor who penned his account in July 1876: Treharne was making 'a praiseworthy effort to open it up as a seaside resort for the "toiling masses" of Cardiff'. This was obviously still a work-in-progress, but the author was confident that Barry Island was destined for success. 'I shall be surprised', he declared, 'if, when Mr. Treharne has matured the scheme he is now carrying out, it does not become one of the pleasantest and most attractive suburban resorts of Cardiff'.[5] Many others agreed with him, for, in the mid-1870s, it was widely thought that a select suburb would rise up on the sand dunes and the headlands and that the wealthiest Cardiffians – the merchants, the industrialists and the professionals – would soon be living there. The *Cardiff Times*, for one, could not wait for such a development. The newspaper was sure that Barry Island's elevation into a residential suburb would be the making of Cardiff. The coal owners and shipping magnates would be encouraged to settle at Barry instead of scuttling away to their villas in Clifton, Cheltenham and Bath. As a result, they would begin spending their considerable incomes locally. Cardiff would quickly become a cultural capital par excellence: its 'splendour . . . would outrival that of ancient Venice and Pisa, Genoa and Leghorn'. A 'constant stream of fashion' would pass between Barry Island and Cardiff, all because 'the sands of Barry Island [had been turned] into a watering place'.[6]

THE 'ISLAND OF THE FUTURE': DEVELOPMENT SCHEMES IN THE 1860S AND 1870S

In the mid-Victorian period, many south Walians were bewitched by the idea of what Whitmore Bay might soon become, if only it were connected to the railway network. As a report in the *Western Mail* put it in 1877, it was 'hard to conceive a pleasanter suburban residence than, in the railway times, will be found here'. It was the 'island of the future' and was bound to become a select marine suburb: 'nothing now remains but for enterprising men to develop the great natural resources and beauties of the island'.[7]

In fact, some 'enterprising men' had already tried. In the later 1860s and early 1870s, local landowner Captain Jenner from Wenvoe sought to build a coal port at Barry Sound, run a railway into the district and develop an estate of superior villas at Whitmore Bay. After purchasing the island from Francis Crawshay, Jenner assembled a team of investors, engineers and architects to help him realize his grand vision. One of his key supporters was J. P. Seddon, a highly respected London architect and friend of several pre-Raphaelite artists. Seddon had an illustrious reputation, having recently worked on a renovation project at Llandaff Cathedral. He was also involved in the design of the new university buildings at Aberystwyth. Of especial relevance to Jenner was the fact that Seddon had a niche interest in the seaside. He had already done work at Southerndown in Glamorganshire, for instance, and he went on, in the early 1880s, to design an innovative bungalow development at Birchington-on-Sea in Kent.[8] The involvement of a figure of Seddon's pedigree underscores just how determined Jenner was to turn Barry Island into a modern, fashionable seaside suburb.[9]

No one could doubt Jenner's commitment to the cause, but his scheme failed in the early 1870s because of his inability to raise the necessary capital. Constructing a railway and a dock was a hugely expensive business and any such project required substantial backers. In Jenner's case, his inability to convince leading figures in the south Wales coal trade to support the initiative proved to be his undoing. Despite growing concerns about the lack of dock capacity in the region, many coal owners and coal merchants still pinned their hopes on Lord Bute making the necessary investment in his dock at Cardiff. Why pay for a new port at Barry if Bute was willing to spend his own money? However, even as Jenner's scheme was failing, it became clear to many that a new dock might yet be the only long-term answer. This is where J. D. Treharne stepped in.

Treharne, a 'remarkable entrepreneur', was a Cardiff chemist with interests in a Rhondda coalmine.[10] He purchased Barry Island at auction in July 1873 for £7,200.[11] Undaunted by Jenner's recent misfortunes at Barry, Treharne set about promoting his own dock and railway scheme. He, too, was keen to see Whitmore Bay become a select suburb and watering place. The island's transformation clearly mattered to him every bit as much as the building of a dock. Before he had signed the deeds to his new parcel of real estate, he announced a competition with a prize of £40 to be awarded to the architect who came forward with the best plans for a fully developed island.[12] The winning scheme included high-class villas (all situated in ample gardens and enjoying sea views), generous roads, a church, 'ten croquet lawns, a bowling green, archery butts, a lake, a music conservatory and a band stand'.[13] This salubrious suburb was to have been connected to Cardiff by a railway branch line. By the summer of 1877, Treharne secured a parliamentary act that authorized his new company, the Penarth, Sully and Barry Railway, to begin work.[14]

Notwithstanding his energy and his prodigious abilities as a businessman, Treharne also failed to turn his dream of an improved Barry Island into reality. In his case, it was a run of bad luck that scuppered the project: some of his key supporters were hit by a string of financial disasters – a flooded mine, a sudden depression in the iron and steel trade and the collapse of a Welsh bank were just some of the calamities that befell them. Within a few weeks of securing parliamentary approval for his railway, Treharne had no option but to abandon his scheme and put the island back on the market.[15]

It is easy, when contemplating Jenner's and Treharne's plans for the future of Barry Island, to dismiss them as the overblown products of two fevered imaginations. A Whitmore Bay of music conservatories, croquet lawns and archery butts seems so far removed from the 'Kingdom of the Chip' that it became in the twentieth century, that it can be difficult to see it as anything other than a dream. However, we need to remember just how close both ventures came to succeeding. Importantly, no one at the time dismissed Jenner and Treharne as madcap dreamers. On the contrary, it was widely assumed that it was only a matter of time before the island became a marine suburb. The railway surveyors employed by Jenner had confirmed the fact. They concluded that there was 'no engineering difficulty' posed by the building of a railway. Little wonder, then, that many contemporaries saw Whitmore Bay as a prime investment. As one commentator put it, once a railway was opened, it would immediately 'convert the greater part of the Island into building land of the most valuable character' because it was so 'admirably adapted for a first-class watering place'.[16] Given such optimism, news that workers had begun staking out Jenner's railway hardly seemed surprising. Barry Island, most were sure, was poised on the brink of an exciting future as a middle-class seaside suburb.[17] For our purposes, we need to see mid-Victorian Whitmore Bay through mid-Victorian eyes. If we do, we quickly realize that Whitmore Bay came within a whisker of becoming a thoroughly high-class resort.

It was the proposal to build a coal port at Barry that made both Jenner's and Treharne's schemes truly viable investment options. Only a busy dock could ever justify the huge expense of bringing a railway to Barry. Tourism and suburban development could never cover the immense costs on their own. Both Jenner and Treharne saw the promotion of a new dock as their primary concern. However, at least in the case of Treharne, tourism was also a fundamental part of his vision for the island. It is easy to miss this point. Prothero gives the impression, for instance, that the Cardiff chemist's decision to invest in the Marine Hotel and the little jetty was somehow dependent upon his bigger plans for a dock and a railway. 'Having decided to promote another railway to Barry Island, Treharne went on to develop the place', Prothero notes.[18] Here, a different interpretation is offered: namely, that there was no such causal link between the railway scheme and the hotel – the latter did not depend upon the former. The opening of the hotel and the building of the landing pier were not motivated by hopes of what might happen in the future; instead, they were a response to an existing demand for tourist amenities. As we saw in the previous chapter, Barry Island had long been flourishing as a resort of sea-bathers. For decades, residential holidaymakers had been sojourning in the little bathing villages of the Barry district. Moreover, as we shall discover in what follows, it was also attracting increasing numbers of trippers. By opening a hotel with a licensed bar, Treharne was simply reacting to these facts.

We can be sure of this because of the speed with which he moved to get the hotel ready for business. He placed the winning bid for the island in July 1873, but he had to wait until the indenture of sale was signed before he could take possession of it. The paperwork was not completed until April 1874. Yet the hotel was open by the end of July 1874.[19] In other words, in just a couple of months, Treharne had ripped out the flotsam and jetsam that decorated the interior of Francis Crawshay's former holiday home, made the necessary alterations for it to be able to receive visitors, and found staff to run it as a hotel. This was long before he launched his railway scheme in 1876. Such a quick turnaround strongly suggests that the hotel was not opened primarily to stimulate tourism to the island (although it doubtless had that happy effect); it was to cater for the tourists who were already there. Within a year, further improvements were made – including the skittle alley, the croquet ground and the swings – and he had applied for permission to build the landing pier to accommodate the various pleasure steamers that were regularly heading out to the island.[20] None of these (relatively modest) developments need explaining by reference to the (much more ambitious) project to open a dock, build a marine suburb and run a railway into Barry. They were all about meeting the needs of the tourists who had been milling around Whitmore Bay every spring and summer for years. The rest of this chapter seeks to underscore the extent of Whitmore Bay's popularity with tourists in the 1860s and 1870s.

THE 'MOST CHARMING AND PICTURESQUE SPOT': BARRY ISLAND AS A TRIPPER RESORT IN THE 1860S AND 1870S

The island was more popular with tourists in the 1860s and 1870s than it had ever been. Cadoxton was still fulfilling its decades-long role as a bathing village, accommodating those well-to-do holidaymakers who were able to stay for weeks and even months at a time during the summer season. It will be recalled that, in the mid-1860s, a former mayor of Cardiff, William Alexander, and the current mayor, W. B. Watkins, both expressed their fondness for holidaying in the district. As Alexander explained it, he was 'well accustomed' with the Barry area, having returned there a number of times with his family for lengthy seaside sojourns.[21] However, it was not just resident visitors who were to be found on the island during these years. Whitmore Bay was attracting ever larger numbers of day-trippers, too. When, in September 1870, the *Cardiff and Merthyr Guardian* included a report on Barry Island, the journalist decided that no detailed description of Whitmore Bay was needed. He explained that it was already 'so well known' to readers, thanks to the steamboat services that had been calling there with increased frequency over recent years.[22] The *Cardiff Times*, in 1871, remarked that Whitmore Bay had become a veritable trippers' resort, a 'favourite place' for Cardiff's inhabitants to enjoy their seaside picnics.[23] And it was enough of an attraction to merit inclusion in a *Tourist's Guide to Cardiff and its Neighbourhood*, published in 1870.[24]

We should not be surprised that the island was attracting more visitors at this time, given the growth of south Wales's population. Barry might have been undisturbed in the long decades before the 1880s, but plenty of other districts had been changed beyond recognition. Industrialization and urbanization sucked huge numbers into the coalfield and places such as Cardiff. It meant that there were many more people living within reach of Barry by the mid-Victorian period than there had been in the Georgian era. The development of the 'hills districts' of Glamorganshire and Monmouthshire began in the later eighteenth century with the spectacular rise of the iron industry. It continued throughout the nineteenth century. By the mid-Victorian years, the coal trade began expanding rapidly, too. Between them, iron and coal sparked a demographic explosion. The populations of the two counties most affected by industrialization grew enormously. Glamorganshire's population stood at roughly 70,000 at 1800; Monmouthshire's was about 45,000. By 1851, the figures were, respectively, 230,000 and 160,000. By the late 1860s, an estimated 500,000 inhabitants were to be found in the two counties.[25]

All were, in theory, potential visitors to Barry Island. This, after all, was the age of the railway excursion. Maps of south Wales began to register a new topographical feature from the early 1840s as ribbons of iron started appearing, snaking their way down from the heads of the mining valleys to the ports on the Bristol Channel coast. The first was the line connecting Merthyr – Wales's largest settlement – to Cardiff. It was opened in April 1841, the first train taking just 1 hour and 38 minutes to travel the twenty or so miles from the iron town to the seaport.[26] Others followed, with the 1850s seeing a significant expansion of the network.[27]

The cheap excursion trains proved a hit with the coalfield population.[28] As early as 1844, for instance, the *Monmouthshire Merlin* was pleased to see that the construction of the Taff Vale Railway had already expanded 'the recreations of the labouring portion' of Merthyr and Cardiff.[29] In the 1850s and 1860s, journalists wrote of the 'excursion mania' that had gripped the inhabitants of industrial south Wales. In 1861, the

Merthyr Telegraph revealed that 'thousands' of Merthyrians had 'bene-fited by the advantages of these excursions', exploring rural and coastal destinations in counties as far away as Carmarthenshire and Pembroke-shire.[30] Companies such as the Taff Vale Railway, the South Wales Rail-way and the Vale of Neath Railway led the way in promoting cheap day trips.[31] An 'excursion fever' had 'taken possession of this district', wrote an inhabitant of Carmarthen in 1869: the 'hoardings and blank walls of the town are literally covered with the announcements of the rival railway companies. The question now seems to be, not "where shall we go?" but "where shall we not go?"'[32]

The siren calls of the seaside were soon drawing visitors from the coalfield. In the days before the institution of bank holidays, Whit-suntide was a favourite time to take day trips out of the valleys. Many made a beeline for the nearest port as a way of gaining access to the pleasure steamers that were churning their way up, down and across the Bristol Channel. On Whit Monday, 1868, the first train into Cardiff on the Taff Vale line 'was of unusual length', containing 'a very large number of pleasure-seekers from the hills'. Many of them headed for the pierhead and climbed aboard the waiting steam tugs and pack-ets; 'hundreds' of colliers and their families went to Penarth by such means on that high day.[33] The following year, some 2,000 trippers from the mining valleys arrived in Cardiff on early morning trains on the Whit Monday. Steamers took them onto various destinations including Bristol, Glastonbury, Weston, Clevedon, Portishead, Flat Holme, Steep Holme and Ilfracombe.[34] Thus, even without a railway into the Barry district, the steam packets opened the island up to large numbers of day-trippers. Excursionists from seaside towns on the English side of the Channel were able to get to the island quite easily, albeit at a price that probably put it beyond the means of many: a return ticket from Bristol to Barry Island cost 2s. 6d in 1870, for example.[35] Meanwhile, for inhabitants of the south Wales coalfield who lived close to a rail-way station, a day trip to the island was now a possibility. The first organized trip from Merthyr was probably that of the 350 ironworkers who, in August 1845, travelled by rail to Cardiff and then onto the island by pleasure steamer.[36]

Nevertheless, in the mid-Victorian years, a trip to Barry Island from the valleys was not the easiest of options. Railway timetables had to synchronize with steamboat timetables that were themselves constantly being updated to take account of the ever-changing tides.[37] Precious leisure hours might be wasted if a connection was missed. When, for instance, working-class trippers from Caerleon tried to get to Whitmore

Bay in July 1876, they arrived at Newport at 8.00 a.m. only to find their steam packet had a mechanical fault. They had to wait four hours for a replacement vessel, by which time the tide was too low to use Treharne's jetty and they were forced to endure 'the very tedious business' of being ferried to the beach in small boats.[38] Little wonder, then, that trippers from Aberdare and Merthyr were more likely to be found enjoying the coastal delights of Swansea and the Gower – just a single train journey away – than they were to be seen at Barry.[39]

The days when trippers from the mining valleys would predominate at the island were yet to come. For the moment, the majority of Barry Island's visitors seem to have come from Cardiff and its environs. Demand for trips to the island from Cardiff increased markedly during the 1860s and 1870s, in line with the town's growing population. Powered by its role as a coal-exporting port, Cardiff grew rapidly. Its population nearly quadrupled between 1841 and 1861 (from 11,100 to 41,100). By 1871, it stood at nearly 57,000, making it Wales's largest urban settlement.[40] Cardiff's inhabitants were just as tempted by a cheap excursion as their counterparts in the valleys. Caerphilly Castle, the Garth Mountain at nearby Taff's Well and Bute's picturesque Castell Coch were favourite destinations, all three regularly being 'thickly covered with visitors' from Cardiff during the excursion season.[41] The seaside appealed to Cardiffians too.

The paucity of seaside resorts near Cardiff became a matter of public comment in the 1860s. To the east of the town, there were no bathing beaches to talk of, just thick estuarine mud. 'Rough miners' from Merthyr would come out of the water 'dirtier and blacker even than they went in', quipped one wag.[42] There were more promising options to the west. Bathers from Cardiff were certainly heading for Penarth by the early 1860s, some using the bathing machines that had been rolled onto the beach by 1864.[43] But Penarth's beach was pebble-strewn and sometimes inundated with foul-smelling mud.[44] The opening of a coal-port just around the corner in the mid-1860s dented its appeal further. There were too many sailors 'and others', one well-to-do Cardiffian grumbled. The general feeling was that 'Cardiff people bathed at Penarth because they had no other place'.[45] Barry, in contrast, stood out as a desirable seaside venue. It was 'the most charming and picturesque spot' and had the advantage, for bathers, of a large beach of clean, firm sand. It was the best bathing beach this side of Tenby, declared one of its more enthusiastic supporters in 1866.[46]

Just as important, it was a relatively easy matter for Cardiff's burgeoning population to get to the island. The roads between Barry and

Cardiff were of a poor standard: winding, narrow and obstructed by numerous overhanging branches, they were dismissed as 'bad' by one contemporary.[47] Yet they were good enough for the journey to be made in a horse-drawn vehicle in about two hours. It meant that it was perfectly possible for trippers to get to Whitmore Bay from Cardiff by road and spend a full day on the sands. A substantial number chose this means of transport over the pleasure steamers, some because it gave them more control over when they made the trip (they did not have to worry about the tide times), some on the grounds of cost.

All manner of works parties, Sunday schools, friendly societies and the like trundled out of Cardiff and headed for the island during these years. When, in July 1868, twenty-six well-to-do members of the Cardiff Naturalists' Society spent a day there, the fact that they went in brakes allowed them to stop off to collect butterflies, moths and flowers along the way. They stayed at Whitmore Bay until dusk.[48] In August 1873, twenty employees from a Cardiff engine works were treated to a day on the island to celebrate the wedding of their employer. They travelled 'to the place of festivity' in a horse-drawn brake.[49] In August 1877, horse-drawn saloons took Cardiff shop workers to Whitmore Bay. The party left at 10.00 a.m. and returned to the town at a late hour.[50] Meanwhile, members of Ararat (Baptist) and Beulah (Independent) choirs set out in brakes to the island from Whitchurch, a village just to the north of Cardiff, in August 1878. By lunchtime they were on the beach, playing rustic sports and singing madrigals, glees and other songs.[51] By 1877, Cardiffians' demand for day trips to Whitmore Bay was strong enough to lead to the inauguration of a new brake service. A shuttle service operated between the Fair Oak Hotel on Castle Street and the island on Wednesday and Saturday afternoons during the spring and summer months. Included in the fare was the price of a ferry across Barry Sound if the tide was in.[52]

However, for all the obvious popularity of the road trip to Whitmore Bay, many more Cardiffians were conveyed there by steamer. The larger vessels could each carry between 200 and 300 passengers.[53] Advertisements for 'marine excursions' to the island proliferated in the early 1870s.[54] The steamers were cheap enough to be accessible to the 'masses', tickets being offered from as little as 2s.[55] Sailing times were determined by the tides. Some services left Cardiff as early as 6.30 a.m.[56] Others departed in the mid-afternoon whilst some left in the early evening for those 'bent upon spending two or three hours enjoyment after the fatigues of the week's labour'.[57] Steamers were often seen returning from the island after dusk.

MID-VICTORIAN BARRY ISLAND AS A LEISURE SPACE

We have no detailed descriptions of what Whitmore Bay's Georgian and early Victorian visitors did during their time on the sands. We can surmise that many of them were there for the good of their health and would, therefore, have bathed at least once a day. Those of a Romantic disposition would doubtless have enjoyed the picturesque seascapes, too. But there were no 'artificial amusements' at Barry Island in those days, no assembly rooms, coffee taverns or theatres to head for after a morning's immersion in the chilly Bristol Channel. There was just the farmhouse-cum-bathing house for those staying on the island.

Little had changed in this respect until the appearance of Treharne's Marine Hotel in 1874. There had been the occasional one-off entertaining 'event'. Francis Crawshay, owner of the island in the 1860s, had a number of schooners built and launched from Whitmore Bay. These were interesting spectacles that caught the attention of the press and of locals. Crawshay made sure that villagers who had come out to watch were given refreshments after the bottles of sparkling sherry had been dashed against the bows of the ships.[58] Nevertheless, as exciting as these launches were, they were too rare to be considered part of Barry's beach culture.

Against this rather spartan context, the arrival of Treharne's hotel at Friars Point represented a major addition to the island's tourist facilities. It boasted a large dining room capable of holding more than 100 patrons, a coffee room, bar, bar-parlour, tap, bar-tap, two kitchens and nine bedrooms. In addition to providing accommodation for staying holidaymakers it also offered trippers a selection of wines, spirits and beers 'of the finest brands', as well as dinners and teas, all 'at the shortest notice'.[59] Its croquet lawn, swings and skittle alleys, whilst modest features in themselves, were the island's first amusements. As one visitor observed, the Marine Hotel formed the 'nucleus of a watering place', albeit there was still very 'little in the shape of artificial enjoyment' at the island.[60] It was a fair point. When compared to other watering places, Barry Island was still the most rudimentary of 'resorts'. It remained a simple bathing place, little changed since the first Georgian bathers made their way onto the sands eighty or ninety years before. Yet, therein lay much of its appeal. Whitmore Bay had all that its visitors in the 1860s and 1870s desired: a fine beach on a romantically 'isolated' little island, excellent bathing opportunities and charming scenery.

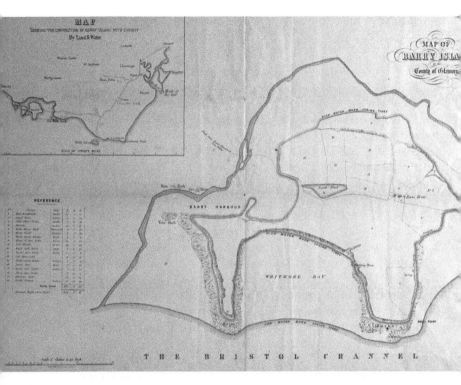

Illus. 9. *Map of Barry Island, 1873. The island as it was in the early 1870s with its farmhouse and leech pool. Tourists had been using both since the 1810s. At some point, a bathing house had been built where the cliffs of Nell's Point met the sand dunes.*

These basic elements provided trippers with a leisure space that they could mould to their own purposes. For some visitors, Barry Island offered an opportunity to engage in uplifting and ennobling 'rational' recreations. Whether it was the amateur geologists who examined the cliff faces and attended lectures delivered on the sand dunes by knowledgeable companions (as happened during a trip of the Cardiff Naturalists' Society in 1868), or the amateur botanists who collected specimens of the island's particularly rich flora, Whitmore Bay was a treasure house of natural delights – a place to be studied and explored.[61] Others collected specimens of a different sort. During the winter months, Treharne allowed shooting parties to pay for the privilege of taking pot-shots at the island's population of wild rabbits.[62]

For yet more visitors, the health benefits of a sojourn at the seaside were still an important motivation. The bathing experience on offer at Whitmore Bay was, all contemporaries agreed, second-to-none. By the mid-1870s, bathing machines were in place on the sands. They joined a bathing house that had been built into the rocks on the eastern side of the beach. Quite when the house appeared is unclear, but its presence on an 1873 map allows us to date it to sometime before Treharne's purchase of the island.[63] And there was the sea air, of course. From the 1860s, the idea gained currency that the atmospheres of coastal resorts were especially blessed with ozone, a rather mysterious gas that was widely assumed to have invigorating properties.[64]

For those visitors who needed reassurance that a trip to the seaside would be a worthwhile use of their leisure time, Barry Island was the perfect choice. Until 1874, devoid of all artificial amusements, it was a reassuringly wholesome place to be. After 1874, as long as one could be trusted to stay out of the hotel's bar, it was still a place remarkably free from the temptations of town life. But, notwithstanding the emphasis on its ability to provide rational recreation, the newspaper accounts of visits in the 1860s and 1870s reveal that, above all else, the island was a place of fun, relaxation and easy sociability: a space where the formal conventions of town life might be loosened just a little. We have already noted that women, as well as men, were seen enjoying a holiday drink on the *Marie Joseph* as it steamed towards the island in July 1876. They did so without raising any complaints in the process. And, for every bather who took his or her daily dips for the health benefits that they would confer, there were probably many more who plunged in simply because it was enjoyable. Even some of the Cardiff's naturalists took a break from chasing butterflies simply for the fun of bathing 'in the cool, clear sea'.[65] Music, singing and dancing were all important elements of the excursions. Pleasure parties frequently brought bands (brass and string) with them on the pleasure steamers from Cardiff.[66] When the Roman Catholic Society of Cardiff went to Whitmore Bay by steamboat in August 1863, their very own Hibernian band went with them, playing during the voyage and again when on the beach.[67] In June 1877, a party of trippers, including workers from a Cardiff boiler-making company, took a brass band with them onto their steam-tug. After landing, a large number strolled around the island, about a dozen bathed, whilst 'others took to dancing on the green sward, in front of the hotel'.[68]

The playing of 'rustic sports' was another popular pastime: some trippers managed to play a full game of cricket on the sands in 1870.[69] Donkey rides were being offered in the summer of 1877.[70] Meanwhile, it is worth underlining how nearly all visitors honoured the practice of taking communal meals, whether they were informal picnics or more formal feasts. At the latter, the rituals of the post-prandial speeches and votes of thanks allowed participants to express their appreciation of each other. 'Respectable' workers praised their 'liberal' employers for kindly organizing the treat, and employers spoke warmly about how the seaside holiday was proof, if it were needed in this age of equipoise, that the agents of Capital and Labour could work together harmoniously.[71] Such exchanges underscored the social bonding that could be fostered by a successful day trip to the island.

CONCLUSION: WHITMORE BAY AT 1877

In 1877, Barry Island was a place of immense possibility. Few commentators demurred from the suggestion that it was soon to become a successful watering place. It had been quietly flourishing as a seaside playground for trippers from Cardiff and, with ever improving rail connections to coalfield communities, it looked destined to attract even larger crowds of excursionists with each passing year. Many were also convinced that it had a bright future as a residential suburb. The *Western Mail*, in January 1877, advanced the island's claims as a place where a 'hygeiopolis' – a 'new City of Health for South Wales' – might be built. Soon a model suburb would surely rise-up on the sand dunes and headlands of Whitmore Bay, the paper informed its readers, 'with some of the latest sanitary improvements, with open spaces, public buildings, avenues and gardens'.[72] Others agreed. With its charming scenery, extensive views and fine beach, the island was perfectly suited to become Cardiff's marine suburb: it was, as one contemporary put it, 'peculiarly adapted for the creation of a fashionable watering place'.[73]

Then there were Barry's claims as the site of a future dock. Viewed one way, the dock project looked ill-starred indeed. There had been a number of serious efforts: all had failed. Nevertheless, paradoxically, each failed attempt only served to emphasize just how suited Barry was to become a site for a major dock. The years of surveys and reports proved beyond doubt that a railway could be run into the district with relative ease (if only the capital could be raised). Furthermore, everyone agreed that Barry Sound was a perfect natural harbour that allowed ships much easier access at low tide than the docks at Penarth, Cardiff or Newport. And the need for a new dock was becoming impossible to ignore. New collieries were opening every year, output was forecast to rise by 4 million tons per annum, and the existing ports were already unable to cope with the huge quantities of coal that were being brought down from the valleys. As one contemporary put it in October 1877, 'there cannot be a doubt but that the estuary between Barry Island and the mainland must in a short time be formed into docks'.[74]

Importantly, it was possible to argue that Whitmore Bay would become a high-class resort and that Barry Sound would be transformed into a booming coal port. Both options, it was averred, could happen at once. In 1877, the notion that Barry Island was destined to be a working-class day-tripper resort – a 'Kingdom of the Chip' – was far from obvious. Most commentators in the know were certain that its future lay as a bourgeois seaside playground.

CHAPTER THREE

VISITORS 'MERCILESSLY' TURNED AWAY

THE ISLAND CLOSED, 1878–1884

IN 1877, BARRY ISLAND'S future as an elite watering place seemed assured. It was, most commentators agreed, set fair to become Cardiff's very own marine suburb. However, within just a few months, all bets were off. J. D. Treharne was quite suddenly forced to abandon his plans to develop Whitmore Bay after a run of bad luck obliged some of his backers to withdraw their support. Just as it looked as if his railway and dock scheme was about to come to fruition, Treharne had no choice but to put the island on the market.[1] It proved to be a turning point of momentous proportions. By the spring of 1878, the isle had been snapped up by the Windsor-Clives, a great landowning family with extensive estates in England and south Wales.

Many observers supposed, quite reasonably, that the Windsor estate would follow Treharne's example and seek to turn the island into a select seaside resort. This, after all, is what powerful landowners tended to do if they had coastal property. Indeed, the Windsor family had pursued just such a course of urban improvement at Penarth, only a few miles to the east of Barry. There, the indefatigable Baroness Windsor had taken an unimpressive little village and transformed it: first, by establishing a coal port and, secondly, by investing in its urban infrastructure. In so doing, she laid the foundations for Penarth's future success as a late Victorian select suburb. Her grandson, the young Lord Windsor, carried on where she left off. From the outset, Robert Windsor-Clive took a keen interest in the growing town, spending his own money on elevating schemes and encouraging other speculators to do the same. It seemed sensible, therefore, to assume that his lordship would look to upgrade Barry Island in the same manner. If the Windsor-Clives could improve sooty little Penarth with its stony beach, imagine what they could do with an unspoilt Whitmore Bay.

However, in a move that shocked contemporaries, the Windsor estate kept developers away from its latest acquisition and let Treharne's plans fall into abeyance. Even more startlingly, Windsor closed the island to all visitors. It is a moment in Barry Island's history that has gone entirely unnoticed by historians. After nearly a century of its functioning as a bathing resort, Whitmore Bay was no longer open to tourists. The certainties of 1877 had dissolved in little more than a year. By the spring of 1879, nothing was certain about Barry Island's future any longer: it had gone from being a place bursting with potential as a seaside resort to one with apparently no chance of becoming a tourist attraction at all. An unsettling peace descended upon Whitmore Bay, a peace that was only occasionally broken by the cracks of the guns discharged by Windsor and his friends when they turned up to indulge their passion for hunting. When the shooting parties had departed, the rabbits and the birds had the island to themselves.

This chapter returns us to this forgotten episode in Barry Island's history. The extraordinary events of the late 1870s and early and mid-1880s underline the great power that landowners could wield. Victorian landlords often acted in high-handed ways. Indeed, in Wales, where the 'land question' was a particularly sensitive issue, such figures, it was averred by many liberals, were two a penny. However, even by the standards of the day, Lord Windsor's readiness to close a popular beach marked him out as highly unusual. All but a few British aristocrats were able to resist the temptation to follow such a provocative course. Beaches, by common consent, were generally kept open to the public. Yet at Barry Island, Robert Windsor-Clive decided to ignore this widely accepted convention and struck out on his own. The effects of the shutdown were to be long lasting, both at Whitmore Bay and, as we shall see, at Penarth. Barry was knocked-out of the running to become Cardiff's marine suburb, leaving the way clear for Penarth to prosper.

SHUTDOWN: THE ENDING OF TOURISM AND THE DELIBERATE NON-DEVELOPMENT OF BARRY ISLAND

There is no mystery surrounding the Windsor estate's decision to purchase Barry Island. As historians have long been aware, it was a transaction driven by the desire to protect the family's interests in Penarth dock. Building that dock had been a costly venture and, at ten years in the making, it had been a tediously drawn-out affair.[2] Much to the chagrin of the Windsor estate, just after the dock opened, in 1865, it transpired that rival parties were actively exploring the possibility of constructing a coal port at Barry Sound.[3] Captain Jenner, Barry Island's owner, was eagerly searching for backers for a dock and railway scheme. He made enough headway to trouble the Windsor estate. The Windsor-Clives found the very idea of dock promoters sniffing around Barry to be deeply unsettling, for, as everyone recognized, Barry was superbly positioned to flourish as a port. Navigating around Penarth's headland was no easy matter, and at low tides ships were required to wait out in the Channel. The approaches to Barry Sound were much easier to negotiate and, crucially, the most heavily laden vessels would be able to pass in and out of a dock there at all but the very lowest of tides.[4] As one newspaper remarked in 1866, just months after the opening of Penarth dock, the

Windsor estate was 'jealous of a competition which might hereafter arise against their dock, on the part of the proposed harbour at Barry'.[5]

Thus, it was fortunate for Baroness Windsor that Jenner's scheme came to naught. However, less than a decade later, the redoubtable Treharne had taken ownership of the island and was energetically promoting his own venture. Worryingly, his plans seemed destined for success, not least because his timing was flawless. The need for the sort of dock that Treharne was proposing was more pressing than ever. As the south Wales coal industry boomed, so the existing ports were demonstrably failing to cope with the huge amounts of coal that were being transported down from the mining valleys. The situation had reached crisis point, with commentators pointing out that the bottleneck at the ports of Glamorganshire and Monmouthshire was already slowing down the trade in black diamond. Empty ships were stuck for days at a time, waiting for their turn to tie up at the harbour side. As the *South Wales Daily News* remarked in December 1875, until the capacity of the region's ports was increased, 'it is a useless expenditure and a waste of capital to open fresh collieries, or to develop in any way the coal resources of the district'.[6]

Against this context, the Windsor estate was acutely aware of the danger that Barry might be developed at any moment. It took the keenest interest in all possible developments at Barry Sound. As Robert Forrest, Windsor's tireless agent, put it in private correspondence in November 1876, he was determined to take 'active measures . . . to try & put a stopper on any scheme for Docks at Barry'. A new port there, Forrest fretted, would be 'a poor look out for our interests at Penarth'.[7] Those 'active measures' included trying to acquire Barry Island, for if they owned it, the Windsor-Clives would be able to stop any rivals from opening their own dock there. Thus, the news that Treharne's great scheme had been derailed was music to the ears of Lord Windsor and Robert Forrest. Even more of a relief was Treharne's acceptance of the estate's offer of £12,500 for the island. The deal was completed in April 1878.[8] After years of uncertainty, the Windsor estate could finally breathe a sigh of relief: it was at last in a position to secure its interests in Penarth by controlling events at Barry.

With Lord Windsor installed as the island's new owner, all talk of the development of Barry Island instantly ended. It was no surprise that the aristocrat did not look to resurrect Treharne's, or anyone else's, dock scheme. Stopping such schemes was the whole point of his family's purchase of the isle. What was surprising was the estate's decision to close the island to all visitors. Unbeknownst to those holidaymakers who came to stay at Barry and Cadoxton in the summer of 1878, they were enjoying their last vacation at the little bathing villages. On the instructions of his lordship, Treharne's Marine Hotel was closed in the late spring of 1879 and journalists were informed that Whitmore Bay was no longer open to tourists. Commentators were suitably astonished. After describing how Windsor's agents were 'mercilessly turning away all visitors to Barry Island', the *Cardiff Times* explained to its readers that 'holiday-makers at this season had better look elsewhere for a place to rest at'.[9] The *South Wales Daily News* was dismayed. It adjudged Windsor's new policy to be particularly hard on Cardiff's inhabitants: 'it diminishes the already too few places of popular resort for holiday makers' from that town, it observed gloomily.[10] Other papers, too, bemoaned the loss of this 'favourite place for excursion parties'.[11]

It is difficult to gauge how complete the shutdown was. Robert Forrest suggested that it was an unqualified success. In a letter penned in 1881, he explained to the Board of Trade that the public no longer used the island 'for walking, bathing, boating, landing, fishing, gathering seaweed or any other purpose'.[12] By this estimation, Barry Island was now entirely deserted. Doubtless, some trespassers (they can no longer properly be called 'visitors' or 'tourists') must have made it over to the beach occasionally. Just a few weeks after the new policy was introduced, a group of Cardiff gas workers visited the island as part of a works outing. Whether they knowingly contravened the ban or travelled there with the estate's permission is uncertain.[13] But, allowing for the fact that there must have been interlopers who sometimes made it over to Whitmore Bay, it seems that the closure of Barry Island was more or less complete from the summer of 1879 through to the mid-1880s. A hundred years of tourism to Whitmore Bay had been brought to an abrupt end.[14]

The island was now peaceful enough for it to become a private hunting ground for Lord Windsor. We know that he went shooting there during the early 1880s for, a decade later, in 1893, he delivered a speech in which he reminisced about happy days spent hunting at his Barry seaside property. He recalled those delightful times when he had the island to himself, and he shared with his audience his memories of 'having walked the best part of a day over Barry Island and brought home, he thought, five brace of partridges and a certain number of rabbits'.[15] Windsor, then, was able to derive great enjoyment from his little isle. So were his close associates. In December 1883, his lordship invited some of his commercial partners over to the island for 'a day's sport' with a sackful of ferrets.[16] No longer a playground for the townsfolk of Cardiff, Whitmore Bay had been turned into a peer's personal fiefdom.

Windsor's decision to shut the island was unprecedented. Certainly, no other nineteenth-century owner had ever enacted such a draconian policy. On the contrary, from the 1850s, they had all gone out of their way to welcome visitors. Francis Crawshay had bought the island in 1856 so that he could enjoy it as a private seaside retreat and indulge his love of sailing. But it never occurred to him to deny others the pleasure of a day spent at Barry's beach. He became well known to excursionists as a beneficent host. For instance, when a party of trippers visited Whitmore Bay in August 1863, Crawshay was there on the sands to greet them. He rowed out to the steamer and ferried the women and children onto the beach, getting his feet wet in the process. One of the excursionists was moved to thank Crawshay publicly in a letter to the *Cardiff Times*. The owner's 'kindness and humility' would not be quickly forgotten, the correspondent explained. Three 'hearty rounds of cheers' had been given for him when the trippers got back onto their steamer, and a brass band struck up 'In a cottage by the sea' in honour of Crawshay's maritime residence on the island.[17] Captain Jenner, Crawshay's successor, was equally keen that Whitmore Bay be well visited. He wrote to the *Cardiff Times* in August 1867 to underline how safe the bathing conditions were and to let it be known that he did not 'at all object to the public visiting Barry Island'. His only request was that visitors leave their dogs and guns on the mainland.[18] After Jenner, there was Treharne, the owner who threw open the Marine Hotel and built the jetty to encourage the steamers to his island.

Lord Windsor was the only owner to close Barry Island to visitors. That he 'mercilessly' turned them away at the very moment when Whitmore Bay was attracting more tourists than ever before, merely made his attack on the public's customary rights of access all the more egregious.[19] Bemused contemporaries were left scratching their heads. They could understand why the aristocrat kept dock promoters and navvies away from his island. His refusal to allow sea-bathers onto his beach just seemed baffling.

MOTHBALLING BARRY ISLAND, DEVELOPING PENARTH

It goes without saying that the impact of the island's closure on tourism at Whitmore Bay was, for as long as the visitor ban lasted, catastrophic. But, at this time, interfering with the pleasure of tourists was not Windsor's primary intention. The sea-bathing visitors were collateral damage.

What he and Robert Forrest were really interested in doing was putting paid to any hope that Barry Island might be turned into Cardiff's marine suburb. We have observed that the Windsor estate's purchase of the isle was motivated by a desire to protect the family's commercial interests at Penarth. This has always been understood in terms of the safeguarding of the trade of Penarth dock. Yet the Windsor-Clives were not merely interested in the dock; they had a stake in the fledgling town's development as an urban centre, too.

The Windsor-Clive family was the main landowner at Penarth and, by the time it purchased Barry Island in 1878, it had already invested heavily in the urban infrastructure of the growing community. Indeed, it had ambitions to turn Penarth into a seaside settlement of high social tone, the first choice for Cardiff's bourgeoisie looking to escape the downsides of living in a boom town. Penarth had one obvious advantage: it was close to Cardiff, perched, as it was, on a headland that overlooked the growing seaport and its great docks. But, notwithstanding its proximity to Cardiff, in the 1870s, it was far from obvious that Penarth would become a fashionable residential centre. This point needs to be fully registered. Barry Island, as we saw in the previous chapter, was well established as the favoured candidate to become Cardiff's seaside suburb. Its natural charms, its picturesque qualities and its status as a romantic island put it far ahead of Penarth.

After all, Penarth was a decidedly uninviting settlement. Indeed, it was only just beginning to shake off its reputation as a breeding ground for fevers and cholera. As recently as 1861, the *Cardiff Times* had complained that Penarth 'bids fair to become one of the filthiest places in the county'. The drainage was 'in an abominable state, the filth in some places actually flows out into the open streets'.[20] Moreover, it was better known as a port that exported coal and iron than as a salubrious marine suburb in waiting. Visitors could miss altogether the fact that it had a beach. When compilers of trade directories arrived in the 1860s and 1870s they saw only a 'rising seaport', a place of industry; they invariably overlooked its beach altogether. They encountered nothing in the rest of the place to convince them that it had the potential to become a refined seaside suburb.[21]

Even its closeness to Cardiff was not necessarily the advantage that it might seem, for Penarth was still difficult to reach in the days before the railway arrived. By the mid-1860s, there was a tolerably good horse-drawn omnibus service from Cardiff to Penarth dock, but visitors to the beach and its environs had to face the 'horrors', as one visitor described them, of the onward journey. In 1865, a disgruntled tripper remarked that 'the waiting, the uncertainty, the disregard of timetables, the cross-ing of steamers, and the descent of frail steps, and then the landing from a rickety stage, and the ascent of the dock hill', made 'the approach to Penarth a task as difficult as the ascent of Mont Blanc to the Alpine traveller'.[22] Matters only improved appreciably when a rail link was extended from the dock to the town. That was not until 1878, the same year that Barry Island passed into the hands of the Windsor family.[23]

That Penarth was even in a position to be considered as marine suburb by the late 1870s was entirely due to the resolute determina-tion of the Windsor-Clives. In the 1860s, Baroness Windsor set about 'improving' the place, at no small cost. Widely seen as the 'patron-ess' of the dock project, her ladyship subsequently proved herself to be a skilled urban developer.[24] Before her death in 1869, she invested large sums in the enhancement of the urban landscape, committing an estimated £10,000 to the building of an impressive parish church – 'a handsome edifice of stone' – and £1,000 to a new national school.[25] And she improved the inadequate drainage and sewerage systems, whilst also laying out 'an excellent system of roads'. As one newspaper com-mented, she had 'done all that an enterprising and far-seeing landowner can do, for the improvement and development of the place'.[26]

If it took a baroness to turn Penarth hamlet into a viable and grow-ing urban community, it took a lord to gentrify it. Robert Windsor-Clive, Lord Windsor, threw himself behind an ambitious development pro-gramme that sought to transform Penarth into a fashionable marine sub-urb. He had already developed a personal fondness for the place. He fulfilled one of his first public engagements there when, aged just eight, he gave a short speech at the ceremony to mark the opening of Penarth dock.[27] More than once, as an adult, he recalled the day that he wit-nessed the dock gates being opened for the first time. He never made an effort to hide his 'great interest' in the town.[28] He was especially proud of the significant growth in prosperity that had occurred under his fam-ily's guidance.[29] Thus, when newspapers wrote, in the early twentieth century, of Lord Windsor's interest in Penarth as having been 'lifelong', they were not exaggerating.[30]

In 1878, Windsor unveiled an expensive scheme calculated to turn Penarth 'into the *beau ideal* of a lovely watering place', one that would compete with the most select resorts in south Wales. The plans included an impressive esplanade, parks, high-quality housing stock, a series of wide streets, a 'commodious' assembly room and reading rooms.[31] A pleasure garden was laid out by estate workers in the early 1880s, and brass bands were engaged to entertain residents and visitors on summer evenings. The *Western Mail* rushed to congratulate Windsor for providing the new resort with its 'greatest attraction'.[32] But his lordship was not content to rest there. In 1882, he paid for experiments to be conducted in the filtration of Penarth's silty seawater so that it could be pumped into a purpose-built complex of 'swimming sea-water baths'. The baths alone cost Windsor £3,000. At the same time, he threw another £10,000 into an extension of the promenade at the seafront.[33] No one could be in any doubt about Windsor's intentions. No longer content for Penarth to be merely a workaday coal port, he was determined to make it 'an attractive summer residence for the wealthier residents of Cardiff and the neighbourhood round'.[34]

This is precisely what happened. Penarth went from strength to strength, especially in the years after the railway arrived in 1878. Villa residences sprang up along the tree-lined boulevards laid out by the estate, and middle-class families relocated from Cardiff in their droves, lured there by its appealing built form and the various resort amenities that Windsor had secured for the town. The 1880s proved to be the pivotal moment in Penarth's journey from coal port to marine suburb. The population doubled from some 5,000 to roughly 10,000.[35] And its reputation as the 'popular seaside town of Cardiff' and 'a fine residential suburb' was secured.[36] The *South Wales Daily News* remarked in 1884 that there were 'few townships where the development has been so rapid, and the transition from a country village to a port, from which sail vessels to all parts of the world, so sudden as at Penarth'. And it lavished fulsome praise on Windsor for his role in its success. 'The noble owner of the estate on whose property these residences are built, and whose income is thereby considerably increased, expends annually thousands of pounds in carrying out improvements of a public character.' It was a telling observation: Windsor was both a cause of Penarth's rise and the chief beneficiary of it.[37]

Doubtless, his lordship would have pursued his urban development project at Penarth whether or not his family had purchased Barry Island. Given his eagerness to see it succeed, Penarth might well have become Cardiff-by-Sea regardless. But we can be certain that once the island was mothballed by the Windsor estate, it was almost inevitable that Penarth would become the favoured seaside retreat of Cardiff's elite. Its only rival – and a superior one at that – was no longer in the running. At a stroke, Penarth went from being second choice to the only choice. Little wonder, then, that Windsor was so keen to close the island in 1879. By doing so, he brought to an end all talk of any urban development at Barry Island. And he ended the search for the location of Cardiff's marine suburb. Whitmore Bay had lost out to Penarth.

Conclusion: landlord power

The late 1870s and early 1880s proved to be a decisive turning point in the history of Barry Island. As late as August 1877, it seemed certain that a fashionable marine suburb would soon spring up around Whitmore Bay. Many commentators were sure that it was poised to become an elite watering place. Yet by the summer of 1879, the island's new owner, Lord Windsor, had closed it – to dock promoters, urban developers and visitors. He did so with the express intention of allowing Penarth to leapfrog Barry Island and take its place as Cardiff's seaside satellite. The impact on tourism was dramatic. Lord Windsor slammed the brakes on the resort development process that had been pursued with such vigour by Treharne. Visitors were turned away, pleasure steamers stopped heading for Whitmore Bay and the Marine Hotel, so recently a popular gathering place of relaxed sociability, stood empty, its doors locked and its windows shuttered. Cadoxton and Barry, for so long thriving bathing villages, were suddenly struck off the list of Wales's little coastal resorts.

Of the two processes – resort development and the construction of a bourgeois suburb – the latter was stymied altogether. A few middle-class villas, overlooking Nell's Point, were eventually built in the 1890s, but the majority of the housing stock that appeared on Barry Island in the years after 1895 was squarely aimed at working-class residents. The dream of a high-class suburb at Whitmore Bay was dead in the water after 1878. This is notable. When powerful landowners with an interest in resort development were in sole control of prime pieces of seaside estate such as Whitmore Bay, they often tried to build resorts of the highest social tone. Eastbourne, as it developed under the Devonshire family in the mid- and late Victorian years, is a good example of such a high-class resort.[38] Windsor was the potentate of Barry Island: he could do what he pleased there. And, as his activity at Penarth demonstrated, he was more than capable of improving a seaside settlement. But he forwent the opportunities to upgrade Barry Island: Whitmore Bay was sacrificed in order that Penarth might thrive.

Windsor was only able to keep the visitors away from Barry Island for a few years. As we shall see in the next chapter, they had returned by the end of the 1880s. However, at the time that the visitor ban was introduced in 1879, no one could count on ever being allowed back to Whitmore Bay again. It looked as if the island was permanently lost to day-trippers and holidaymakers. Windsor was uncompromising on the point: henceforth, it was to be an aristocrat's private hunting ground; pleasure-seeking commoners were not welcome.

As an attack upon popular leisure, Lord Windsor's shutdown of Whitmore Bay has been overlooked by historians. However, it needs to be remembered for what it was: an act of breath-taking arrogance. The public's customary right of access to the island and its beach – a right that had certainly been exercised for a century at least – was simply ignored by the estate. Lord Windsor owned over 30,000 acres.[39] Barry Island's 170 acres were hardly critical to his lordship's ability to indulge his personal interest in hunting. In contrast, Whitmore Bay was a price-less seaside resource for thousands of Cardiffians (and others) who had got into the pleasant habit of visiting each summer.

That Windsor's closure of Barry Island has been forgotten by his-torians is, in large measure, a reflection of how quickly late Victori-ans forgot about the shutdown, too. Relations between tenants and the Windsor estate were generally good and, by the end of his life, Windsor was widely referred to as 'the good earl' thanks to his philanthropic activities.[40] Some of those brought up in early twentieth-century Barry even came to remember the landowner as a friend of the working-class tripper (an erroneous assessment, as will become clear in later chap-ters). His visitor ban had been erased from the collective memory. But that was because, within a few years, it had fallen into abeyance. Tour-ists were back on the island by the end of the 1880s. However, they were not there because of any change of heart on Windsor's part. As the next chapter will demonstrate, he never formally revoked the ban. The return of visitors was an unintended consequence of his decision to allow a dock to be built at Barry Sound.

It was fortunate for his subsequent reputation that the tourists were able to return to Barry Island so quickly. For they made it back onto the sands of Whitmore Bay at precisely the moment when Welsh radicals were gathering evidence for the case against the 'cruel, unreasonable, unfeeling, and unpitying' Tory landowners.[41] Landlords who privileged their love of hunting over the interests of those who lived on their estates were singled out for especial criticism by Welsh Liberals.[42] As the Liberal MP, Tom Ellis put it, there had 'raged amongst some landlords a veritable fever of game-preserving'. He complained of 'the overbear-ing conduct and petty tyranny' of the landlords' game keepers, and he despaired at the 'monstrous increase of rabbits and pheasants' at the expense of the rights of the common people.[43] If the visitor ban had still been operational in the mid-1890s when the Royal Commissioners were compiling their report on the Welsh land question, Windsor's actions at Barry Island would have likely been much commented upon, condemned and better remembered.

As it was, the ban was short-lived and soon forgotten. By the early 1890s, Barry Island was drawing larger numbers to it than ever before. How this turnaround occurred is the subject of the next chapter.

CHAPTER FOUR

RECLAIMED,
1884–c.1890

HISTORIANS OF COASTAL TOURISM have recently reminded us that the relationship between commercial ports and seaside resorts was much more complicated than might be imagined. Peter Borsay and John K. Walton have noted that an older approach to writing about coastal settlements tended either to tell a 'simple story of [a seaside town's] transition from port to resort' or conceived of the resort and port functions as being inimical. In contrast, Borsay and Walton argue that far from working against a town's ambitions to attract tourists, a busy port could sometimes be integrated into an appealing resort image. Fishing ports were a case in point. Holidaymakers frequently responded positively to the scenes of working fishermen mending nets or sorting through their hauls of fish at the harbour side. Such workaday practices were construed as being quaint or authentic.[1]

It is arguably more difficult to imagine how one of the world's busiest coal-exporting ports might be marketed to tourists. Yet, at Barry a busy dock did become an attraction in its own right. The dock was built in the second half of the 1880s, the result of a volte-face on the part of the Windsor estate. Lord Windsor, after being so intent on stopping all development at Barry, joined forces with a group of Rhondda coal owners, led by David Davies, and allowed these wealthy capitalists to develop a dock and railway scheme at Barry Sound. When his family had purchased the island in 1878, the very prospect of promoters trying to build a dock at Barry was only seen as a dire threat to the Windsor-Clives' commercial interests at Penarth. By the time the new dock opened at Barry Sound, in 1889, Penarth was thriving as Cardiff's marine suburb. It was no longer dependent on its own dock for survival. This opened the way for Windsor to become involved in, and profit handsomely from, a new dock at Barry. It was too good a business opportunity to turn down, not least because it was so assured of success. The demand for Welsh steam coal had grown exponentially, and the lack of capacity in the existing ports of south Wales was acting as a brake on further growth. David Davies and his colleagues were increasingly desperate to free themselves from their dependence on the Taff Vale Railway and the Bute Docks Company at Cardiff. Thanks to the support of Lord Windsor, Barry had become their means of breaking the deadlock.[2]

The dock proved to be an industrial dynamo. As far as the Barry district is concerned, it brought one historical era to a close and ushered in a new one. It was also the catalyst for the tourist rediscovery of the Island in the late 1880s. Windsor's decision to proceed with the dock unleashed a series of events that made it impossible for him to keep visitors away from Whitmore Bay anymore. The dock created a town populated by citizens who assumed that they had rights of access to the beach. It also brought a railway into the district for the first time. And that railway ran right up to the Rhondda valleys, home to more than 80,000 inhabitants and growing steadily.[3] The railway was built to convey coal to Barry, but it would eventually be used by trippers. Thus, the dock was directly responsible for connecting Barry to its soon-to-be great visitor heartland. It had another supporting role in bringing visitors back to the Island: in the later 1880s and early 1890s, the dock itself became a tourist attraction and many visitors came from the coalfield specifically to see it. Only after gazing at the great building site did some decide to tarry awhile and head for the beach.

Barry, then, amply bears out Borsay and Walton's contention that tourism could flourish alongside a commercial port. Indeed, at Whitmore Bay, a seaside resort not only blossomed next to the busy dock, it burst back into life because of the port's existence.[4]

'POOR LITTLE CADOXTON': FROM 'PLEASANT VILLAGE' TO A 'PHENOMENAL TOWN'

The decision to construct the dock inevitably had massive implications for the future of Whitmore Bay. For one thing, it ended for all time the possibility that Cadoxton could pick up where it had left off as a bathing village. Its days as a sleepy, isolated place – the perfect holiday retreat for bathers who preferred peace and quiet on their holidays – were numbered.

Late Victorian south Walians were well used to rural communities being urbanized rapidly. Throughout the coalfield, formerly idyllic valleys were turned into lively hubs of industry in no time at all. As pits were sunk, so townships sprang up around them. Meanwhile, down at the coast, the fortunes of little seaports that had been gently declining for generations were dramatically revitalized. Cardiff expanded so prodigiously during the mid- and late Victorian years that contemporaries began referring to it as the 'Chicago of Wales'.[5] Nevertheless, even by the standards of the day, what happened at Barry was remarkable. Centuries of history as a rural community ended quite suddenly. In November 1884, Lord Windsor cut the first sod, symbolically marking the beginning of a period of incessant 'organisation, energy, and activity'.[6] The peace of Whitmore Bay was shattered when the navvies arrived. A camp comprised of a 'large number' of wooden and zinc houses was built on the island to accommodate them. A wharf was hastily constructed to receive the dozen or so vessels that arrived every day laden with plant, bricks and other such hardware. Temporary railways crisscrossed the area to facilitate the speedy movement of the building materials.[7]

As the great dock was excavated, so a town was built from scratch on the hills overlooking the Sound. Speculators swept into the district. 'Enterprising' builders from Cardiff, 'foreseeing a large prospective increase of population in the vicinity', were busy at work by the early months of 1885, constructing shops and dwellings in anticipation of the great influx of workers that was certain to follow.[8] A variety of brick buildings, including beer houses, pubs and a plethora of chapels, came to grace the scene over the next year or two. A hotel, the Royal, opened its doors for business in 1887. One visitor judged it to be 'by no means ugly', a compliment of sorts. Yet the general impression was of a chaotic place. Observers worried that roads were being formed haphazardly. Residential neighbourhoods took shape in a disordered fashion, as the two former little hamlets were expanded 'into a magnitude which is astonishing' but 'without aim or purpose'. 'Poor little Cadoxton looks as if it had been shovelled on one side, preparatory to being removed – a heap of rubbish blocking up the way', remarked the *South Wales Daily News* in May 1887.[9] By 1890, after hundreds of years of pursuing separate careers, Barry and Cadoxton 'joined hands'.[10] There had been approximately 120 houses in Barry and Cadoxton in the early 1880s.[11] By the start of 1887, Cadoxton alone boasted nearly 600. By 1891, there were more than 2,000 houses in the district.[12]

Such breakneck development was necessary if Barry was to accommodate the thousands of migrants who poured into the area, enticed there by the prospect of making a living in Wales's latest boom town. By 1891, the district's population had already risen to more than 13,000. It stood at 20,000 by the mid-1890s; by 1901 it had reached 27,000.[13] Contemporaries marvelled as the quiet, agricultural district was turned into a bustling urban settlement. Barry had become '*the* phenomenal town of South Wales', cried a local newspaper in 1891.[14] Another paper thought that such 'abnormal developments and startling transformations' exceeded even the American experience of explosive growth: Barry's history was like 'a chapter from a Mediaeval romance – a story from the "Arabian Nights"', the *Barry Herald* decided.[15]

Whatever picturesque charms the Barry district had possessed before the mid-1880s, they were soon severely compromised. As one commentator remarked, the urbanization of Barry had been so rapid that 'there appears to have been no time to consider its real requirements, much less to provide for its wants'. The existing sanitary arrangements of the district collapsed under the strain. Most of the new streets were without surface drainage, there was no proper sewerage system, ash pits and middens were allowed to go unemptied for months at a time, and overflowing cesspools throughout the town generated 'offensive smells'. In one street, twenty-six houses were served by just one cesspit which had only been emptied once in twelve months. Cadoxton, that 'pleasant village' of old, was now being referred to as 'Mudoxton' and 'Slushoxton'.[16] In short order, Barry had gone from being a place that sickly visitors headed to for the benefit of their health, to an insanitary settlement in which inhabitants lived in fear of deadly epidemic diseases.[17]

It could no longer be thought of as a tranquil place, either. On the contrary, the sudden influx of large numbers of navvies – 3,000 were in Barry by the summer of 1885, 5,000 by the later 1880s – meant that many commentators regarded the district as one plagued by violence and intemperance.[18] Barry's navvies were 'easily aroused' into a fight, according to one visitor in the spring of 1887.[19] 'Lawless Barry', screamed a headline in the *Cardiff Times*. It portrayed Barry as a place where respectable women felt unsafe on the streets and where there was a generalized sense of disorder. The paper wondered whether Barry was really a small town in Wales or a place in the far west of the United States.[20] Historians rightly point out that the navvies were not necessarily the rough outcasts that they were so frequently portrayed by 'respectable' journalists.[21] Nevertheless, there can be no denying the disturbing effect that the arrival of such great numbers of workers had on the small villages in the district. Even Cadoxton's publicans, the one group that stood to gain unequivocally from the huge increase in thirsty workers, complained of the 'excessive stress' they were now suffering as they struggled to keep the navvies supplied with beer.[22]

The Barry district was no longer a place for those holidaymakers who valued solitude and quiet, rural surroundings. It was a site of steam hammers, raucous workers and earth-shaking explosions.

THE 'GREAT CIVILIZER': THE RAILWAY COMES TO BARRY

The building of the dock triggered not only the urbanization of Barry but also a major improvement in the district's transport infrastructure. This was to be of obvious importance to tourism to the Island. Road users were the first to notice a difference. A new road was run across the Cadoxton Moors to facilitate the movement of building materials to the docks. This had the effect of shortening the journey between Cardiff and Barry by a couple of miles.[23] It was a welcome development, although so busy was the road with works carts heading for the dock that many 'ordinary' users preferred to stick to the old Wenvoe road.[24] Of greater long-term significance was the laying of railway tracks in the Barry district for the first time. The construction of a railway linking Barry with the mining valleys was an integral part of the scheme hatched by the dock's promoters. A 19-mile route connecting Barry with the Taff Vale Railway's line at Trehafod, a settlement in the lower Rhondda, was settled on and 300 navvies were put to work. Their task was a daunting one. Situated in the 'hills district', Trehafod was some 250 feet above sea level. The country through which the line passed was 'attractive to the artist' but it was 'not of that description loved by the civil engineer'. A succession of hills and valleys had to be bridged, tunnelled and cut through. The most impressive structure was a three-quarters-of-a-mile-long tunnel between Treforest and Pontypridd.[25]

In time, this route would become familiar to countless trippers from the valleys. But not yet. Mindful of the need to get a speedy return on its hefty investment, the company successfully reserved this line for the exclusive use of their coal trains, the conveyance of black diamond being far more lucrative than the transportation of day-trippers. Not until the mid-1890s would they be allowed on the tracks from the Rhondda. Until then, they were compelled to travel into Barry on the other new route opened up by the Barry Railway Company. This line, for ordinary goods traffic and passenger trains, headed north-east from Barry and terminated at Cogan where passengers were required to alight and walk a hundred yards or so to pick up a train at the Taff Vale Railway station and journey onward to Penarth, Cardiff and stations beyond.[26]

Contemporaries were certain that the running of the first passenger train into the district in December 1888 constituted a red-letter day in Barry's history. The *Barry and Cadoxton Journal* declared the railway to be the 'great civilizer' for it would end Barry's era as a rough frontier district: 'We have been an exceptional district, more like a town in the Western States of America or a settlement in the Australian Bush, but now we are to become an ordinary town.'[27] The *South Wales Daily News* was not so sure. It thought that the coming of the railway would merely accelerate the process of urbanization already under way. Barry, by its reckoning, would become even more like a boom town in the American West.[28]

Journalists might disagree about the impact of the railway on Barry's status as a frontier settlement, but the inhabitants of the district cared little for such debates. They just celebrated the opening of the line. At settlements all along the railway, huge crowds turned out to cheer as the first locomotive steamed past. In Cadoxton, thousands gathered at the station, local tradesmen closed their shops, brass bands struck up patriotic tunes and children were given a day off school. As the train pulled into Barry Dock station, so the company's directors and honoured guests alighted and took the opportunity to inspect the progress of the dock workings: 'for more than half an hour the quays presented a striking and animated appearance'.[29]

The passenger services were well used from the outset. On the first Saturday of operations between 2,000 and 3,000 passengers rode the company's rails. Amongst them was a 'large contingent' of navvies and other dock workers who decided to pay a pre-Christmas visit to Cardiff.[30] By 1890, fifteen trains ran in and out of Barry station every weekday. Some 1,500 passengers travelled daily between Barry and Cogan in an average week in the early 1890s. More than 1.5 million passengers caught the Barry Railway Company's trains annually.[31]

INDUSTRIAL TOURISM AT BARRY

Not long after work started on the dock and the railway, commentators wondered whether Whitmore Bay might be reopened to visitors. In 1885, the *South Wales Echo* dared to contemplate the prospect of the Island being reinstated as a tourist destination: 'Who amongst Cardiff people has not enjoyed the pleasure of a picnic on Barry Island, bathed on the safe and sandy beach of Whitmore Bay, and rambled over the springy turf of the weather-beaten isle?', it asked. The paper looked forward to Cardiffians being allowed back to Barry Island again soon.[32]

By the time the first passenger trains steamed into Barry Dock station, Cardiff's population was 130,000. The railway gave its citizens another means of journeying to Barry. No longer were they faced with a choice between a road trip lasting a couple of hours or a pleasure steamer trip that was constrained by the tide times. Meanwhile, the railway's journey-shrinking capabilities meant that a day trip to Barry had become a reality for excursionists living much further away than Cardiff. Many more inhabitants of the coalfield could think about spending an afternoon at Whitmore Bay. The numbers in that

Illus. 11. *View of the new dock and surrounding district,* The Graphic, *27 July 1889. Barry Island provided 'industrial tourists' with the perfect vantage point from which to see the great dock. Before long, however, Whitmore Bay's charms began to capture the attention of visitors.*

catchment area were considerable. By the early 1890s, the Merthyr valley had more than 61,000 residents; the Cynon valley had a population of some 43,000. More than 40,000 lived in the Rhymney valley whilst nearly 90,000 lived in the Rhondda, by then 'the most thickly populated valley in South Wales'.[33]

It was all very well having a new railway, but it was still an open question as to whether tourists would be welcomed back to Barry Island. Lord Windsor's visitor ban was still in place and he showed no sign of relaxing it. But this was of no consequence to the trippers, for they returned to Barry uninvited. However, these were visitors of a very different stamp from those who had headed to the island in the decades before Windsor's takeover. These were 'industrial tourists'.[34]

South Walians were fascinated by the dock. So gigantic was this civil-engineering project – it was to be the largest single dock in the country and cost £2 million – that it was regarded as 'the wonder of Wales' and became a visitor attraction in its own right.[35] Newspapers presented

Barry as a place worth seeing, vividly describing the extraordinary scenes that were, day and night, enacted there: the fantastic explosions, the immense clouds of steam and dust that periodically engulfed the area, and the sudden appearance of huge earthworks and deep trenches. 'A man requires a good-sized soul to comprehend Barry in its full acceptance', opined a *Cardiff Times* journalist after a visit to the works in July 1888.[36] There was no shortage of sights to captivate visitors as they looked across more than seventy acres of activity: forty steam cranes were noisily at work; thirty steam locomotives shuttled to and fro; a Cornish beam engine pumped out 270,000 gallons of seawater from the site every hour; more than a thousand trucks and wagons were shunted around the site; five brick kilns were fired up; and there were the massive dock walls, seventeen feet thick, slowly rising up out of the vast hole in the ground. And it was truly enormous: more than 3.5 million cubic yards of earth were excavated during the course of the works.[37] Overlooking this colossal building site was yet one more: that of the new town.

Trippers' interest in industrial Barry was strong enough to prompt the running of a special horse-drawn omnibus service from Cardiff. In the spring of 1888, buses to Barry dockside left Cardiff every 15 minutes, jam-packed with tourists.[38] Even the Cardiff Naturalists' Society – old friends of Barry Island, it will be remembered – temporarily put aside their interest in flora and fauna and allowed themselves to be bewitched by the ingenuity of humans. They were captivated by the 'working of the steam navvies and mud grabbers'.[39] More predictable, perhaps, was the strong interest shown in the new coal port by inhabitants of the mining valleys. 'All up the Rhondda Valley and in the coal districts generally, a great interest is felt in Barry Dock', remarked the *Barry and Cadoxton Journal* in May 1888. The *South Wales Daily News*, too, was struck by the fact that Rhondda miners were eager to see the great transformation of the Barry district.[40]

Hundreds flocked to Barry during the Easter of 1889. The main streets of the brand-new town presented 'an animated appearance' whilst the dock works were 'especially visited'. If any tourists made it over to Whitmore Bay, they went unreported in the newspapers.[41] The same pattern was repeated at Whitsuntide when 'enormous' numbers journeyed to Barry from the coalfield. Crowds, many hundreds strong, came to monitor the progress of the dock, but even larger throngs (measured in the thousands) were drawn to Cadoxton Moors to watch the second annual sports meeting. Once again, the newspapers made no mention of any crowds at Barry Island.[42] Just how much Barry was thought of as a site of 'industrial tourism' was underlined by a newspaper correspondent who paid a 'holiday visit to Barry dock'. Eschewing all thought of a ramble across the sand dunes at Whitmore Bay, this journalist focused only on the modernization of Barry. He wrote about the new train station at Barry Dock, about the hundreds of men he saw toiling at the new graving dock and about his tour around the busy locomotive works. He was oblivious to the fact that Barry's seaside was just a short distance away. For him, at least, there were more compelling sights in Barry in 1889 than a picturesque beach.[43]

But not every industrial tourist left without having paid a visit to Barry Island. The Cardiff naturalists, as one might expect, rounded off their 1886 tour of the dock with a visit to Whitmore Bay.[44] In the summer of 1888, enterprising Cadoxtonians took advantage of the great interest in the dock and began running horse-drawn tours around the site of the works. Some began extending their tours by taking parties over to the Island to see the beach. In this way, some trippers from Cardiff were reacquainted with Whitmore Bay, a place that had been shut to them for the best part of a decade. Others, from the mining valleys, were treated to their first sight of the beach.[45] Thus did the construction of the dock stimulate tourists' interest both in Barry and in Barry Island.

THE VISITOR BAN UNRAVELS

That some locals were able to take visitors over to the Island in the summer of 1888 reveals that, by then, Windsor's visitor ban was no longer operational. Importantly, the ban was never formally rescinded: the Windsor estate never welcomed visitors back to Whitmore Bay. Instead, the shutdown was rendered inoperable by the drastically altered circumstances of the later 1880s.

It is worth noting that the Windsor estate sought to keep the visitor ban in place for as long as possible. Right up to the moment when the navvies arrived, it was expected that anyone hoping to see Whitmore Bay had to ask for his lordship's permission. In July 1884, just a few months before the sod-cutting ceremony, the estate office generously allowed a party of visitors from Trinity Church in the Cathays neighbourhood of Cardiff to land on the island for a few hours. The churchgoers dutifully played their part by publicly acknowledging 'the kindness of Lord Windsor'.[46] Access to Barry Island was still a 'gift' that could be bestowed or withheld. It all depended upon the whim of a paternalistic landowner. In this instance, the fact that the petitioners were, like his lordship, Anglicans living in a south Wales dominated by Nonconformists, undoubtedly improved their chances of a positive response.

Policing the ban before 1885 had been relatively easy. The small numbers living in Barry and Cadoxton were easily kept away from his lordship's private hunting ground and steamship companies could simply be informed that their vessels were no longer permitted to land at Whitmore Bay. That just left any Cardiffians who might have been tempted to come by road. Understandably, few seem to have risked making that journey once it was known that visitors would be turned away. As soon as the works were in full swing, however, the task of keeping visitors away from the beach became impossible. The ban was made meaningless by the intrusion of the works onto the island. Large tracts of land on its northern edge were given over for building purposes, including the laying out of a temporary railway. Early in the proceedings, two steam excavators were placed on the island and 'kept busily going'.[47] Meanwhile, the appearance of a navvy encampment at Barry Island by the early months of 1885 meant that the fields overlooking Whitmore Bay were now well populated: hundreds of labourers were working and living in them.[48]

Barry Island's navvies were the first group to have unrestricted access to the sands of Whitmore Bay since Windsor's ban came into force. Sadly, we have no evidence of how they made use of the beach. Journalists tended only to pay attention to navvies when they were working, fighting and drinking. But we might safely assume that at least some of their number took to the waters to cool off after a day's hard labour. At nearby Aberthaw, in 1896, navvies employed on the new Vale of Glamorgan railway went sea-bathing on a Sunday in late May. (The newspapers only reported that event because one of the party drowned.[49]) There is no reason to suppose Barry Island's navvies were less disposed to taking a dip than their counterparts a few miles down the coast.

The rapidly urbanizing settlements of Barry and Cadoxton quickly filled up with new residents. For the first time, large numbers were living within walking distance of the beach. Once at the site of the docks, it was easier than it had ever been to get to Whitmore Bay, for it was tied to the mainland by a network of embankments, dams and dock walls. Barry Island was an island no longer. Judging precisely when the residents began making their way across to the beach in appreciable numbers is no easy task because of the paucity of evidence.

In the early months of 1888, Barry's population had grown to a few thousand. Because the construction works in Barry Sound were still in progress, few Barrians seem to have made it across to Whitmore Bay at this time. A local newspaper made no mention of the beach being thronged by locals in the Easter of that year. Indeed, Cadoxton Moors, situated to the east of the new town, appears to have been the playground of choice in these early days. A sports meeting held on the moors over the Whitsuntide of 1888 proved popular: navvies joined inhabitants and a large influx of visitors from Cardiff to watch assorted athletic contests including a sack race, a tug of war and a race for men with wooden legs.[50]

Barry's beach could not yet compete with such entertainment. In May 1888, the editor of the *Barry and Cadoxton Journal* lamented the sad 'neglect' of Whitmore Bay by locals. He explained that a 'great many inhabitants of Cadoxton have never seen it [the beach], although it is so close at hand'. Aware that most Barrians were new arrivals and were unfamiliar with the district, the editor helpfully included directions on how to get to the seashore from east Barry and Cadoxton. It was worth the effort, he assured his readers, for it was a 'delightful spot' – 'very pretty' and made of 'real sand', not the 'muddy black sand' found at Penarth.[51] In passing, the editor remarked that he had 'seldom seen many people' at Whitmore Bay. But sometimes, therefore, he had. Critically, some of these early visitors were trippers from outside the Barry district. Steamers from Cardiff and Bristol dropped off visitors at Whitmore Bay in the summer of 1886.[52] The reclaiming of Barry Island by the people was already under way.

By the summer of 1889, we can be sure that many Barrians and excursionists from beyond were exploring the Island for the first time. By that point, there were an estimated 10,000 residents of the new town, far too many for Windsor's men to repel. Moreover, all major work on the dock had been completed. No longer was the channel between the Island and Barry a great building site. Now, Cadoxtonians could access the beach simply by skirting around the east side of the dock, crossing the dock gates and climbing a winding red path to the top of the cliff. Once there, as the *Barry Dock News* informed its readers, 'a splendid view' could be had of 'the whole dock works'.[53] Meanwhile, the numbers of steam packets visiting the Island picked up appreciably. Newspapers reported that many were fascinated by the 'fine dock, every part having a share of their scrutiny'.[54] Many, doubtless, were alerted to the natural beauty of Whitmore Bay for the first time, too.

CONCLUSION

In July 1890, a correspondent to the *Barry Dock News* reported that Whitmore Bay was 'already becoming an attraction'. A 'good number' had been spotted on the beach, bathing machines had been installed on the sands and were 'well patronised'. Even more excitingly, the letter-writer knew for a fact that 'there are already visitors here, staying in the town for the sake of sea-bathing'. So busy was the Island on fine days that he was worried that male bathers who were undressing on the sands (as they had done for decades before Windsor's shutdown) were causing a nuisance. He noticed that ladies and children were being driven away from the rocks at Nell's Point by the numbers of men gathering there to strip off. He urged them to use the bathing machines that had been trundled onto the sands in order to maintain decorum.[55]

It was a short letter, but one bursting with significant information. It reveals that the bathers had returned to Whitmore Bay by the summer of 1890. Some long-stay visitors were holidaying in the town for the purposes of bathing, and there were trippers wandering around the Island's resort spaces enjoying the scenery. The tourists, in other words, were back, their return prompted by the building of a great dock. At Barry, the coal port breathed life back into Whitmore Bay as a visitor attraction. The mammoth building site itself became a tourist attraction whilst the railway that had been built to service the dock brought Barry's beach closer to a huge population in the coalfield. Far from denting its tourist appeal, the port revived the Island's career as a tourist destination. Geography helped enormously, for whilst the dock was, almost literally, just a stone's throw from the Island, it was entirely hidden from the view of beach users. Standing at the water's edge, facing the beach, all the visitors could see were gently rising sand dunes and the cliffs of Friars Point and Nell's Point. There were hardly any signs that 600 yards away was a place of unusually intense industrial activity. The only real indication was provided by the busy shipping lanes, but many tourists seem to have found the coal barques visually appealing. Visitors from the mining valleys were often described as being mesmerized by the impressive consignments of coal that left the dock. Colliers, of course, were looking at the results of their own arduous labour float past.

The dock brought the visitors back to Barry Island. Tourism to Whitmore Bay had been restarted. But there were changes. Barry and Cadoxton's long careers as bathing villages were over. For decades, coastal tourism had contributed to the local economy without sparking an urban expansion. The forces of industrial capitalism were not to be contained so easily. In just a few short years, Barry's history as an agricultural centre was summarily ended. Now there was a busy town just across the way from Whitmore Bay. Its residents would quickly become active participants in debates about what to do with Barry Island. However, it remained to be seen how Lord Windsor would respond to the radically altered circumstances of the late 1880s and early 1890s. No one could yet predict what sort of resort would flower at Whitmore Bay.

CHAPTER FIVE

AN 'EL DORADO . . . WHERE SOFT WINDS BLOW'

RESORT BOOSTERISM FLOURISHES IN THE 1890S

SUCH WAS THE SCALE of the upheaval that convulsed the Barry district in the years after 1884 it was inevitable that its effects would be felt at the Island. In the previous chapter we noted how the construction of the dock, the emergence of the new town and the running of the railway into Barry had the instant effect of making it impossible for Lord Windsor to maintain his visitor ban. By the late 1880s, the first inhabitants of urban Barry were making their way across to the Island to see for themselves its sandy beach, whilst tourists from outside the district were rediscovering Whitmore Bay after years of having to look elsewhere for their seaside pleasures. In this chapter, we will consider another important consequence of the industrialization and urbanization of Barry: the presence of a citizenry that had its own views about what should happen at the Island. For the first time, there was a sizeable group, close at hand and with access to capital, that could shape events at Whitmore Bay. So committed were some to the idea of developing the Island's potential as a resort that they can usefully be labelled 'resort boosters'.

Drawn predominantly from the town's middle class, these boosters argued that Barry's seafront was an asset that should be developed. They pointed out how it could be 'improved' and furnished with the various structures and resort amenities that were such staples at other seaside towns. Their plans frequently involved encouraging Barry's local authority to spend public money on resort development schemes. For a short while, in the 1890s, they appeared to make significant progress in their efforts to transform Whitmore Bay into a leading watering place. Barry, a town created by the exigencies of the coal trade, looked to be developing a 'holiday interest', too.

AN 'UNEXPLOITED GOLD MINE': RESORT BOOSTERS MAKE THE CASE FOR TOURISM

As we have noted, for decades, coastal tourism at Barry Island had not produced any significant investment in tourist infrastructure. The fact that Whitmore Bay was situated in an agricultural district consisting of only small villages helped to keep it in its undeveloped state. With no sizeable population nearby, there were only limited reservoirs of local capital to be devoted to resort development. It consequently fell to landowners like Jenner and Treharne to try to stimulate change. If there had been a small market town at Barry instead of a tiny hamlet, proposals to bring a railway to the island might have found more backers. Furthermore, there would have been more well-to-do inhabitants who could have been called on to help develop Whitmore Bay's tourist infrastructure. By the early 1890s, just such a group had been created thanks to the dramatic growth of the new town.

As Barry urbanized, so a new society quickly emerged. The working class was, by far, the largest single social group, but, from the outset, there was a small but highly organized middle class that took on a leadership role. This propertied elite was comprised mostly of shopkeepers, small businessmen (rarely were they women) and professionals. Some sought to exercise their influence by standing in local government elections.[1] Others preferred to work through one or more of the voluntary associations that flourished in the early 1890s. Some occupied positions in both worlds – the municipal and the voluntary – simultaneously. Between them, these local notables oversaw the growth of a brand-new urban community. They spent ratepayers' money, they agitated for various improvement schemes and, through their public utterances, they helped to construct an urban identity for the infant town. Importantly, in the 1890s, a sizeable number were convinced that Barry should be thought of not merely as a wildly successful dock but also as a promising seaside resort. Whitmore Bay, for the first time, had a group of influential individuals living close by who could press its claims as a tourist attraction.

Barry's residents soon became aware of the Island's potential as a resort. One of the earliest examples of a local commentator pointing out the promise of Whitmore Bay came at the end of 1888. An editorial in the *Barry and Cadoxton Journal* argued that Barry was a 'natural seaside resort'. With just a little development – an esplanade at Barry Island, ornamental gardens at Cold Knap, pleasure boats at Barry Harbour – 'we shall have plenty of visitors', the editor proclaimed.[2] By the early 1890s, the town's opinion-shapers were agreed: the Island would, sooner or later, become a flourishing watering place. As the *South Wales Star* put it in May 1893, 'There are few people in Barry – and they *are* few – who cannot be convinced that Barry is destined to become a seaside resort.'[3] And not just any seaside resort. When they looked across to Whitmore Bay, Barrians saw a beach that could rival the very best. It was Wales's version of Naples Bay, some cried; others decreed that Whitmore Bay would soon be crowned the 'Queen of Welsh Watering Places'.[4]

As these immodest epithets indicate, Barry Island became the focus of a burgeoning civic pride. This first generation of urban Barrians resided in a settlement that simply had not existed just a few years earlier. Yet they quickly came to think of Barry town as their home. The creation of an urban identity helped the new residents settle down. One story that inhabitants could unite behind concerned their dock's runaway success. Another was Barry's explosion onto the urban scene. Living in '*the* phenomenal town of South Wales' was something that everyone could get excited about.[5] Given Barry's striking accomplishments as an industrial and an urban place, it was hardly a wonder that Barrians soon developed a reputation as being a supremely self-confident, and occasionally arrogant, lot.[6] Some of its more zealous advocates averred that Barry would eventually overtake Cardiff and become the region's capital.[7] When they contemplated Barry's future, they only envisaged boundless success. Thus, when the Island's boosters trumpeted Whitmore Bay's great promise as a tourist resort, they were merely giving expression to a wider set of beliefs about Barry's essential greatness.

However, boosters' calls for resort development were not merely the result of a spasm of overconfidence. There was more to it than that. Underlying their argument was the contention that the young town's economy was in urgent need of diversification. The dangers of relying on just one industry – even one as buoyant as the south Wales coal trade – were evident from very early on. Even during the prosperous 1890s, Barry's inhabitants were reminded of just how dependent they were on King Coal for their livelihoods. Stoppages in the coal trade had a chilling effect on the town's economic life and could not be ignored. A six-week dispute in 1893 created havoc in south Wales's coal ports. At Barry, by the end of the strike, the supply of coal had been so severely reduced that on one day only twelve barques left the dock fully laden; ninety-five vessels, meanwhile, were laid-up in the approaches to the harbour. It made for a sobering spectacle.[8] Even more disruption was caused by a much longer lockout in 1898. That five-month stoppage affected 'all grades of society in the Barry district', from tradesmen to railway workers, from dock pilots to coal trimmers. 'There are but few exceptions in our district where the strike has not inflicted frightful loss, and in many cases deprivation of the necessaries of life', the *Barry Dock News* noted darkly.[9]

Strikes and lockouts were, fortunately, only occasional events in the 1890s. But even go-ahead Barry could not maintain its dizzying growth rates for ever. Indeed, as early as 1892, trade slackened palpably. The numbers flooding into the town fell back for the first time, resulting in a glut of housing. At that year's annual regatta dinner, shipper Robert Duncan delivered a widely reported speech urging the townsfolk to do all they could to break the hold of the coal trade: 'Barry should not depend entirely upon the exportation of one article, and that article coal', he advised. He argued that an import trade should be developed, and efforts made to ensure that Cadoxton Moors be filled with a variety of factories and workshops.[10] The hope that industries might be attracted to Barry was oft expressed by late Victorians and Edwardians. Periodically, newspapers excitedly reported rumours that major companies were considering moving to the district. Major engineering firms, a mineral-water producer and a steel manufacturer, all were said to be on the brink of setting up operations in the town at different times.[11] However, various obstacles – including the hardness of its water and the steepness of its business rates – meant that Barry consistently struggled to attract new manufacturers.[12]

Against this backdrop of uncertainty, Whitmore Bay stood out as a ready-made asset just waiting to be developed for the good of the town. A correspondent to the *Barry and Cadoxton Journal* pointed out that the Island's popularity as a beauty spot meant that 'in time' Barry's seafront 'should be a sourse [*sic*] of profit to all alike'.[13] Others concurred. Investing in the Island's resort infrastructure 'would be as good as the establishment of ironworks on the Moors at Cadoxton', asserted a local board member in 1892.[14] Whitmore Bay was nothing less than a 'golden casket' on Barry's doorstep just waiting to be unlocked, explained one commentator in 1893.[15] The *Barry Dock News*, in poetic mood, described it as 'an El Dorado close at hand where soft winds blow'.[16] The *Barry Herald* put it more bluntly: it was 'a practically unexploited gold mine'.[17]

Such assessments encouraged the notion that it was worth promoting and developing the Island as a tourist destination. In 1894, the *Barry Dock News* went so far as to declare that it was the 'duty' of townsfolk to do what they could to 'render the district as attractive as possible to visitors'. 'Private interests' should 'develop the Island . . . for the reception and entertainment of the thousands more who would undoubtedly come to Barry at every opportunity when it is fully realised that due preparations are being made for the convenience and reception of the public'. The paper pleaded with members of the local board to do all they could 'in the direction of popularising the Island'.[18] In 1896, the *Herald* argued that 'we will be blind to our own interests, blind to the interests of the public and the town', if steps were not taken to develop and advertise the Island.[19]

'[T]O MAKE BARRY AN ATTRACTIVE SEASIDE RESORT': BARRY CHAMBER OF TRADE AND BOOSTERISM IN THE 1890S

In the 1890s, the most enthusiastic promoter of resort development at the Island was the Barry Chamber of Trade. Members of the town's business community formed the chamber in 1892. Its main objective was to do 'everything that could possibly be done outside the province of a Local Board . . . to encourage and facilitate the trade of the district'.[20] The development of Whitmore Bay's resort potential became an integral part of the chamber's economic strategy from the outset. In these early years, most of the chamber's members took it for granted that a busy seafront would unleash a powerful tourism multiplier that would boost the town's economy. By 1896, the organization had decided that one of its primary aims was 'to make Barry an attractive seaside resort'.[21] The proposition that tourism at the Island would generate spin-offs became an article of faith. As one member explained it in 1898, it was simply essential 'for the general welfare of the town' that 'suitable provision should be made for visitors'.[22] Another argued that the promotion of Whitmore Bay was 'the most important thing we do'.[23]

The most eloquent advocate for resort development at Barry Island in these years was solicitor F. P. Jones-Lloyd. Jones-Lloyd had moved to Barry in 1890 from the Pembrokeshire resort of Tenby. As he was quick to point out, he had been able to witness at close hand the 'advantages to be derived from a large number of persons visiting a town'. Convinced that a properly developed Island would be a money-spinner, he put forward a compelling case. The benefits of tourism to Whitmore Bay would be widely shared, he insisted: shareholders in the Barry Railway Company would see their dividends rise thanks to the increased passenger traffic to the Island; traders who met the holidaymakers' needs would obviously profit; and Barry would attract more middle-class residents when the Island was 'improved'. A fashionable seafront would encourage house builders to construct a better class of housing. This would, in turn, allow landlords to charge higher rents. The town's rateable value would rise, and the council would have more resources to spend on further improvements to the town's infrastructure. Barrians would find themselves caught in a virtuous circle. Every pound of ratepayers' money spent on Whitmore Bay's seafront amenities would inevitably bring even more money back into the town's coffers. All it would take to trigger this beneficent chain of events was a neatly laid out and properly promoted Whitmore Bay.[24]

Inspired by Jones-Lloyd's vision, chamber members took on the role of resort promoters with gusto. When they could, they sought to effect improvements in the resort infrastructure. For example, the first public seats on the Island were paid for by Chamber of Trade members.[25] However, with only limited resources at their disposal, they were obliged to concentrate their efforts on less costly activities. The chamber functioned as a formidable pressure group, taking the message of resort development to Lord Windsor's estate office and to the council chamber. And it acted as a champion of visitors' rights. Thus, in 1894, when it was felt that the cost of hiring a bathing machine at Whitmore Bay was too high, a deputation of chamber members met with the proprietor and urged him to lower his prices. Likewise, councillors were routinely encouraged by the chamber to do all they could to improve the visitor experience at the Island – whether that meant laying on musical entertainments in the summer months or providing shelters to protect the tourists from the elements.[26]

The chamber's greatest contribution was in the marketing of Barry Island. Jones-Lloyd led the way. In 1893, he set up an advertising fund to which all residents – but especially property owners and hotel proprietors – were invited to contribute.[27] In keeping with ideas about the recuperative powers of the seaside, the chamber's initial efforts at resort marketing involved placing advertisements in periodicals such as the *British Medical Journal*, the *Lancet* and *Hygiene*.[28] However, it soon broadened its approach. In 1897, it produced a seventy-three-page illustrated guide. The guide contained two maps and assorted images of the town and its environs including photographs of Whitmore Bay ('The People's Playground'), Pebble Beach, Porthkerry Park, 'old' Barry village, various places of worship, Barry dock, the railway embankment across to the Island and nearby picturesque villages. The *Barry Herald*, initially at least, was unimpressed. It adjudged it 'mildly preposterous' to think that all the attractive features of the district could be adequately promoted in such a slim volume.[29] But the paper soon changed its mind. Remarking upon the 'unprecedented number of visitors' who arrived in Barry during the summer of 1898, the *Herald* decided that the Chamber of Trade's guide was largely responsible.[30]

In the 1900s, under Jones-Lloyd's guiding hand, the campaign was intensified. The chamber routinely spent between £40 and £50 a year on promotional material. Sometimes the figure was as high as £60.[31] It agitated successfully for Barry to be included in the tourist guides of several leading railway companies.[32] Meanwhile, it placed advertisements in various newspapers in towns and cities throughout England, including London and the great conurbations of the Midlands. In 1906, the chamber distributed some 20,000 leaflets and 3,000 special circulars 'setting forth the advantages of Barry as a seaside resort'. Lists of lodging houses in Barry were sent to clergymen, doctors 'and men of position' living in various English cities.[33] By 1907, its annual guide to the district was fifty pages long.[34] In 1909 and 1910, it arranged for thousands of its guides and pamphlets to be left on trains run by the Great Eastern and the Great Central Railway Companies.[35] Chamber members also oversaw the production of promotional posters to be displayed in railway stations 'throughout as large an area as possible'.[36] The first appeared in 1904 and consisted of a montage of pictures including photographs of the landing stage at the Island, three local hotels, Pebble Beach, Romilly Park and Broad Street. These images were arranged around 'a splendid view of Whitmore Bay'. The *Barry Herald* was thrilled by the campaign: it 'must inevitably attract visitors who seek a holiday near the "sad sea wave"', it concluded.[37]

SWIMMING WITH THE TIDE: THE COUNCIL, THE RAILWAY COMPANY AND THE LANDOWNER PROMOTE TOURISM

Champions of resort development were not confined to the ranks of the Chamber of Trade. Barry's town leaders were just as likely to be supporters of the cause in the 1890s. Indeed, often, because there was such a large overlap in personnel between the chamber and the local authority, a booster might make a speech in a chamber meeting a few days before making the same points in a council committee room. One of the most prominent early boosters was Alderman J. C. Meggitt. Meggitt had the distinction of being 'the first merchant to commence business at Barry', having moved to the district in the mid-1880s from the English Midlands and set up as a trader in timber. He threw himself into the public life of the young town and soon made a name for himself as someone 'prominently connected with every good work in the district'.[38] In the context of Barry in the 1890s, 'good work' included nurturing tourism at the Island. During a visit to the beach in August 1896, he had noticed 'hundreds of people . . . with no place to go to shelter from the wind and rain'. This prompted him to encourage fellow members of the council's Public Works Committee to consider investing in Whitmore Bay's resort amenities. Public lavatories were essential, he argued; so were shelters, a landing stage and a swimming teacher based on the beach. He hoped his colleagues would look at this in 'a broad, liberal spirit, so as to make the town attractive for visitors from the Rhondda, Cardiff, the Vale, and the Rhymney Valleys. They must make provision for them.' Committee members welcomed Meggitt's observations and agreed that they should approach the Windsor estate.[39]

Meggitt had fired the starting pistol. Over the next few years, the council began to engage in resort development activity. Some of its initiatives were substantial. In 1900, for example, it applied to the Local Government Board for powers to raise a loan of £3,300 in order to build a cloakroom, a public lavatory, a reading room and a museum on the Island.[40] Councillors also paid for a bathing pool on the western side of the beach. It was a rudimentary structure – just a low concrete wall that retained water left by the outgoing tide – but it proved a popular feature after it was opened in 1902.[41] Ratepayers' money was spent on two 'bathing houses' at Whitmore Bay. From the outset, the council ran them at a profit: at the end of the summer season of 1902, it was reported that the cloakroom, lavatory and bathing-houses had generated a healthy surplus of £69.[42] In 1903, councillors applied to borrow a further £1,500 to pay for more lavatories and extend the cloakroom facilities.[43]

Boosters took heart from these early examples of municipal involvement in resort development. They were also encouraged by the actions of the Barry Railway Company in the mid-1890s. In March 1896, the company announced that it was to allow passenger trains onto its mineral line from the Rhondda to Barry. This was an event of great significance.[44] Passenger trains had been running into Barry since December 1888, but they were restricted to the line from Cogan. This was a far less convenient route, particularly for visitors from the coalfield: they had faced a difficult journey with multiple changes and complex ticketing arrangements if they wanted to get to Barry Island. Now, from the spring of 1896, there was a direct service down to Barry from the most populous of all the great mining valleys. Whitmore Bay had, at a stroke, been brought closer to the inhabitants of the Rhondda. We shall return to this development in a later chapter. For the moment it is simply enough to notice it.

The second positive railway development of 1896 was the opening of a new rail link from Barry to the Island itself. This was a considerable undertaking on the part of the company. It necessitated the construction of a purpose-built embankment, a 280-yard tunnel and a 500-foot steel viaduct.[45] When the line opened in August 1896 it stimulated a further surge in visitor numbers. No longer would excursionists have to endure a three-quarter-of-a-mile hike from Barry Dock station, around the great port, to the beach.[46] Now, trains deposited trippers just 250 yards from the beach. One Rhondda miner was so impressed with the new arrangement that he declared to a friend that the railway carriages could double-up as bathing machines, so close was the platform to the water's edge.[47] Local newspapers were delighted to learn that some 35,000 trippers had poured through the turnstiles on the opening day. This was a considerable increase on the Easter Monday and Whit Monday figures which had both been around 20,000.[48] Another transport improvement was completed in 1899. The Island's new Pierhead Station allowed passengers to access easily the pleasure steamers waiting to take visitors on to resorts elsewhere along the coasts of the Bristol Channel.[49]

There was yet one more significant reason for the resort boosters to feel optimistic. Lord Windsor signalled that he might be coming around to their way of thinking. After years of repelling visitors, now there were signs that the great landowner was ready to welcome tourists back to Whitmore Bay. The first indication that the old policy had been abandoned came in the summer of 1889. Quite suddenly, the Marine Hotel advertised its services again. It had been forced to shut when Windsor closed the island. Now, newspaper advertisements proclaimed that the hotel had reopened its doors to 'visitors to the docks and the seaside'.[50] This was a relaunch that could only have occurred with the estate's approval. The following year, 1890, it was announced that the Windsor estate had given two 'gentlemen' – one from Cardiff, the other, Edwin Hullin, from Penarth – 'the exclusive use of the beach for bathing purposes during the coming season'. These budding entrepreneurs wasted little time ordering a set of bathing machines of the 'newest and most approved type'. Windsor also gave his permission for a single refreshment room to be thrown up 'within easy distance of the beach, where visitors can be supplied with tea, coffee, &c.'[51]

They were, in themselves, minor concessions, but they were freighted with great significance given Windsor's previous hostility to visitors. They confirmed that the dark days of the shutdown were over. Then, in 1893, came even more exciting news. It was rumoured that the landowner planned to build a summer residence on the Island.[52] Although initially denied by the estate, it soon became an 'open secret' that his lordship intended turning the Marine Hotel into a holiday home. The makeover of Friars Point House, as it was now to be called, was highly impressive. It was also extremely expensive. The interior was remodelled in the fashionable Arts and Crafts Jacobethan style, whilst in the grounds a 'magnificent garden' took shape.[53] In all, the project cost Windsor the considerable sum of £17,000.[54] Well-established trees and

Illus. 12. *Aerial view of Friars Point House, 1921. Windsor spent much more money on his private holiday home at Friars Point in the mid-1890s than he did on any other resort project at Barry Island. It is a striking example of social zoning at the seaside with railway sidings to the north and a working-class beach to the south-east.*

shrubs kept much of Windsor's new property hidden from the prying eyes of visitors, and imposing gates and fencing took over where the Scots Pine and the hawthorn trees petered out.[55] The construction of this aristocratic enclave, just a few hundred feet from a beach that was regularly crowded with tens of thousands of working-class visitors, stands as yet one more notable example of social zoning at the British seaside.[56]

Windsor and his family first stayed at their new seaside retreat in the summer of 1894.[57] During the summer of 1897, the nobleman's children were seen bathing at Whitmore Bay, an experience they reportedly enjoyed 'immensely'.[58] Robert Forrest, Windsor's agent, also took advantage of the luxurious seaside retreat. He proved to be an even more enthusiastic visitor to the Island than his employer, bringing his family to Friars Point House every summer from 1895 until his death in 1910.[59] Some commentators hoped that the mere presence of the aristocrat at his 'palatial' residence would boost Whitmore Bay's profile and have the effect of attracting a higher class of visitor. Their hopes were partially borne out, for between them, Windsor and Forrest played host to a string of distinguished guests during the late Victorian and Edwardian periods.[60] The daughter of an Archbishop of Canterbury, assorted peers of the realm and various high-ranking military officials all holidayed at Barry Island in the years before the First World War.[61]

Windsor's hefty investment in Friars Point House was accompanied by what boosters took to be an important policy statement. During his chairman's speech at a meeting of the directors of the Barry Railway Company in August 1894, Windsor made a few brief comments about the Island. He reassured Barrians that he did not wish to 'exclud[e] the public in any way from the enjoyment of Barry Island'. He was glad to note that the new branch line would soon run across to the Island – a development that would be welcomed, he was sure, by 'all those who desired to get a breath of fresh air at Barry, as well as those who hoped to make Barry Island a place of residence'. Finally, he underlined that he was 'doing all he possibly could to make Barry Island attractive to both visitors and residents' in order that everyone may 'get the full benefit of the advantages of the bay and open sea, which were already thoroughly appreciated'.[62] This was more than enough to convince local reporters that Windsor had been converted to the cause of resort development at Whitmore Bay. As the *Western Mail* put it, his remarks proved that 'his lordship [was] determined to make Barry Island an attractive resort'.[63]

There can be no doubting his determination to make Friars Point House as attractive as possible. Estate workers began improving the land around his lordship's new holiday home. Specifically, a temporary promenade was laid out that ran from Friars Point across to the sand dunes. Some paths were laid out on the headland, a bandstand appeared in 1896 and some benches were installed.[64] In November 1896, Windsor even gave his permission for the first fairground ride to be set up on the Island: a switchback railway that had proved to be a big hit at that summer's Cardiff Exhibition.[65] In the spring of 1897, his lordship's workers built a zig-zag pathway – 'with here and there a sheltered nook for seats' – that ran from the beach up in the direction of Lord Windsor's holiday home.[66]

Commentators were unanimous in their assessment of Lord Windsor's recent activity on the Island. According to the *South Wales Star*, his change of heart meant that Barry was now a 'rising watering place'. The *Dock News* agreed: the Island's future was unambiguously 'as a holiday resort', now that the landowner was lending his support to the boosters.[67] In 1897, the *South Wales Echo* praised his lordship for 'preserving natural beauty whilst utilising the land': 'The pretty little bay is safeguarded from the sight of even a single chimney pot; to the right is the reserved ground of Treharne's [i.e. Friars] Point, at the centre the sandhills have been levelled and turfed, and a garden promenade will crown the slope'. Even the new railway station 'is hidden in a hollow, central and commodious', whilst 'wide roadways sweep the whole course of the island'. The peer who had dismayed contemporaries when he closed Whitmore Bay to visitors was now being lauded for his tasteful approach to the development of the Island. 'Here the autocratic power has done public service', the *Echo* concluded.[68]

CONCLUSION: THE MID-1890S – A SHORT-LIVED MOMENT OF GREAT POSSIBILITY

In the mid-1890s, the promoters of resort development at the Island were certain that the future was theirs. They had identified Whitmore Bay's potential as a watering place, they had put the case for developing the Island in compelling terms, and they were already reaping the reward. In no time at all, the tides of history had turned in their favour. First, the Chamber of Trade had become a vehicle for resort boosterism. Secondly, the town's local politicians showed themselves to be supporters of the cause. Thirdly, the Barry Railway Company had, independently, invested in schemes that only made it more likely that tourism to the Island would flourish. And finally, the Windsor estate had executed a striking about-turn. No longer determined to turn visitors away, now it seemed committed to bringing them back to Whitmore Bay. Any lingering doubt about his lordship's intentions evaporated when news broke of his expensive plans for a holiday home at Friars Point. Clearly, the boosters were not the only ones who were seduced by the charms of Whitmore Bay: Lord Windsor was, too.

In hindsight, this perfect moment when all the major forces – the boosters, the landowner and the Barry Company – were pulling in the same direction, was more mirage than reality. The railway company, as we will see in chapter 7, cannot be described as a keen supporter of tourism at Barry Island in the 1890s. If it sometimes acted in ways that facilitated resort growth – and it undoubtedly did in the mid-1890s – it was often unintentionally, or only grudgingly, helpful. Likewise, Lord Windsor's influence at the Island was far more complicated than it might appear. For a short while, between 1894 and 1896, some of his actions suggest that he was genuinely interested in developing Whitmore Bay's resort potential. What we can say with certainty is that he was deeply committed to developing his own private holiday home. Some other improvement projects were incidental spin-offs from his Friars Point scheme. However, as the 1890s wore on, any enthusiasm that he may have had for resort development at the Island dissipated. By the turn of the century, boosters were increasingly viewing him as a deeply unhelpful figure.

Of the three groups of actors, it was the boosters whose motives are the easiest to divine. They were consistent in their support for resort development. A burgeoning pride in all things Barrian fuelled many inhabitants' desire to see Whitmore Bay transformed into a thriving watering place. Nevertheless, there can be little doubt that underlying their calls for resort development was a far less sentimental reason: boosters believed that the Island would increase their material prosperity.[69] The most vocal supporters of municipal involvement in 'improving' the Island were members of the town's business community. Just as at other seaside resorts, it was a 'transparent self-interest' that led to traders' calls for public funds to be spent on resort infrastructure. In almost every other type of town, leading ratepayers strained every sinew to keep rates down; in seaside towns, the opposite was true. At Barry, in the 1890s, figures such as J. C. Meggitt and F. P. Jones-Lloyd behaved as if they were spokespersons for a holiday interest.[70] They pushed for the council to involve itself in expensive schemes calculated to boost tourism, and they did so without attracting any criticism. However, it was to be a short-lived moment. As we shall see in the next chapter, it was not long before resort boosters found themselves operating in a much more unfriendly environment. By 1900, many were already looking back to the mid-1890s, wondering if their moment in the sun had passed. A holiday interest was never again able to set the agenda in Barry in the way that it did in the last years of the nineteenth century.

CHAPTER SIX

'[A]WAKE
YE SLUGGARDS!'

RESORT DEVELOPMENT
FLOUNDERS, c.1900–1914

EMBOLDENED BY THE encouraging developments of the mid-1890s, Barry Island's boosters promoted the cause of resort development energetically. Throughout the Edwardian period, they continued to push the idea that Whitmore Bay was a cash cow that could, if properly looked after, bring significant sums of money into the town. However, despite a promising start, there followed a remarkably long fallow period. Not until the early 1920s was there any substantial investment in the resort infrastructure at the Island. A whole generation of town leaders had come and gone, yet the boosters had precious little to show for all their proselytizing. It was, by any standards, a notable record of repeated failures. As we shall see, in seeking explanations for their lack of progress, supporters of a developed Island frequently pointed the finger of blame at the town leaders: they stood accused of being hopeless prevaricators. However, it is argued in this chapter that this was a misunderstanding of the problem facing resort boosterism at Barry. Boosters, including those in the council chamber, were stymied by a conjunction of unhelpful factors – from the geography of the Barry district to a landowner who, despite assurances to the contrary, was far from being a supporter of tourism at the Island. The history of Whitmore Bay in the early twentieth century is, amongst other things, a reminder of the continued power of landlords to shape events at the British seaside.

'MUCH TALK: LITTLE WOOL': COUNCILLORS' LACK OF ACCOMPLISHMENT AT WHITMORE BAY

One indication of the boosters' dynamism throughout the Edwardian period is their success in keeping resort development on the agenda of the town's councillors. Between 1903 and 1914, town leaders gave serious consideration to at least eight separate development schemes. A couple were relatively modest. If they had been passed, one or two small shelters would have been built at Whitmore Bay.[1] But most of the projects brought before councillors were much more ambitious. In 1903 and 1904, for example, the council considered plans to build a gigantic shelter capable of accommodating 20,000 visitors.[2] Later, in 1907, it was announced that members of the Public Works Committee had given their support to plans drawn up by W. T. Douglas, an architect of national standing who had an impressive track record in seaside developments. His vision for Whitmore Bay included a permanent promenade, seawall, bandstands, new paths at Friars Point, drinking fountains and seven shelters, one of which was to hold 6,000 visitors.[3] In the event, not all the councillors were as bold as those on the Public Works Committee. Balking at the eye-watering price tag of £35,730, town leaders came up with their own watered-down versions of Douglas's plans. The permutations were endless. Some schemes did away with the seawall; some cut the numbers of shelters; some made do with just one, much larger shelter. One proposal would have led to such a diminutive seawall – it was to be just two feet high – that it would have been overwhelmed by the dunes in no time. One set of plans prioritized the construction of shops at Whitmore Bay. Another set privileged the laying out of the ornamental gardens. And so the different iterations kept coming.[4] The constant mulling over of initiatives did not, in the end, lead to any lasting material changes at Whitmore Bay during the Edwardian years, but it certainly encouraged the sense that Barry's seafront was always poised on the brink of development. Indeed, at least once during this period, builders were sent over to the Island to begin preparatory work.[5]

News of each new proposal re-energized the forces of boosterism. When councillors engaged W. T. Douglas in the spring of 1907, the *Barry Dock News* breathed a sigh of relief. This was the moment when Barry would become the 'Biarritz of Wales', the paper announced.[6] A few months later, a reporter interviewed the architect on the beach. Having listened to Douglas wax lyrical about the Island's natural beauty, the journalist was certain that Whitmore Bay's future success was at last assured. 'Give the Barry Council plenty of money', he remarked, 'and our town, not many years hence, will be unexcelled by Blackpool or Bournemouth, and our welfare will depend, not solely as at present on the black diamond, but will be largely augmented by the advantages of a thriving seaside resort'.[7]

Yet, for all the talk, the much-anticipated grand schemes never materialized. Meggitt first mooted the idea of municipal improvements at the Island back in 1896, but it took nearly three decades before Whitmore Bay was graced with a permanent seawall and its first shelter. It was an extraordinary track record of procrastination. The boosters' frustration grew with every passing summer season. In July 1900, a Barrian wrote to the *Dock News* warning that Whitmore Bay was 'doomed' as a pleasure resort unless councillors grasped the nettle and invested in resort amenities and artificial amusements. Natural attractions were no longer enough to draw visitors, he declared: the public would 'become disgusted with it' and stop coming if town leaders did not act soon.[8] In 1905, E. B. Sawyer, a teacher of plumbing at the Barry Technical Instruction Classes, became so disillusioned with the local politicians that he worked up his own development scheme. A reproduction of his plan appeared in the *Dock News*. It included a pleasure pier (complete with a band stand, a look-out, wind shelters and a handful of lock-up shops), a pavilion and a public shelter. The paper thought Sawyer's scheme was 'most excellent' and suggested that it be submitted for consideration to the council.[9] But like all the other initiatives, it was left to gather dust.

By the later 1900s, after years of inconclusive debates, supporters of a developed Island were in despair. 'Vox Populi', a columnist in the *Herald*, pilloried Barry's local politicians. 'Once a year, without exception, for the last fourteen or fifteen years, our District Council awake to the possibilities of the development of Barry Island', the journalist complained. Precious time was squandered on desultory discussions that always seemed to lead nowhere. 'As usual, at the very last minute, they will take the matter up, rush like a bull at a gate, and decide on the spur of the moment, with the result that they will land themselves into difficulties before they are halfway through their scheme'. Barry Island was being held back by the 'curse of local government', he declared.[10] In March 1912, after an especially drawn-out evening which saw councillors argue for hours about the pros and cons of yet one more resort development project, the editor of the *Herald* dismissed the proceedings with the judgement, 'Much talk: little wool'.[11] Throughout these years, the correspondence columns of the local papers became a place where Barrians vented their anger at the way that the Island question was being mismanaged by councillors. As one disgruntled inhabitant pointed out in 1912, other resorts had a surfeit of 'up-to-date attractions' such as pleasure piers, pavilions, winter gardens and amusement parks: Barry, in contrast, did not even have a seawall.[12] The *Herald*'s editor sympathized with the 'misguided holiday trippers' who kept returning to Barry every summer in spite of the lack of development. He blamed the town leaders. 'In the name of St. Baruc', he fumed, 'awake ye sluggards! Look to your laurels, or you will be whooped from your gilded Chamber!!'[13]

THE TIDE TURNS: RESORT BOOSTERISM FLOUNDERS IN AN ERA OF FINANCIAL CRISIS

Ineffective councillors, incapable of delivering the improvements so urgently needed at Whitmore Bay – it was a powerful criticism and one that chimed, no doubt, with the opinion of many of the *Herald*'s readers who had utterly lost faith in the ability of the town's political elite to make the most of Barry Island's great potential as a tourist attraction.

However, for all its populist appeal, the 'incompetent councillors' thesis is a very poor explanation for the stalling of resort development at Whitmore Bay.

Far from being a collection of bungling politicians unable to cope with the challenges of a major development project, Barry's town leaders consistently proved themselves to be effective operators. Since the later 1880s, they had overseen the rapid growth of a substantial urban community. The building of Barry depended upon the completion of a wide range of costly capital projects – from the installation of drainage and sewerage systems to the construction of schools and libraries and the laying out of public parks. These projects had to be agreed upon, organized and paid for by the municipal authority. That councillors were able to achieve so much in the town during the late Victorian and Edwardian years, yet so little over on the Island, suggests that, if we are properly to explain the lack of progress at Whitmore Bay, we should look beyond an argument that casts local politicians in the role of buffoons and sluggards.[14]

For one thing, the boosters themselves need to shoulder some of the responsibility for the lack of progress. After all, their approach to resort development hardly helped Barry's municipal fathers. They were never at a loss when it came to delivering stirring soundbites about Whitmore Bay's huge potential, but they were notably quiet when it came to explaining how their dreams might be materialized. The assertion that the Island was an El Dorado on the town's doorstep – a 'golden casket' just waiting to be unlocked – was certainly alluring, but what were town leaders supposed to do with such an insight?[15] C. Michael Hall has argued that nineteenth-century resort boosterism should properly be regarded as 'a form of non-planning', so heavy was it on hyperbole and so light on detail.[16] It is a criticism that can be fairly applied to the Barry experience. Claims that Barry could become the Scarborough of Wales, the future Queen of Welsh Watering Places, a Blackpool, a Brighton and a Bournemouth of Wales were all well and good, but what, precisely, did they mean? And how were such diverse outcomes to be realized?[17] Blackpool was an entirely different type of resort from Bournemouth. At one level, such evocative labels were just rhetorical devices, deployed to whip up support. But, in the absence of any more substantial plans, they were all that councillors had to go on. Should they concentrate on trying to raise Whitmore Bay's social tone? Or should they aim to attract more working-class visitors? It is unsurprising, given boosters' often vague and contradictory statements, that Barry's civic leaders struggled to turn empty marketing slogans into properly costed development policies.

Barry's councillors had other problems to wrestle with, too. Of critical importance was a deteriorating financial context. Barry was a boom town. However, by the turn of the century it was teetering on the edge of financial meltdown. This might seem paradoxical. The dock, the mainspring of the town's economy, was outperforming even the most sanguine forecasts of its promoters. Indeed, it was about to replace Cardiff as the top coal-exporting port in the world. Nevertheless, building a town's infrastructure from scratch in just a decade placed a huge strain on the council's finances. From its earliest days, the local authority was required to go into debt to pay for all the costly schemes that it was obliged to undertake. In 1892 alone, the local board had to secure a loan of over £13,000 to pay for street improvements, sewers and water pillars. This prompted a board member to explain that 'the district was at present a poor one, and an enormous expenditure had been forced on the district . . . the place was a new one, and the burdens had fallen heavily on a few'. The board had been compelled to pay for the improvement of some forty streets in just eighteen months.[18]

By the eve of the Great War, the town's indebtedness reached critical levels. Councillors were forced to raise the rates in order to service the debts. The 'high rates' question dominated local affairs in the Edwardian period and focused the public's attention on how town leaders spent ratepayers' money.[19] In 1900, rates stood at a record high of one shilling and nine pence in the pound, causing many residents to call on councillors to embark upon a period of strict municipal economy.[20] It was widely believed that the problem lay with the town fathers and their reckless approach to spending. In a number of wards, ratepayers' groups sprang up with the express purpose of keeping a careful watch on the council's 'wastrel tactics'.[21] The complaint of one Cadoxton ratepayer was typical: 'There was no town in Wales with four times the population of Barry that had such [an] elaborate pile of buildings for the fire brigade as there was in this district, and there was only one other town that possessed a refuge destructor'.[22] Barrians, so this argument ran, were suffering because of the devil-may-care attitude of their councillors. Local newspapers, to prove the case, published league tables that contrasted Barry's public spending levels unfavourably with those of other towns. The *Barry Dock News* castigated councillors for being too 'lavish' in their handling of the ratepayers' hard-earned cash. The only way forward, the paper informed its readers, was for the town to become 'very thrifty in the expenditure of its money'.[23]

It was a significant turnabout. In the mid-1890s, when support for resort development was at its height, Barry's business community acted as a holiday interest group, happy to countenance expensive resort schemes being paid for out of the rates. Now, in the early 1900s, it behaved more like its counterparts in other industrial settlements. The growth of a retrenchment party in Barry tells us something profound about how its social elite viewed their town's economy. For the briefest of moments, a majority of its traders had been willing to see themselves as living in a port that might, soon, become a successful seaside resort. Once it became clear just how difficult it was going to be to profit from tourism at Barry Island, increasing numbers turned against the idea of pursuing the dream of a highly developed seafront and concentrated their energy on keeping public spending down.

The '"mob" . . . from the hills': anti-tripper sentiment in Barry

In such a climate, town leaders were acutely aware that every spending decision they made was subject to intense scrutiny. During municipal elections, candidates across the political spectrum felt obliged to declare their strong opposition to 'spending Ratepayers' Monies on needless and unproductive schemes'.[24] Resort boosters were required to justify their claims: it was no longer enough to make sweeping statements about Whitmore Bay's great promise as a watering place. Most troublingly, doubts grew about the accuracy of the boosters' central claim – namely, that tourism would be good for the town's economy. It became glaringly obvious that, even as the Island attracted ever greater numbers of visitors, few of them seemed to be heading into Barry town. As one journalist noticed in the summer of 1905, the town 'wore quite a deserted appearance' on days when the Island was at its busiest.[25] Another commented that trippers showed 'little or no inclination to visit other parts of the town'.[26] And in 1907, a councillor wondered whether the much-vaunted tourism multiplier effect would ever kick in at Barry, for, as yet, 'no tradesman was much better off for the sojourn of the day trippers in the town'.[27]

In part, critics' disquiet stemmed from a realization that Barry might be drawing too many 'low-value' day-trippers and not enough high-spending resident visitors. Furious arguments occasionally erupted over the social tone of Whitmore Bay. John Stapleton – a nurseryman and Chamber of Trade member – emerged as a scourge of the resort boosters. In his view, too much attention had been focused on catering to the needs of an unremunerative class of visitors. As he put it in

May 1906, he 'would be glad to see the day when day trippers would cease to come to Barry, for then they would get a better class of visitors into the town'.[28] Only when Barrians began courting holidaymakers of a higher social class would they begin to see a return to the town's coffers. The following year he poured scorn on plans to spend £23,000 on a shelter at Whitmore Bay. It was a 'wild goose scheme', he thundered, that would only benefit the '"mob" of trippers'. They should stop looking after the day excursionists and concentrate instead on improving Porthkerry Park and the Cold Knap. These were resort spaces that would attract the 'respectable people' who currently were staying away because of 'the "mob" that came from the hills'.[29]

Stapleton's disparaging descriptions of the visitors from the coalfield drew fierce criticism from many of his colleagues in the Chamber of Trade. They condemned him for his insensitive language and countered that Barry, of all places, should welcome the colliers upon whose back-breaking work the town's prosperity was based.[30] Many Barrians had, for long, been of this opinion. As the *Herald* had observed in 1896, Barry owed everything to those 'sons of toil in the bowels of the earth' and the least the town could do was give them 'a right royal welcome when they visit us'.[31] Later, in 1907, in reaction to Stapleton's attack on the colliers, a correspondent to the *Dock News* reminded him that Barry would be 'only a desert waste' if it was not for the colliers.[32] Nevertheless, it was possible to appreciate all that the inhabitants of the mining valleys had done for Barry whilst still worrying about their economic value as tourists. By 1913, even the *Dock News* had reluctantly reached the conclusion that the trippers were proving to be 'of very little use to the Town'.[33]

Stapleton was right about one thing: the day-trippers dominated Barry's resort spaces. It is impossible to know for certain how many holidayed in the town for a few days or longer because precise information on them was rarely recorded. However, we can be sure that there were some resident visitors and that they always constituted the tiniest minority of Barry's tourists. There are references to 'hundreds of respectable visitors' having expressed an interest in vacationing in the town in the mid-1890s.[34] A few years later a journalist suggested that as many as a thousand visitors had stayed in the town 'for several weeks at a time' during the previous holiday season.[35] In 1907, the council alone had dealt with about 250 enquiries from outsiders who were keen to holiday in Barry.[36] By then, the Chamber of Trade, local newspapers and the town council were all fielding accommodation enquiries from 'intending visitors' who hailed from various parts of the United Kingdom.[37] Some of them could be surprisingly well-to-do. In 1907, a London bank manager brought his family to Barry for the summer. His son, a mathematics undergraduate at Cambridge drowned whilst bathing at Whitmore Bay.[38] The Blow family from Cardiff stayed at the Island for two months every summer in the early years of the century.[39] Other staying visitors were from more modest backgrounds. For example, Arthur Maxworthy, an assurance superintendent from Pontypool, brought his wife and four children for a week's holiday at the Island in 1905.[40]

Thus, when one Islander remarked in 1910 that 'We don't get class . . . here – only colliers and [their] families', he exaggerated.[41] But only slightly. The resident visitors were such rare birds at Whitmore Bay that it was easy to miss them. At a time when the Island was drawing an estimated half-a-million trippers, probably only a thousand stayed for a few nights or more.[42] This was not enough to placate the John Stapletons of the world. Attracting more of them, and fewer day-trippers, became a burning ambition for some Barrians over the coming decades.

A WEAK TOURISM MULTIPLIER EFFECT

Boosterism hit another problem: the unhelpful geography of the Barry district. At resorts where town centre and beach were cheek-by-jowl it was certain that at least some traders would benefit from large numbers of trippers. But at Barry, the beach and town were separated by a great dock and a walk of nearly a mile. Before Barry Island station opened in 1896, those who came by train were compelled to alight at either Barry dock or Barry town station. It was reasonable to hope that some of them might have wandered into the commercial heart of Barry before or after their few hours on the beach. However, after 1896, they were whisked past the town in their trains, straight over to Whitmore Bay. What should

Illus. 13 (top right). *Map of Barry town and the Island, 1898.*
The beach and town were some distance apart. Trippers tended to stay on the Island and not venture into the town. The dock, with its extensive network of railway tracks, merely added to the sense of disconnection between town and seaside.
Illus. 14 (bottom right). *Aerial view of Whitmore Bay with the dock and the town behind, May 1933. It was a long walk from the Barry's beach to its town centre.*

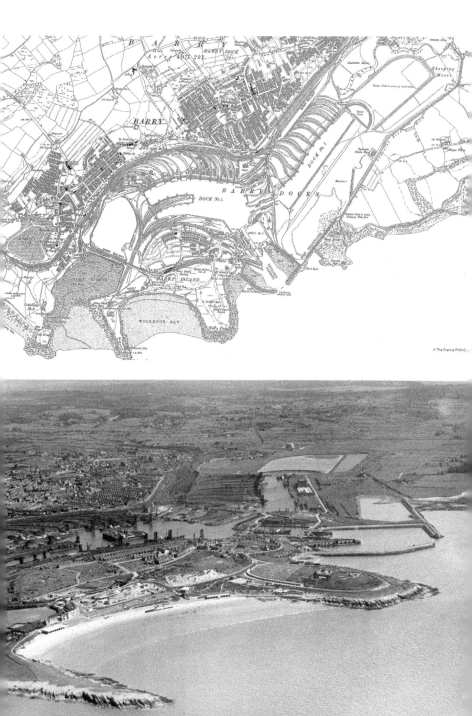

have been a good news story about an upgraded transport link bringing more visitors to Barry had become a disaster. A correspondent to the *Dock News* spotted the problem early on. Responding to the news that the new branch line was to be built, he observed in 1894 that it would doubtless be 'the making of Barry Island', but it would 'injure the trade of Barry Town very much'. Trippers would 'not think of coming back to the town once they have got to the seaside'.[43]

He was right. Trippers, realizing that a trip to the town was out of the question, quickly got into the habit of bringing their own provisions with them. The piles of rubbish that they left behind them told the story: 'empty bottles, remnants of alfresco meals, and greasy papers' – the Island's visitors were keen picnickers.[44] Many even brought kettles to prepare hot drinks. Observers often commented on the number of small fires that were started on the sands. A reporter from the *Herald* was impressed by the 'frequent thin columns of smoke ascending to the welkin' that he saw when he visited Whitmore Bay on Whit Monday, 1910. He took them as proof that 'al fresco teas were still as popular as ever'.[45]

Thus, separation of town and beach meant that the day-trippers were rendered even less 'valuable' at Barry than they were at many other resorts: it kept them on the Island and encouraged them to bring their own refreshments. For the likes of John Stapleton, the solution was clear. If the trippers were not paying their way, efforts should be made to attract a more lucrative class of visitor. But how feasible was this proposition? By the 1890s, it may already have been too late. Whitmore Bay's environs were no longer conducive to the development of a select watering place. Peter Borsay has noted the importance of a rich architectural heritage in seaside resorts that catered for long-stay visitors. Tenby, for instance, was comprised of a medieval built form replete with ageing structures that could appeal to tourists' gothic sensibilities.[46] Tumbledown abbeys and crumbling medieval town walls were noticeably thin on the ground at industrial Barry. It was, as one observer put it, essentially 'a utility place' rather than a tourist attraction.[47] Even the Island – with its railway cuttings, tunnels, roads and working-class houses – had not been spared the developer's spade. One visitor from London found Barry's urban landscape so repugnant that, in 1914, he went into print to express his contempt for the place: he could not 'imagine a worse fate for any human being than to be condemned to live in Barry'.[48] The comment revealed much about his metropolitan prejudices and his pitiful lack of imagination. Nevertheless, it also revealed how Barry's proletarian character might deter those tourists who sought a more refined, urbane setting when taking a seaside holiday.

In 1896, whilst ruminating on the future development of Barry Island, the *Herald* decided that the game was up as far as hopes of making Whitmore Bay a select resort were concerned.

> A *fashionable* watering-place it will never be. There is far too much coal-dust and too many snorting and shrieking steam-engines rushing about all day to make it a desirable seaside resort for those who have the means to go elsewhere; but *popular* it probably will become.[49]

It is undeniable that Whitmore Bay's proximity to the world's leading coal-exporting port did have an impact on boosters' ability to market it as a 'Biarritz of Wales'.[50] Coal dust could be a problem. With nearly 4,000 barques leaving the port every year, colossal clouds of dust were thrown up as they were loaded.[51] When the young Russian writer Boris Pilnyak visited Barry in the early 1920s, he was startled by the polluted atmosphere: 'The coal dust settles on the ships in Barry dock deeper than a centimetre in a day; the sun stands in dust like a copper pan; and it is possible to look at it with the naked eye.'[52] The prevailing winds usually took most of it away from the Island – but not always. Islanders complained of the difficulties of drying clothes outside when unfriendly winds blew in from the north.[53]

Other forms of pollution associated with the dock were more troublesome. When, in March 1894, the *Vanduara* ran aground at Whitmore Bay, it dumped 3,000 tons of coke on the sands. It remained there for months, every high tide dispersing it across an ever-larger area.[54] On other occasions, large deposits of inches-thick mud inundated the beach. '[P]ositively alarming' quantities of the sludge were sometimes swept onto the sands as a result of dredging work that had to be done to keep the channel into the docks clear for shipping. In the estimation of a council official, the filth had 'practically destroyed the bay for pleasure purposes'; bathing had been rendered undesirable and the trade of pleasure boats at low tide had been 'ruined'. Whitmore Bay, he announced, had been well and truly 'besmeared'.[55] Little wonder that the more realistic of the boosters were forced to concede that the Island's appeal to more well-heeled visitors was probably limited by its industrial surroundings. 'Barry cannot expect to be more than a local resort' because of the nearness of the dock, declared one commentator in 1907.[56]

All the above factors meant that it became increasingly difficult for boosters of Barry Island to make the case for resort development. In the more optimistic 1890s, it was enough for them to assert that Whitmore

Illus. 15. *The S.S.* Valsesia *stranded at Friars Point in August 1926.*
Sometimes it was impossible to ignore Whitmore Bay's proximity to
a world-leading coal port. Shipwrecks became tourist attractions in
their own right.

Bay was a gold mine just waiting to be exploited; now, such a claim
seemed vacuous. Years of having to watch as tripper numbers rose substantially whilst the town reaped no obvious reward had taken their toll.
And now that Barry was struggling with its debts, glib assertions that
more visitors would necessarily benefit Barry no longer went unchal-
lenged. Ratepayers living in wards furthest away from the Island were
particularly suspicious of expensive development plans. They were ever
more likely to argue against such schemes.[57] In 1909, it was reported that
voters in Cadoxton viewed 'any huge expenditure' on the Island 'with
great alarm'.[58] Costly projects to upgrade the seafront were now as likely
to be derided as being 'moonshine scheme[s]' produced by 'local gossip
and midnight dreams' as they were to be lauded for their ambition.[59]

By the eve of the Great War, some critics questioned whether it was
worth pursuing the dream of a developed resort at Whitmore Bay at all.
'It was as feasible for Blackpool to try and ship 10,000,000 tons of coal
per annum' as it was to transform Barry into a leading seaside resort,
proclaimed one journalist in 1913.[60] Others argued that the answer to

Barry's financial woes were new industries, not more holidaymakers.[61] Given such scepticism, it was no surprise that councillors thought twice before spending heavily at Whitmore Bay. They were not sluggards. They were merely astute local politicians reflecting their constituents' wider concerns about the viability of resort development at Barry Island.

A DESTABILIZING PRESENCE: THE WINDSOR ESTATE'S ROLE IN STALLING RESORT DEVELOPMENTS

By the early years of the new century, then, boosters faced both a crisis in municipal finances and a growing recognition that tourism at Whitmore Bay was not delivering the long-awaited economic benefits. But their problems did not end there. Lord Windsor, the Island's owner, became increasingly disruptive. As we saw in the previous chapter, in the mid-1890s, there was a moment when his lordship appeared to be a possible ally of the boosters. Sometimes he did take on a supportive role. When, in 1900, town leaders brought forward proposals to build the bathing pool and the changing rooms at Whitmore Bay, Windsor contributed £1,000 to the scheme. He also provided sites for the public urinals at Whitmore Bay and for the museum to house the various archaeological finds that had been discovered on the Island in recent years. The landowner's largesse was noted approvingly by a Local Government Board inspector who proclaimed that 'Lord Windsor has behaved very liberally'.[62]

However, these were to be unusually generous displays on his part. More commonly, the Windsor estate showed itself to be uninterested in resort development. Sometimes, it was just plain obstructive. Windsor's enthusiasm for resort development peaked in the mid-1890s – at precisely the same time as he was lavishing huge sums of money on his private summer retreat at Friars Point. Once that project was completed, his interest ebbed away faster than a falling spring tide.

The contrast with the estate's approach to Penarth is highly revealing. At Penarth, as we have noted, the estate saw the improvement of the seafront as a critical part of its plans to create a fashionable marine suburb. As the *South Wales Echo* explained it, Windsor 'laid out a great deal of money to make Penarth a seaside resort', and he encouraged other 'men of capital' to do the same.[63] When not spending his own money, he happily played the role of facilitator, creating the conditions that made significant investment possible at Penarth's seafront. Thus,

Illus. 16. *Penarth pier, c.1900. Lord Windsor owned Penarth and Barry Island. Penarth showed that, if he willed it, he could oversee the development of a fashionable watering place.*

he persuaded a group of capitalists to set up the Penarth Pier Company and spend £35,000 of their own funds on the pier and its assorted attractions by granting them use of the necessary land at a nominal rent of just £25 per annum.[64] At the same time, the estate cultivated a close relationship with Penarth's local authorities. Local leaders often commented on the 'characteristic generosity' of his lordship, whilst Robert Forrest, his agent, was applauded for 'always [having] been a good friend to Penarth'. The two figures were frequently praised by newspapers for their philanthropic gifts to the town: £100 for a new public clock; £500 towards a new church organ; £1,000 towards a new school building, and so on.[65] Such strong ties meant that councillors felt empowered to embark on various improvement projects. Forrest dined with Penarth's local representatives and discussed how best to 'enhanc[e] the natural attractiveness' of the town 'as a residential centre and health resort'. He made 'generous offer[s] of land' to the local authority. For their part, councillors repaid the estate's confidence in them by spending thousands of pounds of ratepayers' money on a variety of projects that improved Windsor's beloved town. As the *Cardiff Times* remarked, such schemes were only able to proceed because of the active cooperation of Lord Windsor – the landlord's support 'was absolutely necessary'.[66]

When it came to improving Barry Island, however, the estate sought no such close relationship with local leaders. On the contrary, Barry's councillors increasingly felt that they were dealing with a most unpredictable force. On occasion, the estate did not even attempt to hide its capriciousness. Councillors had control of the foreshore – which they leased from the Crown – but the rest of the Island, including the area of the beach above the high-water mark, belonged to Windsor. Windsor and Forrest seemed determined to keep reminding Barrians of that fact. How else can we explain the repeated instances of landlord power being exercised arbitrarily at the Island's resort spaces? For example, when councillors brought forward trifling plans to extend the bathing houses at Whitmore Bay in 1912, the estate rejected them on the grounds that the alteration to the men's house would limit the view from Friars Point – a risible suggestion given the size of the headland and the modest nature of the proposed extension.[67] Even more unfathomable was the news that Windsor's men had, in September 1904, prevented young mothers from taking their prams onto the beach.[68] It was a move that left an apoplectic *Herald* almost lost for words: 'Why! Why!! Why!!!' it spluttered.[69]

These were but minor examples of the estate intervening unhelpfully at the Island. There were more significant instances, however. Most obvious, was his lordship's opposition to any significant development of Whitmore Bay's resort facilities. He clearly had no interest in doing for Barry Island what he had done at Penarth. Apart from some small gifts here and there, Windsor spent little of his own money at the Island. The contrast with his heavy expenditure at Penarth is certainly instructive. By the same token, and even more importantly, his lordship stopped others from investing their capital at Barry Island. True, he allowed Edwin Hullin and his associate to run their single refreshment hut and their bathing machine operation. He let the proprietors of a switchback railway onto the Island in the late 1890s. And he did not object when a troupe of Pierrots set up a little stage on the dunes in the early 1900s. Jimmy Shields – the 'world's greatest comedian and one-legged dancer' – and his Happy Valley Pierrots were regular summer visitors in the early years of the century. They performed on the sands and became firm favourites with the trippers.[70] Great crowds gathered three times a day during the season to watch a mixture of 'choruses, sentimental and comic songs, creole ditties, dances, comic sketches, lantern views – loyal, patriotic, historic, and funny – selections from grand opera, and a pleasing shadow pantomime'.[71] It was all unimpeachably respectable stuff – 'Fun without vulgarity', as a local newspaper put it.[72]

It would be inaccurate to say that Windsor blocked all development at Barry Island, then. But no one could claim that he presided over even the most gradual evolution of Whitmore Bay's resort facilities. Compared with the leading British working-class resorts, with their surfeit of artificial amusements, their commercialized entertainments and striking architectural features, Barry looked woefully underdeveloped. Indeed, if set alongside other medium-sized Welsh resorts, hardly pathbreakers, Barry still looked decidedly third rate. They at least boasted hotels, piers, promenades, pavilions and seawalls. Yet at the Island, the key resort space, Whitmore Bay, remained almost untouched. Even when it came to the most basic facilities, it was severely lacking. His lordship did nothing to provide adequate toilet facilities for the tens of thousands of trippers who routinely gathered on the sands, just a matter of yards from his holiday home. Nor did he throw up a shelter to give the trippers a fighting chance of staying dry during an August downpour. And he refused to allow traders, other than Hullin, onto the Island to provide the visitors with food and drink. The demand for such refreshments was unprecedented, but the estate remained adamant: no traders were to be allowed on the Island. Even as late as 1905, Forrest still insisted that there should be a blanket ban on the sale of food, fruit, toys and all other goods.[73]

We will consider how Windsor's deadening policies affected the tripper experience in the following chapter. For the moment, we need merely wonder why he adopted such a regressive approach. Why not let others cater for the hungry, thirsty playful crowds? Why not let others build a pier (as he had done at Penarth)? Why not let a gaggle of entertainers onto the sands? Why not at least provide an adequate supply of toilets or a shelter or two? Or let mothers with prams onto the beach?

Perhaps part of the answer is to be found in Windsor's continued concern to protect his interests at Penarth. As we have noted, it was just beginning to establish itself as a bourgeois watering place. A prettified Barry Island with a full panoply of resort amenities would have undoubtedly drawn visitors and potential residents away from Penarth. That goes some way to explaining why the estate did not want

Whitmore Bay to become a resort of high social tone. But it does not tell us why Windsor and Forrest were so reluctant to see it develop as a working-class playground. A plebeian Island, after all, should have posed no threat to a genteel Penarth.

Some of the Island's boosters increasingly felt that Lord Windsor was being difficult simply because of his dislike of the trippers: class prejudice, they opined, may have explained his unfriendliness. They may well have been right. We have an advantage over those late Victorian and Edwardian Barrians. Unlike them, we can read a piece of private correspondence written by Robert Forrest in the mid-1870s. In the letter, Forrest revealed his utter contempt for excursionists from the coalfield. He had become alarmed by the numbers heading to Penarth during the summer months from the mining valleys. As he put it, a 'perfect rabble from the hills' had descended upon the place. Tellingly, he went on. '*We cannot stop the rabble coming to Penarth but we can throw obstacles in the way.*'[74] The centrepiece of his plan to keep trippers away involved a ban on the sale of refreshments on, and near, the beach. This was the very policy that Forrest reprised at Barry in the 1890s and 1900s. Indeed, at Whitmore Bay, the estate went further, restricting the supply of toilets and entertainments, too.

The true depths of Windsor's and Forrest's contempt for the Island's visitors and the townspeople of Barry only became fully apparent in the early years of the twentieth century when they closed Whitmore Bay's key resort spaces, the beach included. For those with long memories, it was an unpleasant reminder of the unhappy days of the first great shutdown of the island. The circumstances that prompted the closure were themselves a disturbing example of landlord power being used to undermine the right of visitors to enjoy the Island's spaces. In August 1903, Forrest informed councillors that Windsor was about to charge visitors to access Friars Point. As Forrest explained it, his lordship wanted to 'withhold its use from everybody in order that residents might enjoy the greatest benefit from it'. Locals, Forrest reassured town leaders, could expect to have 'practically free access' (there would be a 'nominal' charge for a season ticket) but 'outside people' would have to pay one penny each. This would 'preserve it from damage by the big crowds from the hills'.[75]

The explicitly anti-tripper message was troubling enough for those who wished to see the Island flourish as a tourist destination, but the stakes were raised dramatically in the summer of 1904 when news broke that the estate had decided simply to close Friars Point to the public.[76] Apologists for the landowner tried to see it from the aristocrat's point of view. The Island was private property, they reasoned; the public had only ever been allowed there 'not as a prescriptive right, but merely as a matter of courtesy'.[77] Most were not prepared to adopt such a supine position, however. The attack on the customary rights of Barrians and tourists constituted 'a gigantic public question' according to the *Herald*: 'Barry Island will lose its attractions for the visitor if it is going to have wire entanglements like Port Arthur'.[78] In the paper's view, the matter of public access to Friars Point was 'the foremost question' of the day. 'On all hands the public are set at defiance by the land monopolists who control the Island, the beach, and the trade of that part of the town, and some determined action must be taken.'[79] Barry's councillors were equally unsettled. They unanimously agreed that the landowner's new policy be referred to the council's parliamentary committee.[80]

At a stroke, Windsor had politicized the Island's resort spaces. It was a remarkably crass move at a time when the 'land question' was a sensitive issue. Wales had become a stronghold of Liberal politicians, many of whom had made a career out of drawing attention to the tyrannical attitude of great landowners.[81] Yet Windsor's disregard for the rights of citizens and trippers did not end there. After months of being criticized in the press and the council chamber for their handling of the Friars Point affair, Windsor and Forrest had their revenge in January 1905. They ordered estate workers to close down the Island. The beach was roped off, holes were dug in the approach roads to prevent vehicles gaining access, and an 'iron unclimbable fencing' was put up at a major junction on the Island 'thus effectively blocking a means of public access to [it]'. The men engaged in erecting the fencing told the council's surveyor they were 'acting according to instructions from the Windsor Estate'. Councillors were outraged.[82] Windsor had reneged on his promise not to exclude the public 'in any way from the enjoyment of Barry Island'.[83] He had also left the town's inhabitants and tourists in no doubt of who was in charge at Whitmore Bay.

It is easy to dismiss the closure of the beach in the depths of mid-winter as mere sabre-rattling, an empty display of machismo. The number of visitors turned away on those chilly January days was probably tiny. But the ropes strung across the entrances to the beach possessed a symbolic power all of their own. As John K. Walton has pointed out, although public access to the foreshores of Britain's beaches 'was guaranteed by convention rather than by law', it was very unusual for landowners to try and interfere with the customary rights of visitors in this way. 'Such attempts were known to be productive of controversy and opprobrium, which helped to discourage them.'[84] Windsor was a truly exceptional case. Not only had he successfully closed the beach to visitors in the late 1870s and 1880s, but he had also managed to repeat the act in 1905.

Apart from infuriating public opinion in Barry, his actions had a discernible impact on the Island's popularity over the short term. The shutdown came at the end of months of wrangling over the rights of trippers to access Friars Point, and word had filtered up to the mining valleys that excursionists from 'the hills' were no longer welcome at Barry Island. In the summer of 1904, an inhabitant of Merthyr Tydfil wrote to the *Barry Herald* expressing his dismay. By erecting a turnstile at Friars Point, Windsor had revealed himself to be the worst kind of landowner – the sort who 'in addition to barb-wiring every pleasant spot, would fence off the pure air and sea shore had they ability'. The correspondent wondered what visitors from the coalfield had done to offend the aristocrat. Colliers visited Barry Island simply to 'revel in the bracing air on the downs, and the grand prospect of the Somerset and Devonian coast' after long months working underground producing the very coal from which his lordship – as chair of the Barry Railway Company – profited so spectacularly. The Merthyrian closed his letter with an appeal to Barry's councillors to do all they could on behalf of the trippers. And he issued a warning: Whitmore Bay was a beguiling spot, to be sure, but there were other beaches nearby.[85]

For a while, at least, some visitors did look elsewhere for their seaside sojourns. Windsor only closed the beach for a day or so in January 1905, but the impression lingered that the ban was still in force. In the early summer, the numbers of visitors at Whitmore Bay were noticeably depressed. According to one estimate, 'many thousands' of visitors had stayed away. The Liberal-supporting *Barry Herald* – no friend of the Tory landowner – argued that the Island was 'losing ground as a pleasure resort for daily trippers' because of his lordship's 'Keep-off-the grass' policy.[86] It reported gleefully that one councillor had gone so far as to call Windsor a 'bloodsucker' because of his actions at the Island.[87] And even the *Dock News*, a Conservative paper, found Windsor's actions indefensible. Barry Island was 'one of the most beautiful of natural watering places in South Wales', but this season it had become 'about as unattractive as it has been for many years'. The town was now 'sustaining a severe loss' thanks to the landlord's intransigence. The 'deplorable deadlock' had to be broken and the *Dock News* was glad to learn that a deputation of councillors was to meet with Robert Forrest. For a paper usually loyal to the great landowner, this was withering criticism indeed.[88]

The closure of the beach in January 1905 and the events leading up to it constituted a low point in the relations between town
and landowner. In September 1904, despairing of the estate's obstructive actions at Whitmore Bay, the chair of the council remarked that
he thought that the Island was 'gradually slipping out of their hands
entirely'.[89] Yet, just a few months after the roping-off of the sands,
Forrest suddenly announced that Windsor was prepared to lease two
sites for shelters as well as the beach above the high-water mark and
the approaches to the sands. It was a breath-taking turnabout. The
land for the shelter was to be leased for 99 years at a nominal rent
of £1 per annum. The same terms were to be applied to the beach.[90]
In the event, the offer was not quite as generous as it sounded: notwithstanding the talk of peppercorn rents and free 'gifts', after two
years of tense negotiations, the ratepayers of Barry ended up having
to write Windsor a cheque for £4,500. In all, once associated costs
were added, they had to stump up nearly £7,000.[91] And, true to form,
the estate inserted a clause in the draft agreement that sought to ban
the sale of refreshments and any 'other articles or goods'.[92] Champions
of resort development gnashed their teeth in frustration, one arguing
that the offending clause 'knocked the whole scheme on the head'.[93]
After further negotiation, a compromise was eventually reached in the
summer of 1907 that allowed limited trading on the sands: six small
booths were to be permitted, and a small area was to be set aside for
hawkers.[94] It represented an important victory for those who wanted
to encourage visitors onto the Island and it offered the promise of a
reinvigoration of the resort development schemes so beloved by the
Island's boosters. But, like most of the estate's concessions at Whitmore Bay, it was only grudgingly given.

CONCLUSION

Whitmore Bay and its immediate environs could, quite easily, have
been transformed beyond recognition by 1900. Elsewhere, landowners, entrepreneurs of leisure and municipal authorities had been busily
investing in resort infrastructure and fashioning resorts out of unruly
sand dunes and windswept beaches. In Lord Windsor, Barrians had
a landlord who had a successful track record in bringing along an
unprepossessing small port – Penarth – and elevating it to the status of
a fashionable marine suburb. One wonders how different Barry Island
could have looked at the dawn of the new century if his lordship had

willed it: if he had allowed capitalists to form a pier company – as he had at Penarth; if he had worked closely with town leaders – as he had at Penarth; if he had invested more of his own wealth into the improvement of the seafront – as he had at Penarth. The one policy that he did transfer to Barry from Penarth was that which sought to make the seafront as unappealing as possible to working-class trippers. At Barry, apart from the lonely switchback railway, there was a near complete absence of artificial amusements and next to no resort infrastructure, not even a basic shelter. There was only one refreshment hut allowed at Whitmore Bay and even public conveniences were few and far between. A day on Barry Island could be an uncomfortable one for the working-class trippers, an important theme to which we shall return in the next chapter.

Not all visitors to the Island were to be made uncomfortable though: those high-class notables who were entertained at Windsor's well-appointed holiday home at Friars Point had every convenience they could wish for – including full access to the headland itself. Windsor's desire to restrict access to everyone else, and especially to excursionists 'from the hills', led to the souring of an already tense relationship between the estate and the town in the 1900s. As criticism of the estate's approach grew, Windsor ordered the beach be closed: a short, sharp reminder to Barrians that he, and not they, were in control at Barry Island. It was a striking instance of landlord power in action and the culmination of years of his riding roughshod over the interests of the visitors to Barry Island from the mining valleys – that 'perfect rabble'.

Barry's resort boosters were much more supportive of the visitors from the coalfield. They colonized the ranks of the Chamber of Trade and goodly numbers were found in the council chamber, too. However, despite their commitment to the cause, they achieved next to nothing when it came to 'taming' and 'improving' Whitmore Bay. Alderman Meggitt first raised the question of a shelter in 1896 but workers would not begin digging the foundations for the first shelter until May 1923 (two months after Windsor's death, as it happened). The dog-in-the-manger approach of the paternalist 'good earl' and his agent did nothing to help the boosters. He was too inconstant a force at the Island for councillors to feel able to proceed with expensive resort development schemes. Councillors would have to wait for Windsor to relinquish power at Whitmore Bay before they could make any significant progress.

Windsor's handing over of the beach and the approaches to the town of Barry was perhaps the most unforeseen of all the estate's

actions at the Island. It is difficult to fathom given the unhappy relationship between the aristocrat and the citizenry. Perhaps we should
see it as just one more example of great landowners retreating from
their seaside estates in the early twentieth century in order to concentrate on more lucrative urban development schemes. Perhaps Forrest and Windsor had simply tired of the aggravation that came with
trying constantly to resist the incursion of the trippers. Forrest had
certainly not tired of Friars Point House. He had a few more summers
holidaying there with his family before he died in 1910. Whatever
the motivation behind the handing over of key resort spaces to the
council, it came at an inopportune time for resort boosters. Concern
about the town's debts was growing as were worries about the failure
of the tourism multiplier effect to kick in. At the very moment when
Windsor's departure from the stage had given development-supporting
councillors more room for manoeuvre, they found themselves facing ever more vocal critics arguing against unremunerative 'moonshine schemes' at Whitmore Bay. It would take a post-war depression
before circumstances were more conducive to resort development at
Barry Island.

Fortunately for Windsor and Forrest, they were remembered by
later generations of Barrians for their handing over of land – not their
visitor bans or their beach closures. By the mid-twentieth century,
so selective had the town's folk memory become that the landowner
and his agent were even being portrayed as friends of the trippers.
In 1964, a 70-year-old resident, Major Sidney Luen, wrote down his
understanding of the estate's role at the Island. Windsor and Forrest
emerged as kindly figures, who looked out benevolently from Friars
Point House at the excursionists, and responded to their holiday wants
in a philanthropic manner:

> About 1900 Lord Windsor saw the vast amount of Welsh min-
> ers coming down from the hills to recuperate themselves and
> their families on Barry Island. Although he was aware that there
> was a public footpath at the edge of Nell's Point he thought it
> was not enough. Accordingly he approached the Barry Council
> and offered them a strip of land if they would construct a road
> on it and dedicate it to the public in perpetuity. The Council
> gladly accepted, the road was constructed and named after Lord
> Windsor's agent, Forrest Drive. Appropriately it could be called
> For Rest Drive. Other members of the Plymouth family later
> added further gifts of land.[95]

It is a heart-warming account, but, as this chapter has demonstrated, it is not an interpretation that can be allowed to stand. The Windsor estate made it as clear as it could that visitors from the hills were, at most, only tolerated at Barry Island in the 1890s and 1900s. Windsor and Forrest stifled development and dragged their feet when it came to providing even basic facilities such as toilets and refreshment stalls. Yet the trippers from the coalfield came anyway. The next chapter considers this important theme.

CHAPTER SEVEN

THEY 'SWEEP DOWN ON THE PLACE AND TAKE POSSESSION OF IT'

TRIPPERS TRIUMPHANT, c.1890–c.1910

PETER STEAD HAS SUGGESTED that the 1920s were 'the vital decade for Barry's identity as a resort'. After the long years of inde-cision and prevarication, the town's leaders pushed ahead with various resort developments. This was the moment, he argues, when the Island 'assumed a very distinct personality', one that it was to retain for dec-ades to come. Barry had finally decided, in his words, 'what kind of resort it really wanted to be'.¹ It is an interesting interpretation and it has the virtue of identifying the decade after the Great War as a time of momentous change at Barry's seafront. At last, work began on shelters at Whitmore Bay – a seawall was thrown up and a permanent prome-nade laid out, too. A fairground was established a short walk from the beach, whilst, over at Cold Knap, the Marine Lake was constructed and a magnificent lido was opened. Barry Island had finally got the invest-ment that its boosters had been calling for since the mid-1890s.

However, there are two problems with Peter Stead's argument: first, its chronology is faulty and, secondly, it misidentifies the actors who were really responsible for the making of modern Barry Island. It is contended here that the 1890s and 1900s were the vital years in the fashioning of Whitmore Bay as a trippers' resort, not the 1920s. It was an outcome brought about by the trippers themselves. Great crowds of them arrived in the early 1890s and their numbers continued to swell throughout the rest of the late Victorian and Edwardian years. Cardiff supplied many of the excursionists, just as it had in the 1860s and 1870s, but now the coalfield became the greatest source of the Island's visitors with the Rhondda, Merthyr and Aberdare valleys constituting an espe-cially important visitor heartland. This was when Barry Island became a workers' playground.

That inhabitants from the mining valleys developed an attachment to Whitmore Bay can seem so obvious as to need no explanation. Yet, in fact, it does. For in claiming the Island as their very own seaside play-ground, they had to endure many discomforts. The challenges began with the rail journey to Barry and continued once they arrived at the Island. There were certainly more welcoming seaside locations – places that were more comfortable and easier to get to. The Island was devoid of some of the most basic amenities that were taken for granted else-where. A few boosters worried about the lack of a pier at Whitmore Bay, but the majority spent their time agitating for shelters and public lavatories – with good reason.

The boosters' greatest fear was that the visitors would desert undeveloped Barry Island and spend their precious few hours of free-dom at other, more go-ahead, resorts. In other words, the Island's champions knew very well that the excursionists were exercising agency: they were making a choice. What is noteworthy is how the trippers kept choosing to return to Whitmore Bay, notwithstanding its multiple shortcomings and deficiencies. By the early 1890s, 150,000 or so visitors were making that choice every holiday season. Together, they became an irresistible force. Their numbers mattered, for they settled the question of the Island's resort identity. By the 1920s, some Barrians might have thought that they still had the power to influence the social tone of the Island, but most realized that it had already been fixed. Whitmore Bay had become the 'Trippers' Mecca' and there was nothing anyone could do to change it.[2] Far from Barrians being able to choose what sort of resort they wanted to see blossom at Barry Island, the die had already been cast – and it had been cast by the visitors, not the townspeople.

They 'swooped down from the hills': The trippers seize Barry Island

Late Victorian and Edwardian Barrians were in no doubt about the character of their seaside resort. Whilst some visitors might come to stay for a few days or even longer, by far the lion's share were day-trippers from the coalfield. According to one estimate, as early as 1892 the Island was attracting 150,000 visitors in the summer months. They came 'mainly from the hills districts', explained the *Barry Dock News*.[3] By 1897, a regional paper announced that Barry's seafront was 'the miners' paradise'.[4] Others styled it a 'picnic ground' of the valleys.[5] Struck by the large influxes of visitors from the mining district, occasionally reporters took it upon themselves to provide details of the trippers' points of origin. When, on a showery Monday in July 1907, 9,000 excursionists poured through the turnstiles at Barry Island station, the *Cardiff Times* disclosed where they were from: 1,500 hailed from Ynsybwl, 1,200 from Ferndale, 700 from Senghennydd, 600 from Tylorstown – and so the roll call of valleys townships went on.[6]

Working out the precise size of the holiday crowds that gathered at Barry Island in the 1890s and 1900s is an impossible task. Journalists are our best source of information, but their estimates often varied significantly. For example, one reporter spied a thousand trippers on the Island on the August bank holiday of 1894; another, on the same day, thought there were 'thousands' on the sands.[7] In the end, the lack of precision does not matter much, for all commentators were agreed on the important point: Barry Island's popularity increased every year throughout the 1890s.

In the early 1890s, particularly busy days at the Island saw crowds in their thousands congregate at Whitmore Bay.[8] They looked very insignificant, indeed, when placed against the gatherings of the mid- and later 1890s. Nearly 30,000 visitors were in attendance on August bank holiday, 1896.[9] Two years later, the same holiday saw an estimated 40,000 head for the sands of Whitmore Bay.[10] And the increases continued into the new century. By the beginning of the Edwardian period, a normal year saw 'at least' 50,000 choose Barry as their August bank holiday destination.[11] Every summer season saw commentators note that 'record-breaking' crowds had arrived at the Island. In 1905, some suggested that Whitmore Bay had become the most popular bank holiday destination in south Wales.[12] One indication of the scale of the Island's increased popularity is provided by this simple fact: in the early 1890s, it took an entire holiday season for Whitmore Bay's visitor figures to reach 150,000; by the early 1910s, this figure was being reached in just a couple of the busier weeks.[13] By then, the Island was playing host to half a million trippers every season.[14]

Why did Barry Island become a trippers' playground rather than, as at Blackpool, a resort where working-class families stayed for a week at a time? The answer lies in the leisure culture of south Wales. Even at the end of the nineteenth century, leisure time was still a scarce resource for workers in the south Wales coalfield. Blackpool's great source of visitors was the cotton district of Lancashire. There, a custom had evolved which saw workers take a week's (unpaid) holiday in the summer. It suited their employers for them to do so, because it provided the masters with an opportunity to carry out maintenance work on their machinery. All the factories in a town would close in the same week. Critically, different towns took different weeks off. As a result, throughout the summer months, there was a constant supply of workers willing and able to head for the coast for a few days at a time. It was a situation that powered the dramatic rise of Blackpool.[15] But, as Hugh Cunningham has explained, the Lancastrian experience was unique: workers in most other districts had to make do with the odd day off here and there.[16] This was certainly the case in south Wales where it made no economic sense to shut a mine or blow out a blast furnace. From the early nineteenth century, coal owners and ironmasters waged a vigorous, and largely successful, campaign to eradicate irregular work habits.[17] In the late Victorian years, industrial workers in the 'hills district' had much less leisure time than their counterparts in Lancashire.[18] Working-class women had even less free time than the men, so punishing was the routine of domestic chores that often began before husbands left for work and continued long after they had returned home.[19]

Against this context of a leisure-starved workforce, the importance of the bank holidays, only introduced as recently as the early 1870s, is readily apparent.[20] Whilst it is difficult to be sure how many miners were able to enjoy all of the bank holidays, it is certain that many collieries were idle on the August bank holidays in the 1880s.[21] Whit Monday, according to one commentator in 1882, was 'the great holiday for the colliers in the year. All collieries are closed, and to work on that day would be regarded almost as a national sin.'[22] In 1886, the *Cardiff Times* declared that the bank holidays were 'almost religiously observed' in south Wales.[23] A few years later, the August bank holiday had become the most cherished of all the public holidays. The *Pall Mall Gazette* averred that it marked 'the zenith of the year's recreation-days for those to whom a day's recreation means so much'.[24] The *Western Mail* described it as the one day of the year when citizens 'wholly abandon themselves to enjoyment', whilst the miner and novelist Jack Jones thought it was 'the greatest holiday of the year'.[25]

Because leisure was in such short supply in the coalfield, workers displayed a strong desire to get more of it. Their habit of absenting themselves from work without their employers' permission was never entirely stamped out. A general manager of the largest producer of coal in south Wales in the 1900s, the Powell Duffryn Coal Company, grumbled that 'such a lot' of his colliers were guilty of this practice: they were 'very irregular' and liked nothing better than to 'get on the spree'.[26] Absenteeism of this sort was most pronounced during the summer months, especially when wages were high. In August 1916, for example, notwithstanding the war, the absenteeism rate stood at almost 17 per cent.[27] Such holidays were taken by individuals, but the workers were also engaged in a collective 'quest for leisure'.[28] Miners' leaders pushed hard for an eight-hour day (a battle that they would eventually win in 1908). And colliers scored an important victory in 1888 when they established the right to take off the first Monday of every month. 'Mabon's Day', as the holiday came to be known, was to be short-lived. The coal owners only ever grudgingly agreed to it and they abolished it when they had the first opportunity to do so, in 1898. But the holiday played an important role in the history of Barry Island. At precisely the moment that Whitmore Bay was being rediscovered by tourists, Mabon's Day gave colliers and their families one day a month that they could spend at Whitmore Bay if they chose. Plenty of them grabbed the chance. During the spring and summer months, the size of the crowds gathered on the beach on the first Monday of the month were noticeably larger than the holiday throngs seen on other Mondays.[29] In the four months to August 1896, the Barry Railway Company carried an average of 5,400 passengers to the Island from the coalfield each Mabon's Day.[30]

The strength of trippers' interest in Barry Island could leave Barrians reeling. The sight of large numbers of 'strangers' streaming out of trains and rushing towards Whitmore Bay was gratifying, but it could also be discombobulating.[31] Observers frequently invoked the idea of Barry Island being under attack by 'hordes of holiday-makers'.[32] In 1897, for example, a reporter on the *South Wales Echo* noted how, 'on holiday occasions', the miners and their families 'sweep down on the place and take possession of it'.[33] The *Barry Dock News* deployed the same image two years later: the great 'multitude of trippers on Barry Island . . . swooped down from the hills, like a wolf on the fold, to get a sniff of the sea'.[34] The trippers as 'hordes', as predatory wolves, invading, 'sweeping' and 'swooping' down on defenceless Barry Island – taking possession of the place: it can easily be dismissed as mere journalistic hyperbole. And so, up to a point, it was. But it also caught an important truth. Barry Island was owned by a landlord who, at best, barely tolerated the trippers from the hills. As we shall see in the following sections, Windsor and Forrest did little to make the excursionists feel welcome at Whitmore Bay. On the contrary, they kept it underdeveloped, devoid of basic amenities and empty of commercialized amusements. They even closed the beach in a fit of pique. The idea that the trippers were seizing the Island's resort spaces, colonizing them against the will of the aristocrat and his agent was not at all far-fetched.

COAL FIRST, EXCURSIONISTS LAST: THE BARRY RAILWAY COMPANY'S DISREGARD FOR TRIPPER COMFORT

The Windsor regime's determination to stifle resort development at the Island makes the holidaymakers' eagerness to visit the Island all the more notable. Whitmore Bay's spartan appearance could have been its downfall if its visitors had not been so thoroughly bewitched by the place. Boosters knew that Barry's success as a resort was far from assured in the late Victorian and Edwardian years. They lived in constant fear of visitor numbers collapsing, so sure were they that the trippers would be driven away by the lack of investment in resort infrastructure. Their concerns were not groundless: a day trip to Whitmore Bay in the 1890s and 1900s could be a decidedly uncomfortable experience.

Getting to the Island was the first challenge that trippers had to overcome – notwithstanding the opening of the railway. Travelling by train anywhere on busy holidays could be a draining experience. Transport arrangements could buckle under the immense numbers of passengers; carefully planned timetables could go awry resulting in lengthy delays; carriages could be dangerously overcrowded; and overstretched staff could inadvertently direct travellers onto the wrong trains. As one tripper put it in 1895, the bank holiday excursion, too often, was an experience marked by 'feverish rushing about'; it was a day of 'noise, horseplay, and fight' and of being 'hustled' on packed platforms.[35] A genteel inhabitant of Penarth thought that travelling on an August bank holiday was all well and good for the 'rougher' element, but the incessant jostling on platforms made it impossible for 'an individual who wishes to maintain a little decorum'.[36] It left some pleasure seekers relieved that the bank holidays were out-of-the-ordinary events.[37]

If being a railway excursionist generally was not for the fainthearted, travelling to Barry Island by train in the early 1890s was even more demanding. For one thing, the Barry Railway Company was set up with the primary goal of transporting coal. In the early years of its operation, passengers were rarely able to forget how low down the company's list of priorities they came. The company's rolling stock was of poor quality, was badly maintained and rarely cleaned. As one female passenger observed, the carriages were 'about the dirtiest lot' she had ever seen – and she had travelled extensively on London's Metropolitan line. Used heavily by dock workers travelling to and from work, the floors of the carriages were often covered in expectoration and their wooden seats were caked in coal dust.[38] The poorer travellers were especially neglected. A customer complained in 1891 that 'To be a third-class passenger on the Barry Railway is sometimes absolutely painful.' To add insult to injury, the company's staff had a reputation as surly and unhelpful. One was so abrasive that he earned himself the moniker 'the Grunting Pigmy'.[39]

Matters were only worsened by the company's insistence that the most direct route from the coalfield to Barry was reserved for the exclusive use of coal trains. The only passenger service into Barry ran on the Barry Railway Company's other line – that which ran from Cogan. The inconveniences involved in getting to Barry from the Merthyr, the Cynon

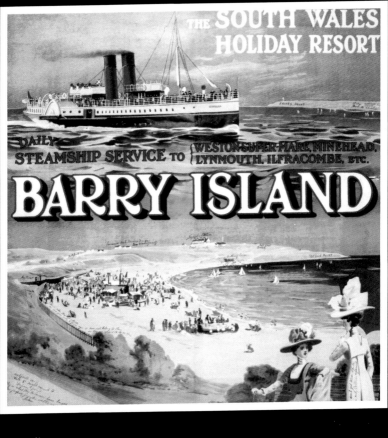

Illus. 1. *The South Wales Holiday Resort*: advertising poster.
*Edwardian Whitmore Bay was a notably undeveloped
leisure space. Most visitors were working-class trippers, but
Lord Windsor's guests could be as genteel as the 'ladies' in
the foreground.*

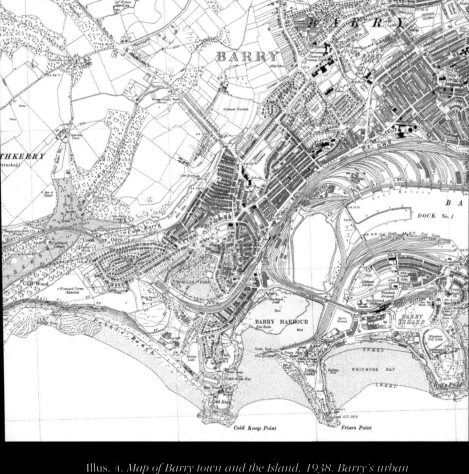

Illus. 4. *Map of Barry town and the Island, 1938. Barry's urban history began with the building of the dock in the later 1880s. Whitmore Bay had a much longer history as a seaside resort.*

Illus. 10. *Lord Windsor: Robert Windsor-Clive (1857–1923),*
The County Gentleman, *18 April 1891. Lord Windsor had a
decisive impact on Whitmore Bay's development as a resort.
By closing the beach to visitors, he achieved something that
few other British landowners did.*

Illus. 17. *View of the sands and Nell's Point, early twentieth century. The contrast between Barry's undeveloped seafront and Penarth's (see illus. 16) is clear from this view of the sand dunes at Whitmore Bay. Not until the mid-1920s would a seawall and shelters be built at Barry.*

Whitmore Bay, Barry Is

Illus. 18. *Barry Island pleasure pier: cartoon,* Barry and District News, *14 December 1945. Barry's resort boosters had long hoped that the Island's seafront might be 'properly' developed. Even in the mid-twentieth century, some were still fantasizing about a pier at Whitmore Bay.*

The Donkeys, Barry Island

Illus. 20. *The donkeys and the boat traders, c.1908. Lord Windsor tolerated donkey rides. The boat traders (their 'shops' can be seen in the background) were not tolerated. The council waged a vigorous campaign against the* ...

Illus. 22. *The bathing pool and the western shelter in the mid-1920s. The western shelter was opened in 1924. The fairground, in the background, was another recent addition to the beachscape. In the foreground, the children's bathing pool was a reminder that some – albeit modest – resort development occurred earlier.*

and the Rhondda valleys by this route were many and varied. Trippers had to travel down from Pontypridd to Cardiff and change onto a train for the Taff Vale Railway's station at Penarth dock. Once there, they had to walk a hundred yards or so to the Barry Company's Cogan station where they could, usually after a wait, catch a Barry Company train to Barry town. As one traveller remarked, 'the inconvenience of crossing over from Cogan station to Penarth Dock station, sometimes with a considerable amount of luggage, or a baby in arms and little children, is . . . felt by many as a real and unnecessary hardship'.[40] Even then, the poor excursionist's plight was not over, for upon alighting at Barry, they faced nearly a mile's walk around the great dock before they were rewarded with their first sight of the beach.

Because the different railway companies had not agreed to offer through-fares, the ticketing arrangements were fearsomely complicated. Passengers from the coalfield had to purchase another set of tickets at Cardiff and yet one more at Cogan. On busy days, they could be queuing for half an hour or more at each ticket office.[41] On bank holidays in the early 1890s, waiting rooms at Cardiff were converted into temporary ticket offices just to serve passengers bound for Barry – but still the crushes could be unbearable.[42]

Enduring the multiple discomforts of getting to Barry via Cardiff and Cogan was bad enough, but passengers' frustration was exacerbated by the knowledge that there was a much easier route to Barry Island – the one taken by the coal trains. The line from Trehafod, near Pontypridd, was direct and quick, but the company did all it could to keep passenger trains off that line. Its reason for doing so was obvious. The millions of tons of coal that were carried on that line to Barry every year generated huge profits. The company routinely paid shareholders a dividend of 10 per cent throughout the 1890s. It was hardly a wonder that directors did not want any disruption to the freight timetable.[43] In 1892, one expert estimated that the amount of coal carried by the company would fall by 13 per cent if even a few passenger trains were allowed onto the line.[44] Trippers' shillings could never make good the deficit, and it was an open secret that the company wanted to 'preserve as long as possible an undisturbed use of the line for mineral traffic'.[45]

No one could fault the financial logic that lay behind the company's decision to keep passengers off its Trehafod to Barry line. Nevertheless, the directors had given assurances when the company was formed that some passenger trains would be allowed onto the mineral line. Their failure to honour that agreement soon became a burning political issue. As early as May 1890, a campaign was launched in the mining valleys and in Barry to get the line opened. Public meetings were held at which leading figures from the coalfield and the port emphasized the importance of improving access to Barry's beach. From the outset, it was framed as a moral crusade waged on behalf of excursionists. The difficulties inherent in travelling on the Cogan to Barry line meant that it was 'easier to get to London from the Rhondda Valley than to get to salt water', explained one campaigner. The public 'had a right to claim this concession as a fair and honourable debt', urged one speaker; it was 'right that something should be done to enable the poor toilers who exhausted their time and energy in producing the black diamond to come down to Barry', commented another. One local notable pointed out that the colliers provided the company with immense profits and it was time, therefore, that directors gave them some 'consideration'. If the company made a loss on the passenger services, they should bear it.[46] A petition was presented to the directors with nearly a thousand names on it.[47]

The directors were not unaware of the storm of controversy that their actions had whipped up. They assured campaigners that they would give the matter serious consideration. But, with no action forthcoming, campaigners kept agitating. More public meetings were held; more deputations were sent to wait upon the company's directors; more angry speeches were delivered imploring the company to discharge its responsibilities under the Company's Act and provide a 'reasonable means of access to the seaboard at Barry'.[48] The directors issued further mollifying announcements but still they refused to act. By the end of 1895, local newspaper editors openly accused the Barry Railway of acting in bad faith – it was 'hoodwinking the public'. Matters came to a head when the local authorities in Pontypridd, Barry and settlements along the mineral line agreed to oppose the company's forthcoming parliamentary bill.[49] This produced the desired result. The directors instructed workers to begin building a string of new stations along the coal line.

Once the decision had been taken, it took just a few months to complete the necessary alterations. On 16 March 1896 passenger trains began running down to Barry direct from Pontypridd.[50] The *Pontypridd Chronicle* was thrilled at the prospect of there being, at last, 'a short route to the sea shore from the Rhondda Valley'.[51] The *Barry Dock News* was similarly delighted. No longer would visitors have to endure the 'long and tedious journey' via Cardiff and Cogan. For the first time, the 'teeming population of the Rhondda, Aberdare, and Merthyr Valleys' would be able to 'reach a lovely seashore in a short time and enjoy to the full a well-earned holiday near the briny'. Barry Island would surely 'become, as it deservedly should, one of the most popular seaside resorts in South Wales'.[52]

The battle to get the mineral line opened for excursionists compels us to reappraise the company's role in the development of Whitmore Bay as a resort. D. S. Barrie has argued that Barry Railway Company 'largely created a popular holiday resort at Barry Island'.[53] This assessment cannot be accepted without significant qualification. For all that the opening of the railway from Cogan to Barry in December 1888 had clearly made a day trip from the coalfield to the Island a possibility, inhabitants of the mining districts were still faced with a journey that was far from straightforward. For more than seven years, the company directors consistently privileged their shareholders' interests over those of the travelling public. That Barry Island was being visited annually by 150,000 trippers in the early 1890s, the majority coming by rail, was a testament to the excursionists' determination to put up with the numerous inconveniences of travelling on the Barry Company's trains from Cogan. They came despite the company's policies, rather than because of them. As it was, contemporaries were certain that many thousands were put off by the unsatisfactory arrangements.[54] As such, we can add Barry to the list of resorts whose expansion was 'neither caused . . . nor actively encouraged' by a railway company, even if it may have been facilitated by its presence.[55]

After 1896, it was a different matter. The company's decision to open the mineral line to passengers coincided with the completion of the short branch line from Barry across to the centre of the Island.[56] Taken together, they acted as powerful stimuli to the growth in visitor numbers. When, in November 1893, the company let it be known that it wanted to construct the branch line, hopeful commentators interpreted the announcement as a sign that it was determined to do all it could to 'bring the teeming population of the Rhondda direct to the seashore'.[57] In truth, boosting tourism to Whitmore Bay was not the only, and indeed not the primary, reason why the railway was extended. The project was driven by Lord Windsor's wish to profit from the urbanization of the northern and eastern sectors of the Island. (Windsor, it will be remembered, was the chairman of the company.) Even as the paint was drying on the new Island station, his lordship began letting nearby land to house builders.[58]

Nevertheless, once the new arrangements were in place, the Barry Company can be said to have played a much more positive role in the development of the resort. It gradually adopted a much more tripper-friendly approach, experimenting with various ticketing strategies specifically aimed at visitors from the coalfield. By the early years of the twentieth century, the company offered a variety of ticketing options: in addition to full-day excursions from Porth and Pontypridd, it sold week-end tickets, tickets that allowed an overnight stay during the week and half-day excursion tickets for those who had just a few hours to spare.[59]

A 'SCANDAL AND A SHAME': DAY-TRIPPERS' DISCOMFORTS AT THE ISLAND

Getting to the Island got much easier after 1896. Nevertheless, resort boosters were still deeply concerned about the discomforts that awaited visitors upon their arrival. If Lord Windsor had simply been uninterested in developing Barry Island's resort amenities himself, that would have been one thing. His unwillingness to let others – be they councillors or private investors – cater to the needs of the visiting public was quite another matter. It had significant consequences for those early trippers. It meant that a day out at Barry Island in the 1890s could be an uncomfortable, and even miserable, experience.

As we noted in a previous chapter, Windsor had spoken in 1894 of his eagerness to do 'all he possibly could to make Barry Island attractive to both visitors and residents'.[60] However, his subsequent inactivity spoke louder than his words. Take, for example, the matter of beach traders. The estate showed itself to be remarkably resistant to the idea that traders should be allowed on to the Island. After allowing just one refreshment room to be set up in 1890, Windsor and Forrest were resolute in their efforts to keep others away from the Island. All hawkers, including those hoping to sell toys, food and drink to visitors, were banned, and so were traders who might have wanted to set up stalls or shops on or near the beach. Forrest made it clear in a number of public statements that, 'on no account' would his lordship allow an expansion of refreshment facilities.[61] Vendors of ice creams and drinks were repeatedly thrown off the Island and prosecuted.[62] Stories circulated that children and even poor widows 'desiring to gain an honest livelihood by providing refreshments on the beach' had been turned away by Windsor's men.[63] One inhabitant felt so hard done by that he wrote not only to Lord Windsor pleading for his rights as a respectable trader to be respected, but also to Lord Bute (who had nothing to do with the Island) and King Edward VII (whose relationship with Whitmore Bay was even more tenuous).[64]

Windsor's policy incensed those townsfolk who wanted to profit from the pleasure seekers: 'In every other place there was absolute freedom in these matters, while in Barry there was not', complained one observer.[65] Meanwhile, the restrictions also angered those who worried that excursionists would not want to come back to such a poorly provisioned beach. A *South Wales Echo* reporter described the scenes he encountered on the Island on the August bank holiday of 1897: 'The *one* Refreshment Room was besieged, eaten out, and all day long there was a frantic dance round the one water standard which does duty for a drinking fountain.'[66] This was not an unusual occurrence.[67] Local politicians, only too aware that they were often being blamed for Whitmore Bay's shortcomings as a resort, issued a public statement pointing out that it was the Windsor estate that set the rules, not the council.[68] Observers grumbled that the estate made it impossible 'even to sell a pennyworth of apples' at Whitmore Bay.[69] There were dark mutterings in the town about how his lordship was 'stifling local enterprise' at the Island.[70]

Not all of Barry's entrepreneurial class were to be put off by Windsor's zero-tolerance approach to beach traders. A handful of the town's poorer inhabitants, desperate to make money from the great holiday crowds, took advantage of the fact that Windsor's writ only extended down to the high-water mark. Knowing that they would be blocked from taking refreshments onto the beach if they approached by land, they took to the sea instead. Beginning in the early summer of 1904, these innovative traders sailed their little boats, loaded with refreshments, into Whitmore Bay, and beached them on the sands. By all accounts, they did a 'roaring trade'.[71] Most trippers welcomed the boat traders, but councillors took a different view of the matter. Hopeful that Lord Windsor might consider handing over control of the Island's resort spaces to the town at some point in the near future (with good reason, as it turned out), town leaders were keen to show him that they could be trusted to keep an orderly beach. Accordingly, they embarked upon a vigorous campaign to clear the sands of the boat hawkers, taking them to court and charging them with breaking various beach by-laws.[72] But the traders were a persistent group. Year after year, during the months between Whitsuntide and September, they were brought before magistrates, fined and lectured on the need to observe the by-laws. Year after year, they returned to Whitmore Bay and continued their trade in refreshments. Not content with simply ignoring the by-laws, the hawkers decided to challenge the legality of the council's action against them. Remarkably, they took the council to the High Court where, in February 1908, the Lord Chief Justice found in favour of the boat traders, deciding that the by-law was 'bad'.[73] Emboldened by the ruling, they kept sailing their little vessels into Whitmore Bay into the early 1910s.[74] Barry's councillors were equally stubborn, though. Armed with a new, improved, by-law, they kept harrying the hawkers. By the outbreak of the war in 1914, the last of the boat shops had been banished from the beach.

That the boat traders were able to hang on for so long in the face of such determined opposition reveals just how strong demand was for their goods. Their little boats could only carry limited supplies of mineral water, fruit and sweets, but every little helped at a time when Windsor was so determined to restrict the number of refreshment outlets on the Island. A day trip to Whitmore Bay could be marred by rumbling stomachs and dry throats thanks to the landowner's unfriendly policies. It could also be a wet and chilly affair if the weather took a turn for the worse. We have seen that the lack of a basic shelter had been a perennial concern of councillors since Councillor Meggitt raised the matter in 1896. It took until the mid-1920s for the first structure to appear. We can easily underestimate the consequences of there being no shelter at Whitmore Bay. The rainclouds that scudded in from the Atlantic could ruin a day trip. Getting soaked early on in a visit meant having to wait around for hours in wet clothes until it was time to catch the train home. Local newspapers are full of reports of trippers having been lured onto the sands by the promise of fine weather in the morning, only to be caught out later in the day. For example, on August bank holiday, 1899, a violent thunderstorm broke in the afternoon that 'seriously incommoded' the thousands of excursionists on the sands.[75] A heavy shower on a July day in 1900 'cleared the beach of the invaders' in just a few minutes.[76] In June 1905, trippers had their day on the sands brought 'to a sudden close' by a thunderstorm that 'drenched' hundreds.[77] The following year, a Tuesday in August saw brilliant sunshine all morning followed by 'a deluge of rain ... that would have made Captain Noah take in another reef in the sails of the ark'. So violent was the downpour that 'Mothers with little children to protect looked with helpless dismay at the storm that threatened to drive in the roof of the station' and visitors alighting at Barry Island station turned around and got on return trains without stepping foot on the beach.[78] In 1906, the Pearson Fresh Air Fund brought 500 children from Cardiff's poorest neighbourhoods to Barry Island for a day out. They got drenched within the first hour. The organizer of the trip, Percy Thomas, declared it 'a scandal and a shame' that no proper shelter had been built, notwithstanding the great popularity of the Island with trippers.[79]

Lord Windsor and Robert Forrest could easily have rectified the deficiency if they had wanted to. Forrest, a frequent visitor to the Island, would have known well enough the unpredictability of the weather as it rolled up the Bristol Channel. As he scurried to the safety of Friars Point House, he might even have seen for himself the great holiday crowds scattering in all directions when a raincloud burst, searching, in vain, for a place to shelter. If he did, such an experience clearly did not fill him with the desire to help the sodden trippers.

The lack of public conveniences on the Island was another major shortcoming. The scarcity of public toilets was shocking given the size of the holiday crowds that regularly flocked to the Island. Crowds of 30,000 gathered at Whitmore Bay on the busiest days of the holiday season by the mid-1890s.[80] So packed was the beach that it could be described as looking like 'an ant-hill'.[81] Even a normal week during the summer months could now bring 20,000 excursionists onto the Island.[82] Yet there was no public lavatory on the Island as late as 1897.[83] It was a very serious deficiency that revealed just how apathetic the Windsor estate was when it came to the comfort of Whitmore Bay's visitors. Trippers took to writing to local and regional newspapers to complain about the situation, whilst councillors spoke passionately about the need to provide toilet facilities for the visitors.[84] By 1900, there had been little improvement. A urinal had been installed at the Island's railway station, but it was hardly sufficient. Visitors were forced to answer the call of nature wherever they could, a situation that led to many 'unsightly scenes'. The *Barry Herald* thought it was outrageous that excursionists who were caught committing an 'act of necessity' in public ran the risk of prosecution. The provision of toilets was, the paper opined, 'the least that can be expected . . . in a civilised community'.[85] A correspondent to the *Dock News* agreed: 'Which are to blame, those committing a nuisance, or those compelling the same?'[86]

The patience of some of the trippers wore thin. In 1900, an 'Earnest Well-Wisher' shared with readers of the *Barry Dock News* his experiences on the Island on a July weekend. He had heard visitors grumble about the 'barrenness' of Barry Island. The lack of a ladies' lavatory, the absence of a shelter and the lack of any entertainments were their primary complaints. 'It is really pitiable to see the poor people wandering around aimlessly', the correspondent noted. Barry's future as a pleasure resort was 'doomed' unless the Windsor estate could be persuaded to adopt a more visitor-friendly set of policies. 'With all the numerous attractions – though with fewer natural advantages – that other seaside places offer – Weston, for instance – how can Barry hope to compete when it is so hopelessly in the back ground?'[87]

ONE 'OF THE LOVELIEST HAUNTS OF MAN': THE TRIPPER-MADE PLAYGROUND

When the boosters complained about the underdeveloped state of Barry Island, they were hardly exaggerating. A ten-minute downpour was all it took to turn a pleasurable day trip to Whitmore Bay into an uncomfortable ordeal for tens of thousands of visitors. However, for all that boosters fretted that visitors might soon desert the Island, the opposite was true: the numbers of pleasure seekers increased. Notwithstanding its 'backwardness' – its lack of commercialized amusements and its evident discomforts – Whitmore Bay drew ever more trippers from the mining district and beyond. The Island's hold over its visitors needs explaining.

Above all else, it was the Island's natural spaces that appealed to its late Victorian and Edwardian visitors. It is one of the continuities that bound the Barry seaside experience of the 1890s with that of the pre-dock days. Indeed, ever since tourists had first been coming to Whitmore Bay in the late eighteenth century, they had done so precisely because of its undeveloped condition. Fashionable crowds gathered at Tenby to enjoy the sociability of the assembly rooms and theatre; Barry Island's devotees came because of the absence of artificial amusements. Later, when the mid-Victorian trippers came by the boatload to enjoy seaside walks, dips in the briny and picnics on the headlands and dunes, it was nature – not 'culture' – that attracted them, too. Now, their late Victorian equivalents were there largely for the same reasons.

In the 1970s and 1980s, social historians drew attention to the rise of a leisure industry in the later nineteenth century.[88] They explained how a 'traditional' working-class culture cohered around a set of practices that were increasingly commercialized and ever more standardized. Whereas patterns of popular culture were regionally, and even locally, distinctive in the early nineteenth century, by the century's end workers from Scotland to Cornwall were increasingly 'playing' in similar ways. From the enjoyment of brass bands to the supporting of organized sports teams, from the patronage of music halls to the visiting of public houses, workers' leisure experiences were becoming homogenized.[89] The rise of the 'traditional' seaside holiday was easily incorporated into this narrative. As John K. Walton has demonstrated, from the 1870s, 'heavily-capitalized entertainment companies' moved into the bigger seaside resorts, keen to make money from the ever-swelling playful crowds. By the 1890s, there were the costly pleasure piers and the great pleasure palaces offering 'everything from menageries to music-hall in giant buildings with exotic furnishings and embellishment'.[90] In the early nineteenth century, Romantics valued the beach as a site of nature; at the century's end, the seaside had become a place where 'the motifs of modernity and progress . . . came to the fore'.[91] It was entirely fitting, therefore, that the only place in *fin de siècle* Britain with a tower to rival that of Eiffel's was a seaside resort: Blackpool.[92]

Late Victorian visitors to Barry Island encountered nothing like this, however. They came to a beachscape that was only lightly touched by capitalism. There were the bathing machines and the single refreshment room. There were also the donkeys and the boat trips around the bay. A new Marine Hotel had opened in the working-class neighbourhood (some distance from the beach) by the mid-1890s and, from 1898, there was a single fairground ride – the switchback railway. But it was all a far cry from Blackpool with its amusement parks, pleasure piers, hucksters and freak shows. At Whitmore Bay, 'non-market' activities – such as sightseeing, picnicking, strolling and paddling – remained central to the tourist experience.[93] Late Victorian trippers spent their holidays at Barry Island in much the same way as had their mid-Victorian predecessors.

Appreciating the scenery remained at the heart of the visitor experience. This was a practice that did not depend upon any costly resort development project. Indeed, on the contrary, the fact that the Island's seafront spaces were largely unspoilt by heavily engineered structures was a positive advantage. Writer after writer remarked upon how 'the natural beauty of the place' was the Island's 'great attraction'.[94] Commentators repeatedly pointed out how visitors appreciated Whitmore Bay's 'charming' and 'pretty' qualities.[95] For its part, the *South Wales Echo* thought that Island was 'one of the most attractive spots on the coast of Glamorgan', whilst the *Barry Dock News*, with pardonable exaggeration, went further, describing it as one 'of the loveliest haunts of man'.[96] The *Barry Herald* noted how many of the visitors it saw on the beach in early June 1897 were 'quite happy, after selecting a favourable spot, to sit for hours watching the motion of the waves . . . the passers-by alone serving to break the charm'.[97]

Visitors from the coalfield may have found the visual appeal of Whitmore Bay especially enticing. After all, they hailed from a landscape of rising verticals – steep-sided valleys led the eye upwards. At Whitmore Bay, the views on offer were defined by sweeping horizontals. For the colliers who spent their working lives underground in the most claustrophobic spaces of all, the psychological impact of gazing out across the Bristol Channel to the Somerset coast some thirteen miles distant can only be guessed. A reporter for the *Barry and Cadoxton Journal* tried to do just that when he saw colliers standing 'on the silver brink, while the insidious water was rising to lap their ankles'. He observed that they were 'staring right out with calm eternal eyes, as though the heaving waves . . . had entranced them . . . recalling them from their thoughts of hard labour in the mines and forges, to aspirations after the boundless freedom the ever-changing sea suggests'.[98] One Rhondda collier standing at Friars Point in 1904 put it more prosaically, but no less powerfully: 'gazing with intense rapture' at the seascape before him, he exclaimed to 'his butty', 'Oh, Daio, there's a view, man, for picture postcards'.[99]

At the most intensely developed resorts such as Blackpool, the beach had ceased to be the prime draw by the final decades of the century. At Barry Island, in contrast, the sands at Whitmore Bay remained the 'Great Attraction' – as they had been for decades.[100] As natural playgrounds went, it had much to keep the trippers amused. For those of a geological bent – and there were probably more than we might imagine – the Island's cliffs repaid close scrutiny.[101] Enthusiasts lost themselves for hours amongst the tea-green marls, the red marls, the crystals of gypsum, the Rhaetic black shales, the beds of ochrey, the flaggy micaceous sandstone and the magnesian limestone.[102] Working-class writer Walter Haydn Davies recalled how the cliffs always captivated one of his fellow Sunday school excursionists from the mining village of Bedlinog: 'Dai Rocks' spent his visits 'hammering away at the varied strata so visible in Barry's cliffs so that he might add to his geological specimens'.[103] Newspapers alerted visitors to the importance of the Island's geological features and there was enough popular interest to prompt a lecturer from the university at Cardiff to produce a geological map of Barry Island to aid those keen to decipher the mysteries of Whitmore Bay's rocks.[104]

No such specialist knowledge was required to enjoy the beach. It was a highly adaptable leisure space. In the hands of the late Victorians, it became a site of family-centred fun. It was especially valued as an unrivalled 'children's playground'. The *South Wales Echo* named Whitmore Bay, with much justification, a 'kiddies paradise'.[105] 'The laughter and shouts of boisterously happy boys and girls fill the ozone-laden air', reported one visitor in August 1910.[106] Others noted how the beach was packed full of 'sand-digging children'.[107] It was also full of picnickers. The Friars Point side of the beach was where many of them congregated, for the headland not only protected them from any westerly breezes, but also made it easier for them to light the campfires needed to brew tea.[108] And whilst reposing on the sands, visitors could quaff the health-giving air, enjoy the scenery and watch each other. For the visitors themselves became an integral part of the holiday spectacle: they were simultaneously sightseers and sights. The beach was 'a scene of much animation' on summer days and, as one observer put it, its ever-moving crowds made 'a pleasing picture'. And as the pleasure steamers passed by 'with their decks crowded with trippers', so beach users stared at their water-based equivalents as the floating trippers returned the compliment.[109] Everywhere one looked, trippers could be seen gazing at each other: Whitmore Bay was a veritable seaside panopticon.

In a resort space almost entirely devoid of commercialized entertainments, the purveyors of donkey rides and pleasure-boat trips were kept busy. Both activities served to keep visitors' attention firmly centred upon the beach and the water's edge. From the outset, the pleasure boats were 'extensively patronized'.[110] There was good money to be made from the trade – a boatload of trippers could pay as much as 10s. and demand for the trips was strong.[111] One visitor to the Island on August bank holiday, 1893 remarked that he 'repeatedly saw young people from the Rhondda Valley rushing wildly into the pleasure boats until they were a long way overcrowded, and in one or two cases the boats nearly sank'.[112] It was a chilling observation, for on the same day, at Aberavon beach, a disaster occurred when thirty-six individuals – many of them teenagers on a Sunday school trip from the Rhondda – were packed into a boat just 20 feet long and 5 feet wide. It overturned in choppy waters resulting in the death of twenty-four.[113] Pit villages, only too familiar with mining disasters, were convulsed with grief by this holiday tragedy. It occasioned 'the largest funeral procession ever witnessed in the Rhondda valleys', when 20,000 mourners lined the streets, collieries stopped work and white blinds were displayed in the windows of houses on the route.[114]

Like the operators of the pleasure boats, those in the business of offering donkey rides to trippers needed little in the way of capital. The returns could be good, although the donkeys were frequently treated cruelly in the drive to make money.[115] One lad took 21s. 8d in pennies by offering donkey rides at Whitmore Bay on Whit Monday, 1899. Assuming each ride was a penny each, that was a total of 260 rides.[116] Walter Haydn Davies recalled how he and his Sunday school companions 'spent most of our money on the donkeys' in the hope of being able to encourage the animals to race each other: 'The donkeys knew better', he added ruefully.[117] Adults as well as children queued up for the rides, a sure sign that the beach was no 'normal' space. Dignity had to be preserved at home, but at Whitmore Bay, the formal rules governing bodily comportment could be relaxed a little.[118] When 1,500 Sunday school pupils and 'friends' from Penygraig in the Rhondda arrived in July 1900, scores of children as well as 'a few grown up people' queued for donkey rides. The riders' 'frantic efforts to retain their seats' afforded 'much amusement', particularly when some of the unrulier beasts broke into a gallop leaving one 'young lady . . . on her back on the sands'.[119] When the scholars of Carmel Sunday school, Penrhiwceiber, arrived at Barry Island in July 1904, 'some of the elders developed a strong passion' for the donkey rides. The *Aberdare Leader* understood the situation perfectly: 'We are sure they would be delighted to see their names in print', the paper gently joshed, 'but pressure of space forbids!' Starched collars might be loosened at Barry Island, with no judgement passed by those who had stayed at home.[120]

The water's edge was another place where conventions were relaxed: trousers might be rolled up and skirts hitched as adults and children waded into the sea. Paddling was ever popular.[121] In 1896, the *Herald* carried an alarmist report of the dangers of such a practice. It shared with readers the findings of a Dr Whitfield Perkins who argued that allowing young children to paddle their feet in cold water whilst leaving their heads exposed to the sun's hot rays could result in paralysis.[122] Most brave paddlers at Whitmore Bay sensibly ignored the good doctor's advice. Indeed, so did councillors. For, in 1900, they began work on one of the few municipal 'improvements' that made it from the drawing board into reality in the Edwardian period: the seawater paddling pool for children. The pool drew large crowds of paddlers and watchful parents.

The more adventurous visitors went further into the sea than just ankle-deep. Historians have noted that bathing had come to mean less to late Victorian beach users, and particularly working-class visitors, than it had to their predecessors.[123] The inconvenience of undressing on the sands, often in uncomfortable bathing machines, and having to adhere to a battery of restrictive bathing regulations that segregated

Illus. 19. *Pleasure boats and paddlers at the water's edge, c.1910. Bathing might have been a minority practice during the Edwardian years, but most visitors wandered down to the water's edge, a place where formal conventions might be relaxed a little.*

the sexes and split up families, did little to encourage people into the chilly waters. A downgrading of the supposed health benefits of immersion in seawater also dented the appeal of bathing for some. Many medical authorities now argued that simply breathing in the sea air was at least as good for the seaside visitor as plunging under the waves.[124] As one south Wales paper remarked in 1901, 'to spend a few hours . . . drinking in deep draughts of ozone is better than taking a course of tonic medicine'.[125] Another writer thought that ozone was such a powerful 'medicine' that visitors to the seaside needed to be careful: 'if at any time the system should get out of order – for the sea air has strange effects on different constitutions – it ought to be seen to at once'.[126]

Illus. 21. *Boat traders on the sands, c.1908. The boat traders asserted their rights to trade on the sands. They took the council to the High Court, and won. This photograph was used as evidence in the trial. The 'x' marked the spot of the boat of C. W. Campbell.*

Bathing was always a minority practice at Barry Island in the 1890s and 1900s. In 1892, for example, of the estimated 100,000 visitors who had made it across to the Island in the summer months, only *c.*2,000 had used the bathing machines.[127] The following year, this figure had risen to some 3,300.[128] If these numbers bear any relation to reality, therefore, only a tiny proportion of the Island's visitors entered the water via bathing machines in 1892. Many more headed into the sea without use of the machines, but still, the claim that most visitors stayed on *terra firma* holds true.

Nevertheless, the practice of sea-bathing had a significance that extended beyond those who braved the waves. It always had the potential to bring disruption to the beach and thereby implicate other visitors.

For example, there was the possibility of drownings. Most of those who bathed at Whitmore Bay at this time could not swim. It was frequently remarked that visitors from the coalfield often had little swimming proficiency.[129] The Island was widely regarded as a safe place for bathers – and, mostly, it was. There were no bathing fatalities between 1890 and 1893.[130] However, at low tide, dangerous currents at Nell's Point could sweep bathers into difficulty. When the alarm went up, the entire beach was turned into a 'scene of horror and pathos' at a stroke.[131] Fortunate bathers were pulled to safety.[132] But not everyone was so lucky. Some terrible tragedies took place in front of huge crowds of horrified onlookers. In August 1897, for example, two Rhondda colliers were swept out at Nell's Point. One was rescued, but the other drowned. 'The sad occurrence took place in the presence of several thousands of persons, and there was considerable excitement along the shore.'[133] In June 1904, the 'merry shouts of the early bathers at Barry Island were suddenly hushed' when a 15-year-old girl from Barry Dock cried out for help just before drowning.[134] And when, on an August evening in 1905, a Cadoxton teenager drowned, 'In the twinkling of an eye the sands, but a few seconds ago a scene of delight, [were] transformed into a terror-stricken and seething mass of human beings.' Several female visitors reportedly 'lay prostrate and hid their faces in the sand' as rescuers tried in vain to reach the unfortunate boy.[135] Occasionally, bodies of drowned bathers were washed ashore days, and even weeks, later, causing trippers yet more holiday trauma.[136]

Such tragic events were relatively rare occurrences. However, bathers problematized the beach in other, more mundane, ways every time they took to the sands. Bathing was an act charged with transgressive overtones. After all, fully clothed visitors were brought into proximity with bodies that were (often much) more exposed than usual. True, some beach users positively relished the prospect of seeing bathers in a state of undress. During the summer of 1904, for example, 'certain men' congregated outside the women's bathing house, waiting for female bathers to emerge. One man even climbed on to the roof of the changing rooms, 'molesting the female bathers by throwing missiles at them'. Such shameless behaviour was roundly condemned. These men 'have no idea of morality or decency', snapped one commentator. 'Whatever control we have, we must prevent females from being molested', declared the *Barry Dock News*.[137] It is clear that women bathers were frequently intimidated by groups of men who gathered to watch as they left the water in their wet, figure-hugging, 'sea-dresses'.[138]

Not all the offending voyeurs at Whitmore Bay were men though. When, in 1900, a large contingent of soldiers who were temporarily based on the Island took their daily dip, large crowds of women gathered to watch as the men came in and out of the water: 'it was impossible to keep the women away when the men were bathing', remarked a disapproving observer.[139] Being subjected to the female gaze could be unsettling. A 'Regular Bather' wrote to the *Dock News* in 1906 to complain about the women who sat down 'for hours staring at the male bathers'. Some had even taken to picnicking on the steps of the male changing room.[140] In 1904, Dr Sixsmith, a Barry councillor, tried to undress on the sands at Nell's Point but found he was being watched by a large group of female visitors. Thinking they would take the hint, he explained his intention to change into his bathing costume. '[A]ll he got from them in reply was "Go you on, my boy; go you on, my boy."'[141]

These bathers sought to hide their bodies from prying eyes. Others were more carefree. These 'immodest' beach users could be particularly troubling figures. Exasperated commentators declared, more than once, that Whitmore Bay was in the grip of a full-blown 'bathing nuisance'.[142] One male visitor, in July 1890, was appalled by the sight of men undressing 'all over the sands' and making no effort to cover their nakedness. He contended that respectable beach users were being 'driven away' from the Island by such scenes.[143] The 1892 bathing season was particularly tense. 'Mrs Grundy', the hyper-respectable gossip-columnist of the *Barry Dock News*, railed against the 'most disgraceful' conduct of the bathers she saw at Whitmore Bay on Whit Monday. The problem, she contended, was generating numerous complaints from upset visitors.[144] One such was 'Pater Familias', a visitor from Cardiff. He had a day trip to Whitmore Bay ruined by the 'indecent and disgusting conduct' of some of the bathers he saw on the Island. They exposed themselves in what he thought was 'a shameless manner'.[145] A few months later, the Inspector of Nuisances reported that the Island was plagued by the problem of public nudity. On one day in August he had witnessed twelve trippers bathing 'without drawers' whilst on another occasion, some 200 'excursionists from the hills' were bathing, some of whom 'he saw running in a nude state, after females'. When the man from the bathing machines tried to remonstrate with the boisterous visitors, they threw missiles at him.[146] Later that month, a male visitor was upset by the sight of women bathers changing on the beach. They were 'arrayed only in the garb of Eden' and in full view of bystanders: why, he asked, did they pick a spot 'where there is no shelter to their naked-ness'?[147] It was all too much for the *South Wales Star*. It thought that too many beach users were being upset, annoyed and shocked by 'the spectacle of men and boys bathing without any regard to the rules of decency'. Unless decisive action was taken, the Island would be 'spoiled' and visitors, in future, would be 'restricted to a very rough class'.[148]

In fact, Barry's elite had already begun to grapple with the problem of Whitmore Bay's 'immoral' bathers. In October 1891, members of the Barry and Cadoxton Local Board passed a set of bathing by-laws that prohibited mixed bathing and, in an effort to bring a little decorum back to the sands, decreed that all bathers were to change in bathing machines.[149] The local board's inspector of nuisances and his deputies were given the task of seeing that the regulations were adhered to. As they marched up and down the beach in their 'quasi-nautical' uniforms, they left bathers in no doubt that they were being scrutinized by officialdom.[150] However, as the size of the holiday crowds swelled with every passing season, the nuisance inspector and his team of helpers were quickly overwhelmed. Accordingly, in June 1894, a new post – that of a dedicated beach inspector – was created.[151] There were limits on the inspectors' ability to police the sands: brazen bathers could appear at any time, upsetting sensitive types with their exposed bodies. But Barry Island was no longer an unregulated space of dangerous liminality. Not until the eve of the Great War was mixed bathing finally allowed at Whitmore Bay. And the beach was still being surveilled by the inspectors well into the 1950s.[152]

The Island's bathers proliferated during the Edwardian period. As visitor numbers to the Island mushroomed in the early 1900s, so did the numbers who entered the sea. On August bank holiday, 1904, for example, nearly 5,000 paid to change in the newly constructed bathing houses.[153] In other words, the number of 'paying' bathers on that single day was more than double the number during the entire bathing season of 1892. On Whit Monday, 1914, 'many hundreds' were seen in the sea.[154] Bathing was another example of how, when 'artificial', commercialized amusements were in short supply, the trippers from the coalfield made sure that they got their holiday pleasures from whatever resources were to hand – and that included the bracing waters of the Bristol Channel.

CONCLUSION

By 1900, the trippers had triumphed. They had colonized the Island's resort spaces and made the beach their very own seaside playground. The visitors who hailed from the coalfield now predominated. In the 1860s and 1870s, on high days and holidays, Whitmore Bay had been Cardiff-by-Sea. After the early 1890s, it was turned into a Rhondda-, an Aberdare-, a Merthyr- and a Rhymney-by-Sea. (Not to mention all the other mining communities that sent their pleasure seekers down to Barry's seashore.) The Island had become a favourite playground of the working-class inhabitants of the mining district. The 'tradition' of Sunday schools in the valleys bringing their young scholars down to Barry Island for their annual treat was firmly established by 1900. By then, it was already being referred to as 'the favourite resort' of Rhonddaites.[155]

This chapter has argued that there was nothing inevitable about the valleys inhabitants' warm embrace of Whitmore Bay. It took an effort for trippers to get to Barry Island, particularly in the early 1890s. Once at their holiday destination, they were confronted with an undeveloped set of resort spaces. But they loyally returned, in ever greater numbers, year after year. If Lord Windsor harboured any hopes that the excursionists' numbers could be kept low by his unfriendly policies, they were well and truly dashed by the time he moved into his expensive holiday home at Friars Point in 1894. Indeed, as the years passed, Friars Point House seemed more like a place under siege, so much did the excursionists dominate the rest of the Island.

The trippers came to the Island because they were seduced by its natural charms and because they could make a leisure space out of the beach, sand dunes and headlands that met their holiday needs. Theirs was a beach experience that had much in common with that enjoyed by earlier cohorts of visitors. It was centred on the enjoyment of the place's natural assets above all else. Not for them the commercialized, 'modern' seaside experience of their counterparts in Blackpool. At Barry Island, an older mode of seaside play was still being honoured.

As we shall see in the final chapter, Peter Stead was entirely right to point to the significance of the 1920s in the Island's history. It marked the beginning of an era in which artificial amusements began to play more of a role. But his suggestion that the 1920s was the decade when Barrians reached a decision about what sort of resort they wanted to see at the Island misses a crucial point: that decision was no longer theirs to make. The trippers had already decided the matter.

While the town's middle-class boosters engaged in endless discussion about how best to proceed with resort development, and the Island's aristocratic owner tried to make the Island as unwelcoming a space as he possibly could, the working-class trippers had acted decisively: they had 'swooped down from the hills' and taken possession of Whitmore Bay.

CHAPTER EIGHT

BARRY-ON-SEA?

THE TRIPPER RESORT CONSOLIDATED, 1914–c.1965

THE THREE DECADES after 1914 proved to be a defining moment in the making of Barry as a working-class seaside playground. At last, many of the long-discussed improvements at the Island and at Cold Knap came to fruition thanks to decisions made by Barry's councillors and to funds provided by the town's ratepayers. Much of the seafront infrastructure that can still be seen by the Island's early twenty-first-century visitors was installed in the 1920s. Tellingly, the trigger for this long-delayed development had little to do with the dynamics of tourism at Whitmore Bay itself, but lots to do with the economic crisis that was draining the life out of the south Wales coal industry. The interwar period could have brought about the collapse of the Island as a popular seaside resort. Its visitor heartland was eviscerated by a vicious economic depression that generated unprecedented poverty and destitution. Yet, as we shall see, the trippers from the coalfield kept coming to Barry Island. Neither the privations of two total wars, nor the harrowing experience of mass unemployment could halt the Island's rise as the coalfield's seaside playground. That was the most remarkable of all the developments.

A RESILIENT HABIT: THE DAY-TRIPPERS AND BARRY ISLAND DURING THE GREAT WAR

Once the 'tradition' of an annual day trip to Barry Island had been established in the later Victorian and Edwardian periods, it proved to be remarkably durable. The first great test of the trippers' devotion to Whitmore Bay came with the declaration of war in 1914. The last day of peace happened to be the August bank holiday. It had been a typically jolly affair at Barry Island. An estimated 50,000 visitors descended upon Whitmore Bay, '[n]otwithstanding the war cloud', as the *Dock News* put it.[1] It was a shock, therefore, to see just how quickly the conflict's impact was registered at Barry's seafront. Just a few days later, in the second week of August, it was decided to turn Whitmore Bay into a firing range for soldiers. The beach was closed to the public and a red flag was flown from Friars Point House as a warning to visitors to stay away.[2] However, this was to be only a temporary shutdown. Within weeks, the soldiers had departed and the beach had been reopened. It remained to be seen, however, what effect the war would have on visitor numbers thereafter.

Many commentators predicted that the day-tripping habit would fall into abeyance for the duration of the conflict. A total war made significant demands on the nation's transport system. Travel became costlier and often involved many more challenges than had been the case in peace time. Considerable obstacles were placed in the way of trippers. In the spring of 1915, all rail excursion tickets were cancelled 'due to military exigencies'.[3] Many thought that this development alone would lead to big reductions in the number of visitors.[4] As one journalist remarked, 'The withdrawal of . . . cheap tickets will cause people to stay at home for the difference between excursion and ordinary fare is considerable when a family outing is in question.' It was regrettable, but the reporter thought it was unavoidable: there was 'more important work' for the railway companies to do 'than conveying trippers to the country and the seaside'.[5] A few weeks later, it was announced that the Admiralty had refused to allow pleasure steamers to ply in the Bristol Channel. This decision effectively made it impossible for trippers from the south Wales coalfield to spend a day at the seaside resorts of north Somerset and north Devon.[6] Later, in January 1917, all ordinary rail fares were increased by 50 per cent and many services cut.[7]

These were just some of the practical challenges that had to be overcome by the would-be tripper during the war years. At a more abstract level, there was another powerful reason for thinking that the demand for day trips would weaken, namely, the belief that pleasure-seeking was not appropriate at a time of war. As John K. Walton has expressed it, 'Guilt and holiday-making are uneasy bedfellows.'[8] There was no shortage of opinion-shapers willing to remind 'patriotic workers' that they should forgo the frivolous amusements of the day trip.[9] As the *Dock News* explained it in the spring of 1915, it would 'be a reflection upon our honour if we at home suspended the manufacture of the all-important war material for a single day, in order to indulge in pleasure and amusement . . . Holidays may well be postponed until peace is declared, and suitable celebrations arranged.' After all, '[t]here will be no holiday in the trenches'.[10] A likeminded Barry councillor denounced an entertainer who applied for permission to perform on the beach in May 1915: 'this was not the time to support such tomfoolery on the sands', the civic father snapped.[11]

However, for all that we might have expected the Great War to halt the Island's rise as a popular resort, the trippers continued to arrive in substantial numbers. During the Easter holidays of 1915, cheap excursion trains did not run into Barry, but the newspapers reported a 'large influx' of visitors regardless.[12] A few weeks later, on the Whit Monday, an estimated 25,000 trippers streamed onto the Island.[13] The August bank holiday was marred by heavy rain in the morning which 'damped the ardour of intending holiday visitors', but still 'many thousands' arrived.[14] Some inland beauty spots in Wales suffered a decline in visitor numbers as a consequence of the suspension of cheap tickets, but Glamorganshire's seaside resorts retained their stronghold on the people's affections.[15] Even when the government postponed the Whit holiday of 1916 (in response to the munitions crisis), trippers kept heading to the coast. Some 25,000 visitors 'swarmed' around Barry Island that Whit Monday.[16] And Porthcawl was so thronged that one commentator felt compelled to ask, 'Is there a war on? The streets . . . on Whit-Monday did not give one the impression that such was the case.'[17] During the summer season of 1916, approximately 250,000 excursionists visited Barry Island.[18] On August bank holiday, 1917, an impressive 50,000 trippers gathered at Whitmore Bay. To put that in context, the same number had been on the Island on the last bank holiday of peacetime, three years earlier.[19]

It was not entirely business as usual though. Observers noted that the holiday crowds contained fewer men than those of the pre-war years.[20] Large numbers had left the mining valleys to go and fight in the trenches.[21] Poignantly, some headed to Barry Island, in their new uniforms, for one last time before they left for the battlefields of Continental Europe. One was overheard exclaiming that he was about to go on 'Kitchener's free tour of France' but that he would be 'pleased to see good old Barry again'.[22] The men who stayed behind to carry on the vital work of producing coal sometimes sacrificed their holidays in the name of the war effort. Their absence was noticed at the Island.[23] In addition, in the latter stages of the war, there was a decline in the number of organized Sunday school trips to the Island. This was after the government had requested that chapels discontinue their annual treats in the interests of food economy.[24]

Notwithstanding these changes to the composition of the holiday crowds, the tripping habit proved to be highly durable. Some contemporaries, wondering what it all meant, decided that the popularity of the seaside trip must reflect badly on the holidaymakers. In 1916, for example, a Barry councillor declared that the large bank holiday crowds at south Wales's resorts showed that people were 'not taking the war to heart' in the way that they had done in the early months of the conflict.[25] In May 1917, a correspondent to the *Barry Herald* found it distasteful that the 'crowds given over to pleasure-seeking' were as large as ever at a time when the nation was 'engaged in a life-or-death struggle': 'we cannot expect victory in this, our just cause, unless as a nation we return to God in true humility and deep repentance', the writer warned darkly.[26] The *Barry Dock News* thought that the holiday tripper was 'not necessarily a slacker', although the use of the adverb clearly showed it was worried that some of them probably were. The paper argued that visitors needed to remember that it was not a time for 'frivolous enjoyment or indulgence' at the seaside. If visitors came to the Island for the good of their health, that was one thing; if they came for fun, that was quite another.[27]

It is difficult to gauge how 'frivolous' the wartime trippers were. However, there is no doubt that the purveyors of seaside entertainments were keen to continue offering their services at Whitmore Bay during the Great War, and the local authority was, by and large, willing to let them. Councillors continued to give their permission for entertainers, showmen and the providers of donkey rides to ply their trade on the beach. The council had 138 applications for the renewal of licences for donkey and boat rides in May 1915.[28] In the same month, fairground ride operators Nash and Sons applied to the council for the right to bring a cake walk and a shooting saloon over to the Island.[29] Roundabouts and swings were installed on the sands in the summer of 1916.[30] The bathing machines were being rolled in and out of the water just as they had been in the pre-war years. Deckchairs were being hired out too.[31] Town leaders approved an application for swimming lessons to be offered at Whitmore Bay in 1915.[32] Meanwhile, a pavilion, a rather makeshift structure of wood and canvas that had first appeared in the early 1910s, remained open for business during the war years. A troupe of Pierrots reportedly attracted 'large crowds' during the Whitsuntide holidays of 1915, offering a fare of comic entertainers, singers and ventriloquists. The pavilion enjoyed another 'successful opening' the following year, too.[33]

We do not need to accept arguments that the trippers to Barry Island were unpatriotic slackers or selfish hedonists who forgot, even for a few hours, those loved ones who had been with them on the beach in previous years but who were now fighting overseas. Indeed, the fact that fortune tellers did a roaring trade on the sands of Whitmore Bay during the summer of 1916, after two long years of appalling losses in the trenches, is revealing.[34] We can easily imagine why trippers might have eagerly paid to hear reassuring news of the future at a time when the Battle of the Somme was underway. Importantly, by no means everyone condemned excursionists. The *Glamorgan Gazette* thought that it was understandable that trippers sought a little rest at the seaside, 'war or no war'.[35] Likewise, the *Cambrian News* contended that 'Nobody can grudge the peace and quietness at the seaside which visitors have sought to brace them up if the war continues to bring gloom and sorrow in the autumn and winter.'[36]

'[L]ONGING [FOR] BARRY ISLAND':
THE GROWTH OF TRIPPER NUMBERS
DURING THE DEPRESSION

The war clearly had an impact on tourism at the Island. Amongst other things, it became more difficult for trippers to get there, Sunday school visits declined and there was a marked preponderance of female over male visitors. However, the conflict was certainly not a hiatus in Whitmore Bay's history as a resort. The trippers continued to arrive in large numbers throughout the conflict. It is no surprise, therefore, that the first year of peace saw big crowds descend on the Island. They were merely carrying on a tradition that had never been interrupted. In 1919, nearly 30,000 travelled by train to Barry on Easter Monday, more than 51,000 on the Whit holiday and some 47,000 on the August bank holiday.[37] But these figures understate the numbers at Whitmore Bay that year quite considerably. Large crowds of Barrians, who made their way over to the Island by foot, joined the railway excursionists. In addition, other visitors from outside the district came by charabanc.[38] Thus, on Whit Monday, 1919, there were an estimated 70,000 pleasure-seekers, 'as light-hearted as ever', on the sands.[39] Prominent amongst them were Sunday schoolchildren. More than 180 chapels had sent their young scholars down to the Island from the Rhondda valleys alone by the beginning of August.[40]

Visitor numbers climbed substantially in the 1920s and 1930s. This was when the Island's reputation as an excursionist resort was cemented. By the mid-1920s, it was already being claimed that the Island was the third most popular day-tripper destination in the country after Blackpool and the recently opened Wembley Empire Stadium.[41] The playful crowds that milled around the Island's resort spaces in the 1920s were often twice the size of their pre-war counterparts. From 1920, the numbers travelling by train to Barry on the Whitsuntide and August bank holidays regularly breached the 100,000 mark.[42] The coalfield, as ever, provided the majority of the trippers. Record numbers arrived from the Rhondda and other mining valleys. However, the numbers hailing from further afield also grew significantly during these years. Bank holidays witnessed special trains pulling into the Island's station from a host of English towns and cities including Gloucester, Shrewsbury, Hereford, Birmingham, Birkenhead and Manchester.[43] By the 1930s, Birmingham was regularly sending 2,000 of its citizens to the Island on the bank holidays.[44] Crowds were now immense. No fewer than 250,000 visitors were packed onto Whitmore Bay on the busiest day of the 1933 season. The beach was 'literally black with people', exclaimed the *Barry and District News*. The 'bather who found more than a square yard of sand or pebbles upon which to deposit his or her clothes was unusually lucky'.[45]

Critically, this growth in the Island's visitor numbers took place despite the economic travails afflicting its great visitor heartland. From the early 1920s, the south Wales coal industry, the mainstay of the social and cultural life of the valleys, declined alarmingly as domestic and foreign markets dried up. As Kenneth O. Morgan has described it, the coalfield 'experienced mass unemployment and poverty without parallel in the British Isles'.[46] Whole communities were impoverished as pits closed. Some areas were especially hard hit. The old iron towns at the heads of the valleys suffered particularly high unemployment rates.[47] In the Rhondda, collieries closed at a bewildering rate. Between 1927 and 1936, the number of colliers employed there fell by nearly 50 per cent, from 39,000 to 20,000.[48] To make matters worse, a number of lengthy industrial stoppages, including the national coal strike of 1921 and the General Strike of 1926 with the seven-month lockout that followed it, depleted savings and generated great suffering. The material basis upon which a whole way of life had been built up during the later nineteenth century was, quite suddenly, undermined.[49]

The destitution imposed severe limits on the ability of people to partake in a leisure culture that was increasingly commercialized.[50] Philip Massey's 1937 study of the valley communities of Blaina and Nantyglo underlined how the lack of disposable income shaped the leisure choices of the unemployed. Free time, far too much of which was now enforced, was spent in ways that did not involve spending money: ponds – even those that were 'contaminated as well as treacherous' – were made to serve as swimming baths, whilst walking on the tops of the mountains became a popular practice.[51] In contrast, Massey found that there was 'very little' drinking in pubs and working-men's clubs because 'most people cannot possibly afford anything more than an occasional half-pint if they are to keep their homes going'. A large proportion (one-third) of his interviewees never went to the cinema. Unsurprisingly, for some, a holiday of any sort was beyond reach. 'Never gets away – not even on odd trips', was the sociologist's note against one family's name; 'Never even a day out since married. Wife saw the sea once, children have never been away', he remarked of another.[52]

The most impoverished inhabitants simply had no spare money for a trip to the seaside.[53] Barry's journalists lamented their absence.

During the lockout of 1926, for example, a reporter from the *Barry and District News* remarked that, during a visit to the Island, he had 'missed . . . the usually overwhelming predominance of the musical accent of Cwm Rhondda. It was unmistakably present but was not the force of the previous years.'[54] Nevertheless, Barrians were more often impressed at how many visitors kept arriving from the coalfield, the distress and destitution notwithstanding. During the 1921 coal strike, for example, the *Dock News* had been surprised at just how many charabancs and trains had come to Barry Island from the mining valleys. 'Most of these holiday-seekers were colliers, and there was not the slightest indication that the cruellest strike that South Wales has ever experienced was still on.'[55]

The determination of the coalfield's trippers to safeguard their annual trip to Barry Island is certainly striking. Occasionally, Whitmore Bay's seductive power led those under its spell into trouble. Consider a report that appeared in the *Barry Dock News* in the summer of 1923. Under the headline 'How she longed for Barry Island', it told of how the 'lure of the seaside' had tempted a Tredegar teenager to steal 7s. from the till of a local shopkeeper. 'She pleaded to the police that she was longing to go on a visit to Barry Island, and was tempted to steal.' She was bound over to be of good behaviour for six months, a lenient sentence which suggests that the magistrate sympathized with her plight.[56] Most of Whitmore Bay's devotees were not driven to break the law. Instead, they struggled throughout the year to save enough for the train fare to Barry. Massey's abbreviated interview notes reveal just how much his informants valued their few hours at the Island. 'Day out, for example, to Barry, perhaps once a year', he wrote about one interviewee; 'Holidays never, sometimes a day trip, family goes to Barry', he observed of another. And so the list ran on: 'Day at Barry all he can manage'; 'Day at Barry most he can hope for'; 'Holidays out of the question. Sometimes save to go to Barry for the day.'[57]

Barry Island's experience of the interwar years was similar to that of resorts located in other areas hard hit by the Depression. As was the case with the working-class populations of industrial Scotland and the north-east of England, so the workers of south Wales clung tenaciously to their annual trip to the sea.[58] As Huggins and Walton have observed, far from denting the appeal of the excursion to the coast, 'Unemployment made the seaside trip all the more important in helping to forget the horrors of the depression.'[59]

DECISIVE DEVELOPMENTS: THE COUNCIL'S INVESTMENT IN RESORT INFRASTRUCTURE

The trauma of mass unemployment was not confined to the mining valleys. As the south Wales coal trade faltered, so the effects were registered at Barry, a town where it was estimated that some 90 per cent of the population owed their livelihood, some more directly than others, to the shipment of coal.[60] The early 1920s were particularly difficult years for Barrians, but, ironically, it was the post-war depression that prompted the council to begin spending large sums of public money on Barry's resort spaces.

The downturn in the coal industry's fortunes was soon felt in the town.[61] The dock had exported 11 million tons of coal and coke in 1913. By 1920, this figure had declined by more than a third to 7 million tons.[62] Such a convulsion caused immense hardship. By October 1920, it was reported that there were more than 2,200 unskilled men out of work in the town. Some families were in severe distress.[63] Begging on Barry's streets was one of the clearest indicators of the hardship. When two ex-soldiers, desperate for food, took to begging in January 1921, they wore masks to avoid recognition.[64] Soup kitchens opened in the town at the end of 1924.[65] Several thousand dock workers were unemployed by 1925 and the miners' lockout of 1926 merely intensified the hardship. In June of that year, shopkeepers told journalists that they had 'never experienced such an anxious time'.[66] Against such a grim context, the prospect of developing the town's tourism function appeared especially attractive. As one local remarked, 'Once again we are reminded at Barry how dependent we are upon coal, for as soon as anything stops the shipping of it, everything is at a standstill in the town.'[67]

As early as the autumn of 1920, town leaders were contemplating the introduction of public works schemes for the unemployed.[68] The following year, they applied to the Ministry of Labour's recently established Unemployment Grants Committee for a loan to help finance such schemes.[69] The councillors sought £21,000 to pay men to build a seawall, a shelter and some shops – some of the very improvements that boosters had been calling for since the 1890s.[70] This request was turned down, but a revised bid for £9,300 was approved in February 1922. Eighteen men were put to work immediately. At last, Barry Island was to get its seawall.[71] More schemes were presented to the Unemployment Grants Committee in quick succession, including one to develop the Cold Knap and another to build a shelter at Whitmore Bay.[72] Work started on the shelter and the promenade in May 1923.[73] In February

1924, fifteen men were employed on the improvement projects on the Island and some fifty at Cold Knap.[74]

The impact on Barry's tourist spaces of the Unemployment Grants Committee's schemes was profound. After decades of discussion and procrastination, there was an explosion of intense activity. The shelter, with its shops and flat roof ('an ideal place for concerts and dances'), was opened on Easter Monday, 1924. A promenade, forty feet wide, ran across the seafront and was backed by a rockery. Tennis courts and bowling greens graced Nell's Point. The seawall, at a cost of nearly £30,000, was finally completed in the spring of 1925.[75] Cold Knap, the little headland on the western side of the Island with two beaches of its own, Pebble Beach and a smaller one at Watch House Bay, was transformed almost beyond recognition. The Knap had been a favourite retreat for many late Victorian and Edwardian Barrians. As one local put it in 1922, it was the 'greatest summer resort of Barryites'.[76] Most agreed that the headland's tranquillity, especially when compared with the bustling Whitmore Bay, went a long way to account for its popularity, although its 'rugged beauty' was also cited as a major draw.[77] Yet, notwithstanding its natural charms, in October 1923 work began on improving the area: a garden was laid out; a promenade was built overlooking Pebble Beach; walkways of white concrete framed a large boating lake that was shaped as a Welsh harp; and, most impressive of all, an open-air swimming pool was constructed.[78] The saltwater lido, at 360 feet long, 90 feet wide and boasting a capacity of 1 million gallons, was one of the largest in Britain. Together the pool and the lake cost £49,000, of which the Unemployment Grants Committee contributed £29,000. Some £25,000 had gone in wages to the unemployed.[79]

The 'improvements' did not impress everyone. In February 1923, a crowded meeting of ratepayers told councillors of their fears that town leaders 'were spoiling the already existing beauties of the sea-front by what appeared to be indiscriminate digging and laying of concrete'.[80] These locals liked their seaside spaces to be as undeveloped as possible. But they were outnumbered by those who wanted the seafront to bear more of the hallmarks of civilization. The *Barry Dock News* was thrilled by the developments: 'Barry Island's natural advantages never suffered from lack of eulogy', the paper explained in 1925, 'but only needed developing to make Barry Island as attractive as any seaside resort in the country . . . The visitor cannot but be impressed with the way in which the glories of nature and modern conveniences are to be found side by side.'[81] Thus, Culture and Nature had to be brought together to make a beauty spot even more attractive to the tourist. The *Barry Herald* concurred. Ruminating on the project to upgrade the Knap, the newspaper thought that in the days before it had been 'improved', the Knap had suffered from a 'lack of amenities of civilized existence': 'though delightful in itself, [it] was still in its primitive state, and not at all conducive to the average tripper's pleasure'. Untouched, natural spaces could carry a charge of barbarism at the modern seaside; what a proper resort needed was a natural landscape that had been 'civilized'.[82]

At last, Barry's seafront had been developed. But it took the harrowing experience of mass unemployment to bring it about. The shelters, the promenade, the seawall and the lido should properly be seen as monuments to town leaders' struggles to keep poverty and distress at bay in the town. They were certainly not the result of a sudden recognition that the resort boosters had been right all along. The tourism multiplier had next to nothing to do with the decision: structural shifts in the global demand for Welsh coal were the main drivers of the changes at the Island. Indeed, it was still far from clear whether the tripper resort at Whitmore Bay would ever justify such expensive improvement schemes. The weakness of tourism's contribution to Barry's economy is a point to which we must return later in this chapter.

THE 'GLORIES OF NATURE AND MODERN CONVENIENCES . . . SIDE BY SIDE': THE 'MODERNIZED' BEACH EXPERIENCE

If Barry's resort spaces were subject to some dramatic changes in the 1920s, the same can be said of the way that visitors experienced the beach and its associated leisure sites. True, some key elements remained remarkably stable: the simple acts of walking, appreciating the seascapes, sharing al fresco meals with friends and families, playing on the sand, paddling and bathing. All these practices were staple features of a day out at the Island in the interwar period, just as they had been in the 1890s, and long before. However, there were noticeable changes, too: Whitmore Bay was being 'modernized' and the forces of Civilization – in the form of fairground rides, electric illuminations and blaring megaphones – jostled with Nature for the visitors' attention.

One obvious development was the rise of sunbathing as a practice. Sun-worshippers made much of the health benefits to be had from a 'sun-bath'.[83] It was an idea that encouraged a great undressing at Britain's seaside resorts. It also focused attention on the bodies of Whitmore Bay's visitors to an extent unseen since the controversies prompted by 'immodest' bathers in the 1890s and 1900s. One manifestation of this was a sudden interest in beachwear. For the first time, observers of Whitmore Bay began noticing fashions in swimming and sun-bathing costumes. For example, the *Herald* noted, in 1927, that the 'American bathing costume' had arrived in Barry that year. The 'younger set' had been seen at the lido in black knickers, white vests and neat white belts.[84] Local drapers' shops began selling bathing costumes with built-in corsets in 1928, much to the annoyance of one male commentator who was left wondering whether he had spent his time at the lido admiring women's figures or their corsetry.[85] A couple of years later, in the early 1930s, it was the 'beach pyjama' that was all the rage.[86]

The cult of sunbathing necessarily meant a greater exposure of the body. Late Victorian women had been obliged to turn up to the beach in restrictive Sunday-best clothes that made no allowance for the fact that they were on the sands. Many continued to dress in this way in the 1920s and 1930s, too, but now increasing numbers were to be seen wearing 'the flimsiest summer dresses'.[87] It was too much for some. Those of a sensitive and, often, a voyeuristic disposition began scouring the beach for signs of 'shameless' visitors. One or two kept detailed records of how many women had bare legs and how many men had open collars. In 1929, beaches at the small villages of Rhoose and Fontygary, just a few miles along the coast from Barry Island, became the centre of a national news story thanks to the efforts of one especially enthusiastic social purist. Of the 204 beach users that he encountered on a Saturday in July, 128 were women with bare legs. Such displays, he claimed, were 'greatly criticised by some residents'.[88] So shocking were his depictions of the 'immodest' sunbathers that the story was picked up by the *Daily Express*. When interviewed by one of the paper's reporters, some visitors were unrepentant. One 'Cockney blonde' accepted the charges: 'Yes, I am very, very naughty, and I admit it . . . I have danced on the beach at midnight, and you can say so.' Another, a young woman from the Midlands, explained that she was on holiday, 'not in a reformatory school . . . It is all very well to be penned up for a year without sight of the sea.'[89]

It was this sort of devil-may-care attitude that worried some of Barry's more buttoned-up citizens. And it has led some historians to emphasize the liminal nature of the seaside, seeing the beach as an 'in-between' space in which the normal rules governing public behaviour were suspended, challenged and, sometimes, inverted.[90] There was more than a whiff of the liminal at Barry Island during the roaring twenties, even if occasionally it was only in the way that some beach activities were reported by the local newspapers. Thus we read of the all-night-dancing and bathing 'orgies' that took place at Whitmore Bay during the summer of 1927, for instance. Thousands were said to have spent a Saturday night in August revelling on the beach as a means of extending their stay. Trippers were seen dancing the Charleston 'in the light of many bonfires', midnight bathing was indulged in and gramophones were left blaring on the sands from dusk to dawn. All this, as a shocked *Herald* felt compelled to point out, took place during the early hours of the Lord's Day.[91]

But we should not push the liminality thesis too far. Often immorality was in the eye, and mind, of the beholder. The moralist who spent his afternoons perched on a clifftop counting 'immodest' young female sunbathers on the sands below was certain that he was discharging a public service even if the young women he was ogling invariably disagreed.[92] Indeed, most beach users were able to negotiate the 'informalization' of beach dress codes without fearing that they were living through the last days of Civilization.[93] In any case, far from being a space of dangerous freedom, Whitmore Bay beach was, in fact, highly regulated. Beach inspectors – introduced some thirty years previously, in the 1890s – were still being paid to patrol the sands, enforce by-laws and reprimand those who stepped too far out of line.[94]

The inspectors were not the only guardians of morality at Barry Island. Whitmore Bay beach was a Mecca (or perhaps that should be a New Jerusalem) for Nonconformist Sunday schools, and it was a rare day indeed that did not see ministers and deacons on the sands watching over their flocks – and everyone else. Religious services were frequently held on the sands themselves. The first time that commentators noticed such services at Whitmore Bay was during the Religious Revival of 1904–5, but now, in the 1920s and 1930s, they became a staple feature of the beach experience. In the later 1920s, the Barry Free Church Council used megaphones to broadcast its sermons.[95] By the early 1930s, the Nonconformists had commandeered one side of Whitmore Bay, their thrice-weekly services lasting an hour and a half. The Salvation Army took possession of the other half of the beach.[96] Clearly, the 'immodest', sunbathing, dancing hedonists never had it all their own way at Whitmore Bay.

If the Island's late Victorian visitors could have peered into the future and glimpsed the beach of the 1920s and 1930s, they would have been flabbergasted by the sight of sunbathers and women in flimsy dresses and beach pyjamas. But there were other features that would have surprised them just as much. For example, the way that areas of the sands had been transformed into sites of commercial exchange was a major contrast with the beach as it had been under Windsor's regime. With the withdrawal of the Windsor estate, the beach was opened to traders. It was not a free-for-all though. Permission had to be sought from the council by anyone wishing to sell goods or services on the sands, and town leaders were keen not to let the beach become, as one put it, an 'open market'.[97] Nevertheless, those of an entrepreneurial bent enjoyed a freedom (albeit a regulated one) that was simply unimaginable to their late Victorian and Edwardian predecessors.

The most successful figures were those who already had extensive experience catering for holiday crowds. There was M. W. Shanly, the 'chair king', for example.[98] He was a London-based entrepreneur who began business in the late nineteenth century as a 'chair caterer' in some of the capital's biggest parks.[99] By the early twentieth century, Shanly had taken his chairs to the seaside. Countless pleasure seekers at various Welsh resorts, including Llandudno, Barmouth, Criccieth, Porthcawl and Tenby, reclined on deckchairs hired out by Shanly.[100] He established a foothold at Barry before the Great War, as soon as the Windsor estate released the beach to the council.[101] His first season at Whitmore Bay was in 1910.[102] In 1914, he paid the council £30 for the rights to place bathing machines and chairs on the Island. By the mid-1920s, his interests at Barry extended over Whitmore Bay, the Knap (he had the rights to the rowing boats on the Marine Lake and was given the lucrative rights to running the lido) and some of the town's parks.[103] By 1929, his stock of deckchairs at Barry had reached 8,000.[104] He was doing well enough to be able to pay the council 40 per cent of his gross takings and still make a tidy profit.[105] Shanly was certainly keen to stay in Barry. When, in 1929, his contract with the council was up for renewal, he asked for a new agreement that would have given him trading rights for the next forty-five years.[106]

Shanly was joined at Barry by another business figure of national stature – Pat Collins. Collins was one of the pre-eminent showmen of his day. By the early twentieth century, he had not only established himself as the leading roundabout proprietor in the country, but had expanded into the film industry, too. His willingness to innovate meant that he can be counted as one of those fairground proprietors who 'bridged the gap from the nineteenth to the twentieth century'.[107] He certainly brought Barry Island's amusements into a new era after acquiring the Pleasure Park in 1930. The park had been set up by showmen Sydney White and his brother. They had established a foothold on the Island during the immediate pre-war years, just after Windsor handed over control to the council. In 1909, they set up swing-boats and merry-go-rounds on the sands.[108] An impressive 'Figure 8' rollercoaster was erected in 1912.[109] The White brothers expanded their fairground operation in the early 1920s, installing a greater range of rides and amusements including the obligatory galloping horses, swings, shooting ranges, stalls and a helter-skelter.[110] The fair boomed, its rides particularly appealing to adults.[111] Large, 'good natured' holiday crowds flocked to it, some to be thrown around on the latest state-of-the-art rides (the 'mountain slide' evoked considerable hilarity in the summer of 1922, for instance), some just to enjoy the simpler delights of its shooting galleries and 'win-a-penny' stalls.[112] But whereas the White brothers were content to rely on steam to power their raucous organs, Collins belonged firmly to the age of electricity. Collins ran electric cables across to the Island to flood the amusement ground in bright light. In part, this was to create a tourist spectacle. But it also allowed him to extend the holiday season further into the autumn months.[113]

Collins invested heavily during his first few years on the Island, perhaps spending as much as £60,000 on the fairground. A few hundred men were employed in the construction of the ground; a few hundred more found work running the stalls and operating the rides. A handful of older rides remained – including the Figure 8 – but Collins was always keen to refresh his offering. Some rides were merely new to Barry, but, characteristically, Collins was keen to trumpet the fact that others were new to the United Kingdom. In his first year, he brought two brand-new rides in from America and another two from Continental Europe. Favourites included a ride involving 'original Welsh golden dragons' and the 'Honeymoon Express', which comprised 'a journey by train, through the proverbial honeymoon tunnel, where the "brides and bridegrooms" could enjoy themselves to the full'. Then there was 'The Caterpillar', 'a novel and entertaining ride' that gradually ensconced the cars in a large green cloak that left the occupants in darkness. Strong jets of air, 'quite capable to blowing one's hat off', were released which fanned the faces of the thrill seekers. 'Over the Falls' and the 'Ghost Train' were similarly 'thrilling', the 'Crazy Yo-Yo Ride' threw visitors around, the 'Palace of Sensations' was replete with 'mysterious and marvellous things', whilst the 'Death Ride' offered the spectacle of daredevils riding their motorbikes around a perpendicular track. More sedate pleasures were on offer at a capacious open-air dance floor with its 'fine amplified gramophone to provide the music'. And there was a menagerie full of performing animals. It had ten lions (one of which was allegedly untameable), a troop of 'entertaining' monkeys and a boxing kangaroo that was expected to engage in pugilistic encounters with his trainer.[114] By the summer of 1933, visitors to Collins's fairground could even revel in the sight of a lion 'driving' a motor car on the 'Wall of Death'.[115]

Shanly and Collins were the captains of Barry's tourist industry and were by far the most substantial figures who made money from the visitors. But beneath them was an army of less successful, but no less energetic, petty capitalists: hawkers, hucksters and small-time entertainers. They were to be found on the approaches to the beach as well as on the sands set aside for traders. Stalls were set up above the high-water mark. At just 10-foot square with a corrugated iron roof, a flooring-board floor, a water boiler and bread-cutting boards, and canvas covering the sides, they were basic enough structures but they helped transform the visitor experience.[116] No longer were visitors obliged to go hungry and thirsty during a day trip to the Island. These stallholders had some capital behind them. Not only did they have to stock up with refreshments, but they also had to bid every year for the right to trade from their stalls. Successful candidates might end up paying anything from £80 to £120 for the privilege.[117]

The stallholders were members of the 'retail aristocracy' compared to the rest of beach traders. Most of the latter were familiar enough figures. The donkey boys and the pleasure boat operators had been there long before the First World War. So had the Italian ice-cream vendors, at least on the days when they were not being chased off the Island by Lord Windsor's men. Others, however, were new arrivals: the photographers who roamed around offering to take and develop 'snaps' of the trippers while they waited; the telescope owners who hired their optics out to visitors so that they could gaze even more intently at the seascape (and the bathers); the weighing-machine operators (of which there were twenty at the Island in the late 1920s); the Punch and Judy performers; and the newspaper boys who patrolled the beach 'shouting "Echo" on the sands'.[118] Whitmore Bay's beach certainly was not an unregulated 'open market', but it was a veritable marketplace nonetheless – and a noisy one at that.

By the mid-1920s, Barry Island offered what one local journalist called a 'modernised beach' experience.[119] Its modernity was most evident in the great illumination events that were staged at Whitmore Bay from the later 1920s. The Chamber of Trade was a pioneer in this field. In 1928, it organized an impressive series of carnivals that drew tens of thousands of spectators. The chamber closed the season with a festival of 'liquid fire' with floating electric lights in Watch House Bay and a fireworks display.[120] In the early 1930s, chamber members paid for a small display of lights at Whitmore Bay, but there was general agreement that something more striking was required.[121] At the end of August 1934, town leaders stepped in: their 'Bright Light Nights' saw Whitmore Bay and its environs illuminated in a most spectacular fashion. All the resort spaces were saturated in artificial light. At dusk, the bay was transformed from 'a gloomy and almost dreary place, into a garden of colour'. Novelty illuminations were installed at the promenade gardens including skeletons, 'fortunately not too realistic, made of electric bulbs, jog[ing] up and down'; red arc lamps transformed fountains into showers of 'glowing sparks'; mosaic mirrors, hanging over the fountains, threw 'will-o-the-wisps on the onlookers' faces'; dovecote-like structures were installed along the promenade, out of which flooded 'multi-coloured rays over the lawns and flower beds'. So sophisticated and dazzling was the scene that that some visitors were put in mind of Paris's Place de la Concorde, with its various 'schemes of night illumination'. The Island's lights were a great success, drawing visitors from far and wide. Motorists from various south Wales towns streamed onto the Island, and Friars Point and Nell's Point were packed with spectators, all keen to get the best views. Councillors were pleased enough with the results in the first season to keep the illuminations switched on throughout October.[122]

Barry Island had become a place of 'gaiety and glare', of 'scenic railways, hooplas, merry-go-rounds, whizz-bangs, the blare of music and the raucous voices of those soliciting their patronage'.[123] By the mid-1930s, the Island was drawing more than a million visitors each summer season.[124] Some, it is true, hankered after the good old days. The Island 'was much better in its natural state', remembered one visitor in 1944, when 'we kiddies used to enjoy ourselves for hours playing roly-poly on the sandy banks and never having to worry about someone coming along to warn us to keep off the grass or mind the flowers'.[125] But most of Whitmore Bay's visitors responded positively to its novel mixture of the natural and the artificial. They were happy enough that the sand dunes had been replaced by a modern fairground, with its numerous rides and food stalls, its booths selling 'buckets and spades, balloons, tin trumpets, dolls and paper hats', and its music 'blar[ing] from several different points at once'.[126] In 1937, a journalist working for the *Herald* noted how the huge Easter holiday crowds moved effortlessly from the beach, where many thousands 'romped all over the sands', basking in the early spring sunshine, across to the beautifully manicured gardens at Cold Knap with their fine displays of blooming flowers. They went via Whitmore Bay's promenade and rock gardens. In just a few steps they moved not just from one space to another, but between the categories of Nature and Culture. The water's edge, the wildest of all Barry's spaces, continued to be the primary attraction for most trippers. But the siren calls of modernity were hard to resist. As the *Barry Herald* remarked, 'nearly all were attracted at some time in the day to the show-grounds' to see the new rides that were being advertised by 'loud-voiced showmen'.[127]

'[O]NE OF THE MOST SELF-SACRIFICING TOWNS IN THE UNITED KINGDOM': THE PROBLEM OF BARRY ISLAND

On the face of it, Barry councillors' willingness to invest in Whitmore Bay's tourist infrastructure seems like a gamble that paid off handsomely. Visitor numbers grew year on year and Barry Island had never been so popular. As one visitor from Hereford put it in 1925, 'Barry Island and its amenities have become famous throughout the length and breadth of the British Isles'.[128] And so they had. But its appeal was almost exclusively restricted to day-trippers. Only about 1 per cent of Barry's holidaymakers were long-stay visitors in the 1930s – a proportion that had changed little since the 1910s.[129] When viewed from the vantage point of Barry town, the predominance of the day excursionists was not without its downsides, the most significant of which was the weakness of their contribution to the local economy.

Trippers generally are a much less lucrative type of tourist than their residential counterparts. As we have seen, tripper demand for the Barry Island seaside product remained remarkably strong throughout the interwar years. Nevertheless, it was still subject to unpredictable shocks. It could fall away during an extended spell of wet, cold weather, for example.[130] Because of the way that demand was concentrated not just during the spring and summer months, but also on weekends and, most especially, the bank holidays, a few badly timed rainy days could depress traders' profits substantially. Meanwhile, at Barry, the intractable problem of geography – the distance between town and beach – meant that the tourism multiplier effect was particularly attenuated. Indeed, if anything, it had grown weaker over time. Now that there was a fairground to keep them entertained, the trippers of the 1920s and 1930s were even less likely to find their way into the town than had been their late Victorian predecessors. There were numerous visitors from the mining valleys who were intimately acquainted with Whitmore Bay's topography – even coming to think of particular stretches of sand as 'their own' – but who had never once visited Barry town.[131] To these trippers, Holton Road and Barry's High Street might as well have been a thousand miles away from the rocks of Friars Point and the sands of Whitmore Bay.

The economic benefits that should have come from having a million trippers at the Island each season were further diminished in the interwar period by the poverty suffered by many of the excursionists. That Barry Island's great visitor heartland was one of the most impoverished areas in the country necessarily had noticeable effects at Whitmore Bay. One commentator put it pithily in 1925: because the coalfield 'was practically bankrupt', so were most of the visitors it sent to the Barry.[132] For many, paying for the train ticket to Barry was biggest cost of the day. Once they arrived at the Island, they were careful to restrict their spending. It was oft-observed that 'The large majority of trippers brought their own food with them and spent very little, if anything' whilst on their day trip to the beach.[133] Traders were confronted with the largest holiday crowds the Island had ever seen, yet were still left complaining about having a slack time of it.[134]

The recollections of Edward Evans, an inhabitant of the Rhondda who visited the Island as a young boy in the later 1930s, show how carefully poorer families husbanded their limited resources. Spending was restricted to just a few pence and was often targeted at 'luxuries' – an ice cream, perhaps, or a fairground ride. Born in Ynyshir in 1930, Edward Evans came from a family that was fully conversant with the struggle to make ends meet. His father died in the mid-1930s, and his mother had to rely on 'public assistance' to support herself and her seven children.[135] With little money to spare once rent had been paid and food had been purchased – 'We could hardly live' – Mrs Evans was able to save enough to accompany her children on the annual Sunday school trip organized by Penuel Chapel. There was little left to spend at the Island. The meals for the day were all prepared at home: 'We had hampers of things. Everything you could make, or your mother made, you'd take because you couldn't afford to buy it.' If one of his uncles had a spare shilling, the children would be treated to a single fairground ride each. Edward Evans remembered how the first sight of the donkeys led him to declare, 'Oh, the donkeys! I'm going to have a ride today', but his mother's answer of 'Never mind. We'll see!' was a gentle reminder that there were only so many treats that could be paid for out of the limited budget.[136]

Just how little money was expended by the visitors to the Island bears underlining. It explains why the 'holiday industry' at Barry was so weakly developed. Only a handful of entrepreneurs were able to make serious money out of the trippers. The small traders who were below Collins and Shanly in the economic pecking order managed to keep their heads above water, but only by keeping their costs low. So limited was the visitors' spending power that even seaside entertainers were not guaranteed success. In 1921, one impresario, Stanley Blake, lost £300 when he tried to stage concert parties at Whitmore Bay. The initiative had been a 'failure', he told councillors, when he asked them for permission to sell the building he had erected.[137] When the Barry Silver Prize Band staged concerts at Whitmore Bay in the early 1920s, it drew large enough audiences, but almost all the seats were empty: nearly everyone stood through the performances rather than pay the sixpence extra to hire a seat.[138]

Instead of becoming an integral part of the town's economy, tourism remained incidental to it. Barry Island boomed, but the reverberations were barely registered back in the town. Indeed, in every meaningful respect, Barry was not a seaside town at all. The urban landscape gave few indications that the most popular beach in south Wales was close at hand. There were scarcely any examples of residential houses being built in the modernist style, for example. There had been no great rush to build hotels to cater for the visitors. No impressive music halls or theatres were thrown up to entertain the trippers. There was no obvious boarding-house district. And there were no landmark architectural features (there was no equivalent of the Blackpool Tower, for instance). Barry did not even have its own version of Blackpool's 'Golden Mile'.[139] Indeed, the majority of its inhabitants did not think of themselves as living in a seaside town. When councillor C. B. Griffiths dared to suggest, in 1925, that Barry's best days as a coal port were behind it and, henceforth, they should concentrate on developing its tourism function, he was roundly castigated for his defeatist attitude.[140] Most residents were not ready to give up on the dock, and hardly anyone thought that tourism offered a way out of Barry's current difficulties. It was thus entirely predictable that when, in 1926, another town leader wondered whether they should consider changing the town's name to something with more tourist appeal, such as 'Barry on Sea', 'Barry on the Sea' or even 'Aber Barry', the idea sank without a trace.[141]

A number of inhabitants became increasingly frustrated at the sight of a packed Island failing to deliver any benefits to a town whose economy was desperately in need of a boost. A correspondent to the *Barry Herald* decided that Barry must be 'one of the most self-sacrificing towns in the United Kingdom', for 40,000 inhabitants had provided 'ungrudgingly' for huge numbers of 'people from the outside who can take advantage of its natural beauties and public improvements without spending a penny in the town'.[142] Even members of the Chamber of Trade began to worry about how 'thousands of people visited the town during the summer' with 'no apparent evidence of the community benefiting from these visits'.[143]

Barry Island had become a problem for the town's leaders and a vigorous debate about what should be done with it began in the mid-1920s and ran throughout the rest of the interwar period. Some contended that it was time to turn away from the trippers and encourage long-stay visitors to the town. This argument rested on the assumption that there was a strong pent-up demand for residential holidays at Barry that just needed to be tapped. All that was required was an upgrading of Barry's seafront. Proponents of such a plan tended to downplay the future role of Whitmore Bay – it was too 'downmarket'. They concentrated instead on areas to the west of the town such as Porthkerry Park and the Cold Knap. A marina at Watch House Bay would surely attract the 'right' sort of holidaymaker. A state-of-the-art conference centre would bring professionals and business people into the district. A tasteful development of Pebble Beach would have a similarly uplifting effect. Importantly, by now, most supporters of such schemes took it for granted that private investors, rather than the town council, would finance them.[144] The days of assuming that ratepayers should foot the bill for resort development projects were long passed.

Other Barrians threw their weight behind a more modest proposal to raise the social tone of Barry's resort spaces, namely, through the expansion of the supply of hotels, guest houses and boarding houses. W. T. Ace, newsagent, prominent local Conservative and the vice-president of the Chamber of Trade, contended that 'the future success of Barry as a holiday resort rested entirely with the erection of a number of residential hotels. Their very presence would induce people from all over the country to spend most of the summer months in Barry.'[145] Dan Evans, a leading retailer in Barry and president of the Chamber of Trade in the mid-1920s, thought that an exclusive hydro hotel should be built on the Island overlooking the bay.[146] Others called for skyscraper hotels to be built at Whitmore Bay, or for the Great Western Railway to pay for its own hotel in the town.[147] Councillor C. B. Griffiths declared that the development of hotels and boarding houses was such a critical issue that landowners should be asked to charge lower ground rates to any private investor willing to build holiday accommodation in the town.[148] The editor of the *Barry and District News* agreed. The ratepayers had done enough to beautify the seafront at Whitmore Bay. Now it was time for builders and speculators to take up the challenge. Their reluctance to do so, thus far, had become a 'sore question'.[149] In 1928, the editor returned to the theme, declaring that time was running out: 'The final, real development of Barry inevitably must be the duty of private enterprise, and the hour is almost at hand.'[150]

Yet despite such impassioned pleas, private investors did not respond. They clearly did not see the Island as the El Dorado that an earlier generation of resort boosters had portrayed it. Whether they were right to pass over the opportunity to develop hotels in interwar Barry is probably an unanswerable question. We know that there was some demand for holiday accommodation in these years. By the mid-1930s, an estimated 10,000 visitors stayed in the town for a few days or more during the summer season. This was not an insignificant figure, but it was hardly impressive. If we assume, for the sake of argument, a four-month holiday season, it meant that, on average, some 625 visitors stayed in the town every week. They were easily accommodated in a town of 40,000 inhabitants – even without an overabundance of hotels and boarding houses. A few hundred working-class residents were thought to be renting out rooms in their homes to visitors during the summer months.[151]

Knowing how many residential holidaymakers there were in the mid-1930s tells us nothing about how many more would have come if only the supply of holiday accommodation had been increased. Some Barrians were confident that the demand for holiday rooms was much greater than the supply: the council clerk intimated as much, in 1925, when he announced that he was inundated by enquiries from prospective visitors asking where they could stay.[152] Nevertheless, it seems highly unlikely that, by building a few hotels, the town would have been able simply to reinvent itself into a more select, fashionable resort. Doubtless, Whitmore Bay's natural attractions would have appealed to bourgeois visitors, but they would have found the prospect of holidaying in a depressed south Wales coal port unappealing. Mixing with working-class trippers might have posed problems for some. We do not normally know how middle-class visitors responded to Barry Island – their numbers were so small. But a letter survives that highlights just how alien a week in Barry could seem to someone used to spending time in a more select resort. Mrs Cooke from Cheltenham holidayed in Barry by mistake after being 'lured' to the town by the 'honied words' of the council's publicity brochure. Not realizing Barry's industrial heritage, nor its popularity with working-class trippers, she found the experience upsetting enough to pen an angry letter to councillors. Viewed through her eyes, Barry was an unattractive resort: she had never 'seen such a dingy and depressing place'. For a town marketed by the councillors as a 'seaside paradise', she was appalled to find it 'shockingly dirty and sordid'. There were no entertainments to keep her amused in the evenings and she was angered by the high cost of the refreshments on sale at Whitmore Bay. She left feeling that she had been mis-sold her holiday. This was one well-heeled tourist who was not coming back to Barry – no matter whether it got a hydro or a suite of well-appointed hotels.[153]

Perhaps private investors decided that there were simply too many Mrs Cookes in the world to get excited about the prospect of littering Barry with fashionable hotels. Whatever their reasoning, the fact that no impressive hydros opened and no skyscraper holiday apartments towered over Whitmore Bay meant that the trippers were unlikely to be joined, anytime soon, by increasing numbers of residential visitors. The frustration of those who wanted to see Whitmore Bay's social tone raised was often all too evident. It sometimes bubbled over into anti-tripper statements. In July 1926, Councillor J. R. Llewellyn declared his hope that 'the time is not far distant when the day visitor will be a question of the past'.[154] Just a couple of months later, Dan Evans put it even more bluntly: he explained that he had no interest in boosting the tripper trade, and, 'in fact, he wished this visitor would stay away'.[155] The notion that trippers might actually be an unwelcome burden to an already cash-strapped town was expressed more than once.[156]

A strong undercurrent of resort scepticism surfaced from time to time in interwar Barry. Commentators noticed the disadvantages that accompanied the Island's popularity with trippers. The litter they left behind was a frequent source of annoyance, for example. Residents wrote to their local newspapers expressing their dismay at the 'millions of dirty bits of paper' that plastered railings on the Island. They bemoaned the 'accumulation of filth on the rocks above high-water mark', and they fulminated against the trippers who left behind a 'great quantity of litter and broken bottles' on the sands of Whitmore Bay.[157] Friars Point was described as being left in a 'disgraceful state' after busy days in the summer: 'the smell arising from the litter was most abominable', according to one observer in August 1926.[158] Irritation levels increased when inhabitants were reminded of the cost of cleaning up after the trippers.[159]

Then there were the congestion difficulties posed by the huge crowds. In the early 1920s, most trippers arrived by train – some 75 per cent were thought to be railway excursionists in 1923.[160] On the busiest days, trains arrived every five minutes, each one carrying at least 500 trippers.[161] Because of the distance between the Island and the town, as long as this state of affairs persisted, most Barrians were insulated from the effects of the great incursions of holidaymakers. It was a different matter for Islanders. Anyone hoping to use the bus service connecting the Island to the town could find themselves having to endure lengthy waits at bus stops and uncomfortable journeys on dangerously over-crowded vehicles. One resident of the Island, in a letter to the *Barry and District News*, grumbled about the 'bus problem': 'It is very annoy-ing to have to wait a long time to get back home to cook, etc., and see crowds of holiday makers taking the room up in the buses.' As a sufferer of 'bad legs', she thought it was intolerable. She wondered if a scheme might be introduced that guaranteed residents a seat whenever they travelled on the town's buses.[162]

By the later 1920s, the problems of congestion became more gen-eralized as increasing numbers of visitors arrived in motor vehicles. On Whit Monday, 1929, it was reported that an 'almost endless stream of vehicles' – including thousands of bicycles and private cars plus 'many' charabancs and motor bikes – flooded the approach roads to the Island. The resulting traffic jam was enormous.[163] The Easter holidays of 1928 saw the roads around Barry 'seized by the great god Petrol' and turned into 'long ribbon[s] of noise'.[164] In 1938, a cloudburst on the afternoon of the August bank holiday produced 'one of Barry's great disasters'. Trippers who had arrived by car all rushed to get off the Island at once, jamming the roads through and out of the town in the process. Some trippers, soaked and shivering, were still waiting at midnight for their buses to pick them up.[165]

The great influxes of visitors produced another set of problems, for they had the potential to occasion behaviour that offended the town's residents. We have already noted how some observers were discomfited by the sight of sun-loving visitors exposing themselves 'immodestly' in the 1920s and 1930s. There were plenty of other forms of seaside behaviour that could upset residents in these years. Examples included 'unmanly' 'Peeping Toms' spying on courting couples at Barry's sea-front spaces, drunk and disorderly outbursts, youthful hooliganism (of various descriptions) and vandalism of municipally run buildings and spaces.[166] References to these and other transgressive acts can be found in the pages of the local newspapers. And yet, most observers were more struck by the low incidence of such antisocial behaviour. When describing the scenes at Whitmore Bay, journalists invariably wrote in terms of the holiday crowds being 'good natured' – they were never

DO THE TRIPPERS UNDERSTAND ENGLISH OR ONLY WELSH!!!

Illus. 23. 'Keep off the grass': cartoon, Barry and District News,
23 August 1946. Barry's playful crowds were notably well behaved.
That didn't stop some Barrians complaining occasionally.

threatening; holidays invariably passed off 'very happily'.[167] The sobriety of Barry Island's holiday crowds was commented upon much more frequently than the drunkenness of pleasure seekers.[168] As the *Herald* remarked after the August bank holiday of 1927, given that 60,000 visitors had descended upon the Island, 'the orderly behaviour of the myriad visitors' was most commendable; in particular, 'the sobriety . . . was astonishing'.[169] Of the million visitors who were on the Island in the summer of 1934, not one had been brought before the Barry magistrates for drunkenness.[170] A few commentators suspected that the low rates reflected a more relaxed approach on the part of the police when it came to inebriated trippers, and this may have been a factor.[171] Nevertheless, it is likely that Barry's visitors were, in truth, a very well-behaved lot. As we have already noted, the trippers from the coalfield came with their friends, family members, neighbours, workmates and, often, chapel ministers. For most visitors, the Island was not a place where they were able to escape the supervision of elders and betters. Nor did they want to. After all, the great majority were highly 'respectable' citizens in their own right. As one Barry councillor explained it, 'the greatest proportion of people in the Rhondda were deeply religious' and did not come to the Island to cause trouble.[172] It is perhaps not surprising, then, that so few trippers let themselves down during the few hours they spent each year at Whitmore Bay. A pint or two at lunchtime in the Marine Hotel might be acceptable for the adult males, but the strong expectation was that they would still be in a 'tidy' state when they returned to their families on the beach.[173]

Far more troublesome than the trippers' behaviour was the demand they generated for goods and services on the sabbath. The cause of sabbatarianism was notably strong in interwar Barry. Whilst many Nonconformists were willing to accept the fact that Sunday was a favourite day for trippers from the coalfield to head to Whitmore Bay, they were not willing to do anything that threatened the sanctity of the Lord's Day. Sabbatarians saw themselves engaged in a battle to protect the 'moral health' of the town.[174] Throughout the 1920s and 1930s, a wide range of activities were adjudged to be unacceptable on the 'Welsh Sabbath'.[175] The running of charabancs from the town to the Island on Sundays was campaigned against by the Free Church Council in the early 1920s, for example. So was the playing of ragtime songs by bands at Whitmore Bay during the hours of religious services.[176] The Free Church Council also petitioned the Great Western Railway to stop promoting boat trips from the Island in 1924.[177] Meanwhile, the matter of boatmen being allowed to hire out their little vessels on Sundays became one of the most hotly debated issues of all. One sabbatarian councillor, with no sense of irony, stated that Sunday boating was 'the most important question the Council had yet been called upon to decide'.[178] That was in 1924. They were still debating it a decade later – and the sabbatarians were still winning the argument.[179]

The ongoing battle over whether Sunday trading should be allowed at Barry Island revealed some interesting contradictions in the town's approach to tourism. The town's elite was split between those who hoped that a 'progressive seaside resort' might yet flourish at Whitmore Bay, and those who took it upon themselves to protect the morals of the inhabitants and the visitors.[180] Councillor J. T. Maslin, a Conservative, found the approach taken by some of the more zealous Nonconformists infuriating. He complained that their inflexible stance on allowing visitors a little harmless fun on Sundays was driving visitors away.[181] But for those who were quite open about their desire to see a 'Puritan Sunday' observed at Barry rather than a 'Continental' one, there was little room for compromise.[182] One sabbatarian councillor argued that it was time to stop encouraging trippers to Barry Island altogether: 'The present multitudes of people coming there from all parts of South Wales were disturbing the tranquillity of Barry's Sunday, and he hoped the town would be allowed a little peace.'[183] Even Dan Evans, a figure who was all in favour of developing Barry's specialism in tourism, could find himself supporting policies that sought to make Barry Island less attractive on Sundays. In 1932, for instance, he came out strongly against a suggestion that visitors should be allowed to play miniature golf at Whitmore Bay on Sundays.[184] To complicate matters further, some socialists found themselves lining up with the chapel-goers. For them, it was a matter of protecting the right of workers not to have labour on a Sunday.[185] Others, also approaching the question from the point of view of workers, concluded that the rights of those toiling in the coalfield trumped all other considerations: the colliers and their families deserved the opportunity to be able to enjoy a Sunday at Whitmore Bay – and that included the right to play miniature golf and go boating.[186]

So vexed an issue had the development of Barry Island become, that some Barrians decided that a halt should be called to all further investment in resort infrastructure. In May 1928, Councillor J. R. Llewellyn argued that enough was enough: ratepayers had just watched councillors spend £100,000 of their money on the improvements to Whitmore Bay and Cold Knap at a time when 'so much dire distress and poverty prevailed' in the town. With a thousand dependent poor citizens costing the local authority some £750 a week to support, Llewellyn argued that it was no longer feasible to devote any more funds to the lost cause of tourism. 'There were hundreds of thousands of day trippers coming to the town who left nothing behind save a huge litter of broken bottles, paper bags and fag ends.' Llewellyn urged councillors to suspend all development schemes for a period of three years.[187]

Most councillors did not rally to Llewellyn's battle cry in 1928. Many of his colleagues spoke up in favour of the trippers from the coalfield: they argued that those who worked underground rarely saw the sun and deserved a few hours in the sunshine. Where, one asked, would Barry have been were it not for trippers? Another thought it very unfair 'to throw mud in their faces'.[188] Nevertheless, the question of what should be done with Barry Island never really went away. In 1935, for example, it resurfaced yet again with councillors and irate inhabitants arguing that it was time to 'cease being philanthropic' when it came to dealing with the visitors. Town leaders seriously considered imposing a penny tax on all rail excursionists to the Island. As one supporter of the idea pointed out, they could have raised £625 on the August bank holiday alone by such means.[189] But the most eye-catching proposal of all came in the form of a suggestion that Friars Point could be fenced off and trippers charged for admission. Unknowingly, Barrians were flirting with a policy that had incensed an earlier generation of residents when it emanated from the estate office of Lord Windsor.[190]

MUNICIPALIZATION, THE EASING OF THE DEPRESSION, AND WAR

In the end, Barry's leaders decided that they were better off with the day-trippers than they were without them. There were, on balance, usually more inhabitants who felt well disposed to the visitors than not. Matters improved a little at least as the interwar period unfolded thanks to the successes enjoyed by proponents of greater municipal control of some of the services offered at the seafront.

When anyone discussed the council's role at Barry Island, the conversation soon turned to M. W. Shanly's activities. From an early date, some councillors wondered about the wisdom of relying on a private entrepreneur to hire out deck chairs, bathing machines and boats. The strong impression that Shanly was making a tidy sum from his operations at Barry's seaside led some during the Great War to ask why the town did not step in and deliver the services itself.[191] Every time Shanly's contract came up for renewal, heated debates were ignited about whether the council should take over control.[192]

The idea of municipalizing seaside amenities tended to split the council along party lines. Labour councillors took up the cause of municipal control with enthusiasm. Stan Awbrey and E. C. Gough contended that not only would ratepayers get a better deal if the council stepped in and took over from Shanly, but his employees would not have to work long hours for paltry wages. Awbrey pushed hard for fair wages clauses to be inserted into any new contract signed with the 'chair king'.[193] Gough, in 1934, urged Barrians to ask themselves how it was that Shanly was able to flourish at Barry. Was it because he was a genius possessed with extraordinary organizational skills? 'Or is it that he pays low wages to his employees?'[194] The 'anti-Labour' group on the council took a different view. They argued that 'It was better in the interest of the ratepayers that business should be left to business men.'[195] But such a position left open the question of whether an 'outsider' such as Shanly should be allowed to profit so handsomely from Barry's resort spaces. Dan Evans, for instance, was a vocal opponent of municipalization yet was unhappy that local traders were being pushed off the Island by the likes of Shanly.[196]

In October 1934, Shanly's contract was renewed, without the addition of a fair wages clause.[197] But it was to be a short-lived victory for the cheerleaders of private enterprise. The cause of municipalization enjoyed significant levels of popular support in the town. Barry Ratepayers' Association mobilized its members by pointing out that, after the summer of 1934, Shanly had taken some £7,000, and handed over just £2,000 to the council as specified in the terms of his agreement. As one speaker put it at a public meeting, 'It was no use saying Barry got nothing from visitors' when Shanly was able to walk away with such hefty sums every season.[198] Stan Awbrey fought the council election of 1934 on the principle of municipal control and recorded the largest number of votes for Labour in the court ward.[199] Furthermore, the council was already involved in the provision of leisure amenities. Some of them were at Whitmore Bay. As Labour councillors pointed out to their opponents, the local authority was already running the miniature golf course, bowling greens and tennis courts.[200] And they were already profiting directly from their provision of cloakroom and lavatory facilities at the Island. Over £1,100 poured into the town's coffers from these sources alone in the summer of 1927, for example.[201] It became increasingly difficult to argue against further council involvement at the seafront when income was already being derived from such council-run ventures. The tide was turning in favour of the municipalization party. By the late 1930s, the lucrative deckchair business was taken over by the council. The chair king's reign at Barry Island was over.[202]

The extension of municipal control over the trading that went on at Barry's resort spaces was a significant development. The ratepayers of Barry were at last in a position where they might hope to see some substantial returns from their seaside investments. In time, they did. By the mid-1950s, the council's entertainment and seaside activities committee regularly reported healthy profits. In the golden summer of 1955 – the one considered at the start of this book – the council's income from its seaside interests stood at nearly £35,000 in the nine months to the end of August. In the same period, it had spent a little over £20,000 at

Whitmore Bay and the Knap. Fifteen thousand pounds of profit was not to be sniffed at, particularly in a post-war era that saw council budgets placed under pressure. It was the first year in which the seaside had not only paid for itself but had actually contributed a surplus to the general fund.[203] Whitmore Bay was hardly yet an El Dorado, but at least it was beginning to pay its way.

By the later 1930s, there was a mood of growing optimism in the town. At the annual dinner of the Chamber of Trade in January 1938, members delivered speeches that celebrated both a recent reduction in the rates and, even more encouragingly, the news that the dock was enjoying a revival of fortunes. They pointed out that the town's ship-repairers had noticed a welcome upswing in business, too. Most important of all, they trumpeted the fact that unemployment in the town had fallen by nearly 30 per cent in recent years – from 4,000 to 2,680. Against such a heartening assessment – the 'Possibilities of Barry are Tremendous' crowed a newspaper headline – the passing of the Holidays with Pay Act, and its adoption by south Wales coal owners, was just another welcome development.[204] Miners in the coalfield were now entitled to a week's paid leave – a development that reinvigorated hopes that Barry might yet be able to attract resident visitors.[205] But before anything much could be done in that direction, the Second World War intervened.

As was the case during the First World War, it cannot be claimed that tourism to Barry Island was entirely undisturbed by the 1939–45 conflict. Beach users were occasionally panicked by air raid sirens. Whitmore Bay was thrown into confusion on a June afternoon in 1940 by a false alarm, for example.[206] Some of the resort amenities were closed to the public for long periods. Most notably, the lido was closed from 1941 until the summer of 1944 because the council wanted to keep it as a source of water in case of emergency.[207] Then there was the disruption to the public holidays. The government vacillated on the matter of what to do about the holidays. On the one hand, there were advantages in reducing pressure on the transport system. On the other hand, there was recognition that allowing civilians to take holidays would be good for morale.[208] Resorts on the southern and eastern coasts of the country, where the threat of invasion was greater, were subject to more restrictions than those on the western side. But nowhere was it business as usual completely. Barry was affected by the government's decision to cancel the Whitsun and August bank holidays of 1940, for example. Traders were quick to report the negative impact on their takings. The fairground proprietor told local newspapers that the number of visitors who passed through the gates of the Pleasure Park over the Whitsun weekend was down by two-thirds.[209] Whitmore Bay's donkey men requested that the council cut the cost of their permits by 50 per cent, so badly were they affected by the wartime conditions. Tellingly, councillors were not convinced that trading conditions on the Island were as bad as the donkey men suggested. They only granted a 20 per cent reduction in the permit fees.[210]

They were right to be suspicious. For even on holidays that had officially been cancelled, the Island retained its ability to attract day-trippers. On the non-existent August bank holiday of 1940, for instance, 'many thousands' of visitors from the coalfield were seen milling around Barry's resort spaces regardless of any prohibitory Order in Council. According to one Island shopkeeper, business was 'As good as any normal summer Sunday.'[211] A pattern was established that continued for the duration of the war with trippers arriving at the Island throughout the summer months as usual. Their numbers were not quite as large as their pre-war equivalents, but they were sizeable, nonetheless.[212] On the August bank holiday of 1941, such was the demand from passengers that extra trains had to be put on between Cardiff and Barry and excursion trains pulled into the Island station from the English Midlands.[213] When travel restrictions made journeying by train difficult, determined trippers found other means of getting to Barry. On August bank holiday, 1944, for example, a superabundance of bicyclists arrived at Whitmore Bay.[214]

It was hardly a wonder, then, that John Collins (his father, Pat, had recently retired), felt confident enough to invest in new fairground rides during the war. The Moon Rocket was brought over from New York's Fair in 1940, whilst from the Glasgow Exhibition, a 'Gigantic Scenic Railway' was purchased at a cost of £18,000. It was claimed that it was the largest scenic railway in the world. Weighing in at 800 tons and boasting 1¼ miles of track, it may well have been. In case Barry's visitors needed convincing of its merits, much was made of the fact that a number of celebrities had ridden on it in Glasgow, including Amy Johnson, the pioneering aviator, and, at different times, the Everton, Arsenal, Glasgow Rangers and Celtic football teams.[215] Collins's fairground offered Barry's trippers a welcome moment of escapism. When, in May 1940, the pleasure park staged an armed forces night, it was purposely marketed as providing visitors with the opportunity, for a few hours at least, to privilege harmless fun over the serious business of war. 'Come along next Friday and forget the Sergeant-Major!!!' exhorted the advertisements.[216]

JOHN COLLINS'
ENTIRELY RECONSTRUCTED
PLEASURE PARK
BARRY ISLAND

Telephone : Barry 730.

SEASON : WHIT. SATURDAY TO SEPTEMBER, 1940.

FIRST TIME HERE OF THE FOLLOWING SENSATIONAL RIDES :

★ The World's Largest SCENIC COASTER RAILWAY ★

**The greatest thriller ever presented in the world.
A mile of Dips and Thrills. It's a Wow.**

Also the following Favourite Rides :	THE MOON ROCKET. Shooting to the Moon.
SUPER DODGEMS DE LUXE. Ride 'em and Dodge 'em.	STRATOSHIP. Stunt Flying.
TILT-A-WHIRL. JUMPING HORSES. WATER CHUTE.	OCTOPUS. It's New and Original.
WALL OF DEATH. GHOST TRAIN.	AMERICAN FUN HOUSE The laugh of a lifetime.
JUVENILE RIDES. SIDE SHOWS. EXHIBITIONS, Etc., Etc.	BIG ELI WHEEL. Towering to a height of 70 feet.

The "WONDERLAND" of South Wales

MAKE JOHN COLLINS' PLEASURE PARK
YOUR
HOLIDAY RENDEZVOUS

Illus. 24. *'The wonderland of South Wales': Advertisement for Pleasure Park, 1940. Barry Borough Council Development Committee, Barry (Barry, 1940). Visitor numbers remained high during the two world wars. In 1940, John Collins felt able to invest heavily in new rides such as the Moon Rocket and 'the world's largest' scenic railway.*

CONCLUSION

The interwar years clearly constituted a critical moment in the history of the Island as a seaside resort. This was when it became firmly established as one of the most cherished leisure spaces in south Wales. It was also when commercialized entertainment became an integral part of the Barry Island seaside product. In the late Victorian and Edwardian years, visitors had hardly anything to spend their money on beyond donkey rides and the pleasure boats. By the early 1920s, the fairground had become part and parcel of a day trip to the Island. For the first time, there were entrepreneurs who were willing to invest significant sums in the development of a range of 'artificial' amusements. And Barry's ratepayers contributed to the process, too. With help from the Unemployment Grants Committee, they paid for the lido. And they paid for the much-anticipated shelters, the improvements at Cold Knap and the prettified beach gardens at Whitmore Bay. By the end of the 1920s, most of Barry's resort spaces had taken a shape that they were to retain until the closing decades of the twentieth century – and, in many cases, beyond.

A modern leisure 'industry' burgeoned at Barry Island in the 1920s and 1930s in ways that it simply had not before the First World War. As such, the Island is an example of a seaside resort that conforms to the chronology sketched out by leisure historian Stephen G. Jones. In Jones's view, the commercialization of leisure may have gathered pace in the later Victorian period, but it only reached its culmination in the interwar years, the moment when 'the leisure product was radically altered'.[217] Certainly, we can point to other seaside resorts that attracted leisure entrepreneurs and investors long before 1914 – Blackpool being a prime example. Barry Island was not one of them. It was a resort that was still only lightly touched by capitalism, even in the opening decades of the twentieth century. A commercialized leisure industry was not fully established at Whitmore Bay until the 1920s.

It was ironic. The spending power of its visitors had been much greater in the years from 1870 to 1914 than it was in the 1920s and 1930s, a fact that explains why the commercialization of leisure at Barry Island in the interwar years was, in fact, still a rather attenuated phenomenon. We can only guess at what would have happened if Lord Windsor had been an enthusiast for resort development at Barry Island in the later decades of the nineteenth century. It seems certain that Whitmore Bay would have been much more heavily endowed with artificial amusements, including, doubtless, a pleasure pier, if he had been.

For all that the Island boomed in the interwar years, it caused a number of leading Barrians sleepless nights, as they turned over the problem of how to capitalize on Whitmore Bay's immense popularity as a tourist attraction. It was overwhelmingly a tripper resort, and so many of those trippers came from a coalfield where poverty and distress were endemic. They arrived loaded up with all the essentials needed for a few hours on the beach. If they were lucky, they might afford a 'luxury' or two, in the shape of a fairground ride, an ice cream, or the hire of a deckchair perhaps, but precious little else. Even during the turbulent war years, some commentators found time to mull over the problem of what to do with Barry Island. Their answer was nearly always the same: concentrate on the supply-side. Build upmarket hotels and guesthouses, erect a pier, open restaurants. Perhaps, speculated the more ambitious Barrians, the town might open a municipal airport in order to begin 'attracting the class of public that will come to stay as opposed to the day-tripper'.[218] (The idea that, soon enough, airports would be the means by which many holidaymakers would turn their backs on the British seaside and head for the Mediterranean did not cross their minds.)

It all seemed so simple. But the reverse was true. The private sector did not respond to the exhortations of those calling for hydros and high-class hotels. And councillors, having spent £100,000 on shelters, a seawall, ornamental gardens, lakes and a lido, were in no position to keep on spending. They were managing a town, after all, that had itself been hit hard by the Great Depression. However, Barry Island's success did not depend on the private capitalists nor on local politicians. As we argued in chapter 7, in the late Victorian years, the visitors themselves had been the key actors in the Island's history. They continued to be the critical figures during the interwar period. They demonstrated the depth of their attachment to Whitmore Bay through two wars and a slump that plunged the coalfield communities into destitution. Throughout the 1920s and 1930s, commentators worried that the visitors would be forced to give up their day trip to Barry, forced to stay at home by crushing poverty. Many were dreadfully impoverished, hungry and malnourished. But they returned to Whitmore Bay every holiday season, come rain and shine, war and global depression.

They came because the Island and its simple seaside charm offered a moment's respite from the strains of everyday life. They sometimes did this in the most curious of fashions. In the summer of 1929, for instance, the big attraction at Whitmore Bay was a professional faster, Billie Brown, from Lancashire. In July he was sealed in a glass cabinet at the western shelter with a bed, a stash of cigarettes, a portable wireless and a supply of mineral water. His sixty-seven-day fast, during which he lost forty-five pounds, was long enough to ensure that he beat a rival, Ricardo Sacco, who was starving himself in Blackpool at the same time. Visitors from the coalfield were fascinated by Brown's feat of endurance. It is easy to see why, for his 'act' came out of an experience that many found all too relatable. Brown was an unemployed cotton spinner who, for the best part of a decade, had 'been buffeted from pillar to post', picking up what little work he could find as a 'common pedlar, street vendor and tipster'. Spectacular episodes of fasting were Brown's way out of every-day hunger. As he explained to his supporters at Whitmore Bay, he saw the attempt to break the fasting record as an 'opportunity to make [his] future happier and to earn [his] living in a more congenial manner' than he had been able to do since 1920.[219] Here was someone who, in the liminal, topsy-turvy world of Barry's seaside, was able to voluntarily pit himself against starvation and win. One does not have to be a psychologist to work out why so many of the poor trippers found that an appealing scenario.

But more often, just being at Barry Island was salve enough for visitors. It was a point remarked upon by 'Peplyn', correspondent for the *Barry and District News* after he had spent time with the August bank holiday crowds in 1928. The holiday was 'splendidly free from mishaps and bad behaviour', and Peplyn was struck by how 'all the colours of life . . . unfolded themselves and spun round like an exotic pleasure-wheel' at the Island. He conceded that some of his readers might take issue with him: 'Not much colour, you may say, in sandwich-bags and . . . pale meagre youths from Cwm Rhondda blowing the smoke of extreme rakishness out of the corners of their mouths.' But Peplyn was on hand to put the doubters right.

> Bank Holiday at Barry Island is the occasion when the unconscious selves of these men become conscious. They are men, not of the region of slag-heaps and shafts, but of the world. And so they blow cigarette smoke, and do many other things to show the lively, print-frocked girls on their arms that they are devils of fellows.

Peplyn was convinced that Barry Island provided its visitors with the opportunity to be more than just a worker: at Whitmore Bay they could be fully human. Visitors were temporarily freed from the pressures of everyday life. He noticed how 'Stout women from those towns which produced boxers and coal, laugh, with almost abandon enough to forget the trailing troop of children behind them, and often the willing burden in their arms.' And he remarked upon the 'bold way in which youths and girls, and many middle-aged women wore paper semblances of weirdly checked caps and an occasional fez'. But he decided, at Barry Island, it was 'a thing entirely logical'. After all, he concluded, 'Why be a collier when the blue and gold of the seashore besieges the spirit?'[220]

CONCLUSION

W E OPENED THIS BOOK with a description of the Barry Island seaside experience as it was in the mid-1950s. It was, by then, a classic example of a trippers' resort – catering to the needs and wants of visitors who were able to spend just a few hours at a time by the sea. Some of those trippers made long journeys to get to the Island, from as far afield as Birmingham, Manchester and Birkenhead. However, its great visitor heartland was much closer: the south Wales coalfield. By then, Whitmore Bay had become tightly woven into the cultural life of the mining valleys. Day trips to the Island became treasured memories, recalled years later with fondness. The annual excursion to Barry's seafront had even become a suitable subject for poetry.[1]

For those contemplating the Island's extraordinary popularity from the vantage point of the 1950s, it was almost impossible to imagine that the Island might have developed in any other way. Indeed, from the earliest days of Barry's existence as a town, the idea took hold that Barry was the 'natural seaside resort' for the inhabitants of the Rhondda, the 'playground for the toilers of the Welsh Valleys and the Hills'.[2] Looking back over the previous half-century or so, it all had such an air of inevitability about it. It was a mindset that led to an overestimation of the importance of the later 1880s and early 1890s in the history of the Island. The construction of the dock was, by any measurement, a momentous event: it led to nothing less than the birth of a new town; it brought the railway into a rural, off-the-beaten-track district; and it established a direct connection between Barry and the great mining valleys that were to provide so many of the Island's visitors in the twentieth century. It is hardly a wonder that some writers decided that these years were the moment when tourism at Whitmore Bay finally took off. The railway had, at last, shattered the Island's isolation and, in short order, great crowds of trippers were spied on the beach. The infant town's journalists, new arrivals in the district themselves, thought that they were witnessing something novel. They had 'discovered' Whitmore Bay for the first time themselves just a few months earlier; they thought that the tourists were doing the same. Barry's historians have followed their lead. Thus, we are told that the late 1880s saw some of the earliest pleasure steamer trips to the Island and that 1892 was Whitmore Bay's 'first full season as a holiday resort'.[3] Yet, as we have seen, the story of tourism at Barry Island did not begin with the opening of the dock. It began fully a century earlier. When those busy holiday seasons of the early 1890s are looked at in the *longue durée*, they lose their status as a starting point and become instead a turning point.

One of the effects of giving due weight to the Island's experience of tourism in the century before the 1890s is that it emphasizes the contingency of its subsequent development into a tripper resort. Not only could the Island have become a very different sort of tourist resort, it already had been some of those different types of resort. During its long career as a tourist attraction, Whitmore Bay had attracted the most well-to-do visitors imaginable. In the 1820s, a marquess bathed in its pellucid waters. A new phase was reached in the middle years of the century when it made a name for itself as a resort of Cardiff's social elite: a playground for its town fathers and their families. Cadoxton functioned as a 'bathing village'. As such, it was a very particular type of seaside resort, one that was without the distinctive urban infrastructure that was commonly found at the more developed resorts, and one that was not wildly transformed by tourism. But it should properly be thought of as a seaside resort nonetheless. There was no shortage of such village resorts along the coast of Wales in the nineteenth century and they and their devotees – the tourists who eschewed the crowds and sociability of the bigger resorts – deserve more attention in our seaside histories than they have been given.

By the early 1870s, Barry Island had broadened its appeal, attracting day-trippers from Cardiff and other ports along the Bristol Channel. Its beach was remote if approached from the mainland, but if visited by sea it was easily accessible. Pleasure steamers were able to bring hundreds of visitors at a time to the romantic little island. By that point, it looked set fair to become a marine suburb – a select seaside retreat for Cardiff's wealthy merchants and professionals. In 1875, not only was a working-class Whitmore Bay by no means a foregone conclusion, it was not even thought of as a likely outcome. On the contrary, if J. D. Treharne's plans had come to fruition – and they almost did – in the 1880s the island would have been studded with high-class villas occupied by Cardiff's richest merchants.

It took a powerful landowner – one with no interest in developing the Island's resort function – to set Whitmore Bay on to another historical trajectory. After his family purchased Barry Island in 1878, the young Lord Windsor and his agent Robert Forrest sought to ensure that the island remained entirely undeveloped as a means of protecting the estate's interests at Penarth. It has long been acknowledged that the acquisition of the island was a blocking move to stop rivals building a dock at Barry that would hurt the profits of the Penarth Dock Company. (It was a different matter when Windsor himself was presented with the opportunity of being involved in the construction of a dock at

Barry, of course.) What has gone unrecognized is the degree to which the mothballing of the island helped Windsor and Forrest in their aim to turn their unprepossessing little coal port, with its second-rate beach, into Cardiff's marine suburb. By keeping all developers, resort and residential, away from the island, Penarth's main competitor in the race to become Cardiff's seaside suburb was knocked out of the running.

During the early years of Windsor's tenure as landowner, Barry Island's sole residents were partridges and rabbits, its occasional visitors were aristocrats with their guns and hunting dogs. Its closure to tourists was a remarkable example of a great landowner acting with impunity. At a stroke, the citizens of Cardiff and elsewhere were denied their customary right of access to the beach at Whitmore Bay. Decades of tourism to the Island were ended. This was a shocking turn of events. No other owner in the nineteenth century had acted in this way, and it was entirely unnecessary for Windsor to do so. He had only to keep the developers away: there was no reason to keep tourists away, too.

Windsor's decision to proceed with the dock and railway project rendered his visitor ban meaningless. Visitors were bound to return now thanks to Barry's lightning emergence. It was impossible to keep away the tens of thousands of new Barrians. It was just as futile to try to keep away the hundreds of thousands living in the mining valleys just 20 miles or so from Barry. Their demand for the seaside product on offer at Barry Island was to prove the critical factor in the making of twentieth-century Whitmore Bay.

It has been argued here that the trippers seized Barry Island. As observers noted, they 'swooped down' on the place and took 'possession' of it.[4] They did this in the 1890s. They came despite Whitmore Bay's often unwelcoming environment: no shelters, a woefully inadequate supply of lavatories and refreshments, and little in the way of 'artificial' amusements. They came despite an inconvenient rail journey that entailed multiple changes, lengthy waits and time spent in ticket queues and dirty carriages. They came despite a landowner who flirted with resort development briefly in 1894, who declared his willingness to keep the Island open to visitors and who spent a huge sum of money on the refurbishment of his own private holiday home at Friars Point, but who went on to do nothing to improve the lot of the working-class trippers. At Penarth he proved himself a great facilitator of resort development; at Whitmore Bay, his lack of interest was palpable. At Penarth, the aim was to construct a select watering place; at Barry, the objective was to keep the 'rabble from the hills' away.[5] Occasionally, the depth of the great landowner's contempt for the visitors was revealed for all to see – as in January 1905 when estate workers fenced off the Island with iron 'unclimbable' barriers and roped off the beach. It was a stunning display of landlord power, but it was to be Windsor's last throw of the dice. Within months, he began the process of handing over the sands to the council.

The trippers were the key actors in the making of twentieth-century Barry Island, but they had important allies in the new town. From the 1890s through to the First World War, the Island's boosters tirelessly promoted the idea of resort development. In part, their arguments were driven by altruistic concerns – the sense that Barry owed the colliers and their families a debt of gratitude was strong. In part, the boosters were driven by feelings of civic pride. Barry was a new town in search of an identity. Its success as a dock was important, but there was a concern to demonstrate to the world that there was more to it than just its prowess at shipping coal. The prospect of Barry becoming a successful watering place as well as a dock was enticing. They were also motivated by the hope that a popular Barry Island would further boost the town's economy. They explained why it was worth spending ratepayers' money on expensive capital schemes on the Island. The boosters generated much interest in the idea of developing tourism at Barry. However, in the 1890s and early 1900s, town leaders' room for manoeuvre was seriously constrained by Lord Windsor's opposition to any significant improvement projects at the Island. Despite bringing forward countless schemes – for shelters and promenades and piers – they achieved little. And when, finally, councillors gained control of the Island's resort spaces, the town's indebtedness made it politically difficult to sell resort development to the ratepayers. Attitudes had also hardened against substantial investment at Whitmore Bay when it became clear that making money from the Island's visitors was more difficult than the boosters had thought. The distance between beach and town was too great for appreciable numbers of trippers to make it over to Barry's commercial centre, and Whitmore Bay's industrial setting meant that it was not attracting the more lucrative long-stay visitors.

Historians of late Victorian and Edwardian seaside towns have found that ratepayers' associations and traders were often keen supporters of municipal resort development schemes. This made them unusual. In other towns and cities, these groups were often keen to keep municipal spending – and therefore the rates – as low as possible. Tellingly, in pre-war Barry, after a brief spell pushing for council-led projects at the Island, significant elements of the business community turned against resort development. There was a drive to bring down the rates and curtail municipal spending on costly tourism 'moonshine' schemes at Whitmore Bay. Barrians seemed to forget that they were living in a seaside town. But for a very good reason: tourism contributed so little to the local economy. Ironically, when Cadoxton was just a little bathing village in the 1850s and 1860s, tourism made a real difference to the lives of many of its inhabitants. Visitors' shillings were a welcome addition to families' incomes. In the 1930s, when a million day-trippers visited the Island each year, most of Barry's residents were not a penny better off. Commentators and shopkeepers, newspaper editors and councillors noticed the weakness of the tourism multiplier effect in the Edwardian years. By the interwar period, with the Island crowded as never before, it was a problem that could no longer be ignored. Barry was a town with an immensely popular beach, but it was not a seaside town in any meaningful way. This is still the case. Out of 121 seaside places studied by economists in 2010, Barry emerged as the town in which tourism accounted for the lowest proportion of jobs. Just 1 per cent of Barry's workers were classified as working in the tourism industry. In Tenby, the figure was 53 per cent; at Barmouth, it was 48 per cent; and at Porthcawl, 26 per cent.[6]

The interwar depression in the south Wales coal industry triggered the building projects of the early and mid-1920s: the seawall and shelters, the lido and the improvements at Cold Knap. All this activity can make it appear as if Barry town was finally deciding what sort of resort it wanted to see flourish at its seaside. But in this book a different argument has been advanced. By the 1920s, it was too late for supply-side investments to alter the character of tourism at the Island. Councillors and leading figures in the Chamber of Trade spoke as if they had the ability to make a more fashionable resort by upgrading the resort facilities. If a hydro was built at the Island, or a marina was opened at the Old Harbour, then the day-trippers would simply melt away and be replaced by high-spending residential visitors. However, in truth, the likelihood of this happening was slight. Barry was still a working coal port, and its reputation as a place of coal dust and industry was too great for it to be suddenly reinvented as a select watering place. And, perhaps even more to the point, there was no hint that the trippers would ever give up on the Island in the way that Dan Evans hoped they would.

Eminent transport historian Jack Simmons once remarked that the development of seaside towns 'cannot be discussed adequately in any form of generalisation ... For each of them grew in its own way, and to understand its growth, the town itself must be looked at on its own.'[7] It is a compelling point. Barry Island's history certainly underscores the importance of local factors in the shaping of its development. Never-theless, as Martin Daunton has argued, the danger of an approach that concentrates on what is unique in a town's history is that it can be 'an invitation to antiquarianism'. Daunton contends that variations between towns 'must be placed within a framework which can establish where a particular community stands in relation to others'.[8]

The Tourism Area Life Cycle model, developed by geographer Rich-ard Butler, provides us with one such framework. Based on the idea that tourist destinations are products that are 'subject to the "laws" of product cycles and marketability', Butler sketched out the evolution of a hypothetical tourist resort.[9] He identified various stages through which a resort might be expected to pass. First there was the exploration stage. Small numbers of tourists discover a suitable tourist destination. With no specific tourist amenities these early visitors have to rely on the locals for their accommodation, refreshments and such like. Next comes the involvement stage when some residents begin to specialize in catering for tourists. A tourist season emerges, and tourism begins to have a dis-cernible impact on the local economy. The development stage follows. The resort is marketed heavily, there will be significant investment in tourist facilities, visitor numbers will increase substantially and there will be changes to the physical appearance of the resort. This, in time, gives way to a consolidation era that sees the resort at its most pop-ular, a 'major part of the area's economy will be tied to tourism', and the holiday industry – in all its various forms – will be most evident. A stagnation phase comes next as the resort becomes unfashionable and perhaps rundown. This might be followed by a decline phase or one of rejuvenation.[10]

Butler's model describes an ideal type. As the work of historians has demonstrated, no resort's development can be made to fit its neat schema perfectly.[11] But at least the model has the virtue of describing the broadest outlines of many resorts' trajectories. For our purposes, it is useful in highlighting just how different much of Barry Island's experience was. True, we can identify an exploration phase in Barry's history. Its earliest visitors, drawn to the beach in the 1790s, came to a place that had no specific tourist amenities. Likewise, we can point to an involvement stage, when inhabitants in the hamlets of Barry and Cadox-ton began to cater for the visitors. By the first decade of the nineteenth century, the island's farmhouse had been turned into accommodation for bathers. But what is remarkable is both how long this phase lasted – at least until the 1870s when Treharne began developing the island – and how many of the characteristics of the exploration stage remained intact. When it was a little bathing village, Cadoxton was frequently reported as being 'crowded' with visitors, but it wore its credentials as a tourist destination very lightly. Its mid-Victorian visitors holidayed in a place that still had next to nothing in the way of specialized tourist amenities. This was a major part of its appeal. But it was not how the 'ideal' resort was supposed to develop. Butler's resort is one that is constantly evolving, always becoming more developed (until it reaches the end of its life). At Barry Island, there was nearly a century of hardly any change – no investment, no spectacular upswing in visitor numbers, no tourist-generated urban growth.

Just when it looked as if the island was entering its development phase, Lord Windsor closed it to tourists altogether. The predictive power of the geographer's model breaks down completely at this point for it allows no room for the idea that a budding resort might simply stop entertaining visitors altogether. A deep chill fell upon the island in the early 1880s, and it was only with the industrialization and urbanization of the Barry district that tourists were able to return to Whitmore Bay. From the 1890s, visitor numbers rocketed. Read one way, there might be enough evidence for us to conclude that this was the point at which it entered its development stage. A railway now connected Whitmore Bay to the mainline. Visitor numbers grew strongly year after year, and the Island was being enthusiastically marketed by the efforts of the Chamber of Trade. Yet there was no great investment in tourist infrastructure. This was thanks, primarily, to Windsor's unwillingness to see a holiday industry established there. Once again, Barry's seaside found itself in a curious hybrid-stage – edging towards a new phase of growth, yet unable to make the transition cleanly from a previous stage. Only in the 1920s did it, at last, make the move into the development stage. Entrepreneurs of leisure invested in the resort's amenities. Pat Collins and M. W. Shanly, most notably, made sizeable profits from their operations at the Island. Nevertheless, by this point, the geographers would expect tourism to begin to play a noticeable role in the local economy. So, as we have seen, did contemporaries. But this was not to be the case. Barry Island failed to become the much vaunted 'golden casket'. Even in that blessed summer of 1955, it was only the Island traders who really made any money from the trippers, although at least Barry's ratepayers began to reap some rewards from the Island. This was the first year that the council made a hefty profit on its various seaside activities. Some sixty or so years after the boosters had waxed lyrical about the Island's potential as a cash cow, the townsfolk started to see some returns on their significant investments in seaside amenities.

How to make money from tourism at Whitmore Bay is a question that has troubled Barrians ever since the 1890s. It was of great consequence for inhabitants of a town that faced more than its fair share of economic troubles in the twentieth century. But it mattered little to its visitors – the visitors who made Barry Island into their very own seaside playground. The Georgian sea-bathers who immersed themselves, teeth-chattering, in the chilly waters of the Bristol Channel, certain that it was good for their health; the contra-dancing excursionists who brought a harpist with them in 1824; the trippers from Cardiff who headed for the Island on pleasure steamers at the first sign of sunshine on that sweltering Saturday in July 1876; the countless Sunday school children whose annual trip to Whitmore Bay from the mining valleys became such cherished childhood memories; the young soldiers who visited the Island one last time before heading off to the trenches of the Western Front; the unemployed colliers and their families for whom an afternoon on the sands in the 1920s and 1930s was their one trip out of their impoverished valley in a year. And all the other numberless pleasure seekers for whom Barry Island was the seaside resort of choice. They, more than anyone else, made Whitmore Bay into a special leisure space.

In 1896, a journalist on the *Barry Herald* ruminated on the immense developments that had, over the previous decade, so altered the Island and its environs. He lamented the loss of its 'rural beauty' and its status as an island. The developer's spade was in the process of transforming everything it touched. However, the reporter was struck by at least one great continuity: 'no one can alter "the Severn Sea", called of moderns the Bristol Channel. That still flows and ebbs, even as in the time of the holy (and doubtless dirty) gentleman whose solitary sojourn gave name to the island.' The writer took heart from this reflection. '[S]o long as the sea endures Whitmore Bay will be a pleasure ground', he predicted.[12] We might be tempted to point out that history suggests humans can fall out of love with the sea quite as easily as they fell in love with it. The medievals' phobia of the beach makes the point. Nevertheless, if we apply his observation to the years studied in this book, it captures an important truth. It was Whitmore Bay – its sands, its headlands, its ozone-infused zephyrs and its gently lapping waters – that so bewitched those generations of south Walians who discovered for themselves the charms of Barry Island. And we only need to recast the sage reporter's conclusion a little to arrive at a statement that we can endorse with confidence: so long as humans are drawn to the sea, so Whitmore Bay will endure as one of south Wales's most beloved pleasure grounds.

NOTES

INTRODUCTION

1.   *Barry and District News*, 4 August 1955.
2.   *Barry Herald*, 8 April 1955.
3.   *Barry Herald*, 15 April 1955.
4.   The National Archives, BD28/713, Letter from S. A. Luen to James Griffiths, Secretary of State for Wales, 29 October 1964.
5.   *Barry Herald*, 15 April 1955.
6.   *Barry Herald*, 3 June 1955.
7.   *Barry Herald*, 3 June 1955; *Barry and District News*, 2 June 1955.
8.   *Barry Herald*, 15 July and 5 August 1955.
9.   *Barry and District News*, 4 August 1955.
10. *Barry Herald*, 15 July 1955.
11. *Barry and District News*, 29 September 1955.
12. See, for example, *Barry and District News*, 6 June 1957, for reports of even bigger Whitsun crowds at the Island in 1957 than had arrived in 1955.
13. *Barry and District News*, 11 August 1955.
14. *Barry and District News*, 1 May 1969.
15. *Barry Herald*, 4 February 1960.
16. *Barry Herald*, 21 April 1960.
17. The National Archives, BD28/713, G. A. Jellicoe, 'A landscape design for the foreshore of Barry, South Wales', 1 September 1956, 1.
18. *Barry Herald*, 28 July 1960; *Daily Mail*, 18 August 1965.
19. The National Archives, BD28/713, Application for Permission to Develop Land by Butlin's Ltd to Glamorgan County Council, submitted 16 November 1962, p. 8.

20. The National Archives, BD28/713, Letter from Luen to Griffiths, 29 October 1964; *Barry and District News*, 5 June 1969.

21. The National Archives, BD28/713, Letter from Raymond Gower to Keith Joseph, Minister of Housing and Local Government, 2 April 1963; *South Wales Echo*, 22 October 1964.

22. The National Archives, BD28/713, Butlin's Planning Application, pp. 2–3.

23. *Barry and District News*, 22 May 1969.

24. *Barry and District News*, 22 May 1969.

25. Gwyn Thomas, *A Welsh Eye* (London, 1964), p. 63.

26. *Barry and District News*, 15 August 1957.

27. *Barry Herald*, 5 August 1955.

28. Geoff Jones, *Cardiff Airport at Rhoose: 70 Years of Aviation History* (Stroud, 2011), p. 36.

29. *Barry and District News*, 9 January 1969; John K. Walton, 'The origins of the modern package tour? British motor-coach tours in Europe, 1930–70', *Journal of Transport History*, 32/2 (2011), 145–63; John K. Walton, 'British tourists and the beaches of Europe, from the eighteenth century to the 1960s', in Martin Farr and Xavier Guégan (eds), *The British Abroad Since the Eighteenth Century, Volume 1: Travellers and Tourists* (Basingstoke, 2014), pp. 19–37; Miriam Akhtar and Steve Humphries, *Some Liked it Hot: The British on Holiday at Home and Abroad* (London, 2000).

30. *Barry Herald*, 9 June 1960.

31. *Barry and District News*, 25 August 1955.

32. Thomas, *Welsh Eye*, p. 62.

33. Peter Borsay, 'Welsh seaside resorts: historiography, sources and themes', *Welsh History Review*, 24/2 (2008), 92–119.

34. Notwithstanding Barry's remarkable urban history, it has failed to capture the attention of urban, and other, historians. Thus, Donald Moore (ed.), *Barry: The Centenary Book* (2nd edn, Barry, 1985) retains its position as the most important academic study of the town's (and, by extension, the Island's) history. The chapters by Matthew Griffiths, Iorwerth W. Prothero, Richard W. Thomas, Brian C. Luxton and Peter Stead are essential reading and contain many invaluable insights. Writers of local and popular history have been much more alive to the Island's significance. Mark Lambert and Jonathan Lambert's recent *Secret Barry Island* (Stroud, 2017) is a good example, although also see Barry A. Thomas, *Barry Island and Cold Knap* (Machynlleth, 2010).

35. *Barry Dock News*, 27 February 1914.

36. Dai Smith, *Aneurin Bevan and the World of South Wales* (Cardiff, 1993), p. 2.

37. Brian C. Luxton, 'Ambition, vice and virtue: social life, 1884–1914', in Moore (ed.), *Barry*, pp. 271–331, 310.

38. For historians rightly emphasizing the important role played by the railway in Barry's post-1890 resort history see D. S. Barrie, *The Barry Railway* (Lingfield, 1962), p. 153 and David Bradley, 'The development

of Barry, Penarth and Porthcawl as seaside resorts, 1881–1939'
(unpublished MA thesis, University of Wales, College of Cardiff, 1990), 4,
30. Barrie goes too far in contending that the Barry Railway Company
largely created the resort. Bradley, in contrast, suggests that there were
'scores' of visitors at Barry before 1890 (Bradley, 'Development of Barry',
30). In this book, it is argued that this still seriously underplays the
importance of tourism before 1890.

39.   Luxton, 'Ambition', p. 312.

40.   Iorwerth W. Prothero, 'The port and railways of Barry', in Moore (ed.),
       Barry, pp. 209–69, 213, 217.

41.   Prothero, 'The port and railways', p. 217. Elsewhere, he puts the figure
       at 15,000. (See Barry Library, Iorwerth W. Prothero, 'Barry and its Dock,
       Volume 1: The Schemes that Failed' (1993), 134.)

42.   Prothero, 'The port and railways', p. 219.

43.   Dai Smith, 'Barry: a town out of time', *Morgannwg*, 29 (1985), 80–5, 84.

44.   Although note the perceptive speculative comments of Mark Lambert
       and Jonathan Lambert (in their *Secret Barry Island*, pp. 58–9) when
       they observe that tourism was not 'totally absent' from the Island in
       the nineteenth century. However, after opening up the possibility
       that tourism might have been a feature of the district's economy, they
       conclude that, because it was not connected to the railway network,
       'Barry Island missed out on tourism's formative years'.

45.   Matthew Griffiths, 'Landlords and tenants, 1700–1880', in Moore (ed.),
       Barry, pp. 165–207.

46.   Fred Gray, *Designing the Seaside: Architecture, Society and Nature*
       (London, 2006).

47.   Patrick Mullins, 'Tourism urbanization', *International Journal of Urban
       and Regional Research*, 15/3 (1991), 326–42; Patrick Mullins, 'Cities
       for pleasure: the emergence of tourism urbanization in Australia', *Built
       Environment*, 18/3 (1992), 187–98.

48.   John Hassan, *The Seaside, Health and the Environment in England and
       Wales since 1800* (Aldershot, 2003), p. 19; John K. Walton, *Blackpool*
       (Edinburgh, 1998), p. 3; P. J.Waller, T*own, City and Nation: England,
       1850–1914* (Oxford, 1983), pp. 131–44.

49.   Thomas, *Welsh Eye*, p. 61.

50.   John K. Walton, 'The seaside resorts of western Europe, 1750–1939', in
       Stephen Fisher (ed.), *Recreation and the Sea* (Exeter, 1997), pp. 36–56.

51.   John K. Walton, *The British Seaside: Holidays and Resorts in the Twentieth
       Century* (Manchester, 2000), p. 27.

52.   As P. J. Waller has put it, 'Seaside towns were not homogeneous types'
       (Waller, *Town*, p. 135).

53.   Jens Kristian and Steen Jacobsen, 'Roaming Romantics: solitude-seeking
       and self-centredness in scenic sightseeing', *Scandinavian Journal of
       Hospitality and Tourism*, 4/1 (2004), 5–23; John Urry, *The Tourist Gaze:
       Leisure and Travel in Contemporary Societies* (London, 1990), p. 46.

54. Gray, *Designing the Seaside*, p. 13.
55. Nigel Yates, 'The Welsh seaside resorts: growth, decline, and survival', University of Wales, Lampeter, Occasional Papers, 1 (2006), 1.
56. Borsay, 'Welsh seaside resorts', 100.
57. Richard W. Butler, 'Sustainable tourism: a state-of-the-art review', *Tourism Geographies*, 1/1 (1999), 7–25.

CHAPTER 1

1. Esther Moir, *The Discovery of Britain: The English Tourists, 1540–1840* (London, 1964), pp. 123–38: 129; Jane Zaring, 'The Romantic face of Wales', *Annals of the Association of American Geographers*, 67/3 (1977), 397–418: 401; Hugh Dunthorne, 'Early Romantic travellers in Wales and the Netherlands during the late eighteenth century', *Dutch Crossing*, 24/2 (2000), 208–21; Kathryn N. Jones, Carol Tully and Heather Williams, 'Introduction: travel writing and Wales', *Studies in Travel Writing*, 18/2 (2014), 101–6: 101; Prys Morgan, 'Wild Wales: civilizing the Welsh from the sixteenth to the nineteenth centuries', in Peter Burke, Brian Harrison and Paul Slack (eds), *Civil Histories: Essays Presented to Sir Keith Thomas* (Oxford, 2000), pp. 265–84: 274–7.
2. Henry Penruddocke Wyndham, *A Gentleman's Tour through Monmouthshire and Wales, in the Months of June and July, 1774* (London, 1775), pp. i–ii.
3. Richard Hayman, '"All impetuous rage": The cult of waterfalls in eighteenth-century Wales', *Landscapes*, 15/1 (2014), 23–43.
4. John R. Gold and Margaret M. Gold, *Imagining Scotland: Tradition, Representation and Promotion in Scottish Tourism Since 1750* (Aldershot, 1995), ch. 2; Alastair J. Durie, *Scotland for the Holidays: Tourism in Scotland c. 1780–1939* (East Linton, 2003), ch. 1.
5. Mary-Ann Constantine, 'Beauty spot, blind spot: Romantic Wales', *Literature Compass*, 5/3 (2008), 577–90: 577; Hayman, '"All impetuous rage"', 32.
6. John Davies, *A History of Wales* (Harmondsworth, 1993), p. 347.
7. Hywel M. Davies, 'Wales in English travel writing 1791–8: the Welsh critique of Theophilus Jones', *Welsh History Review*, 23/3 (2007), 65–93: 65.
8. Lena Lĕncek and Gideon Bosker, *The Beach: The History of Paradise on Earth* (London, 1998), pp. 41–2; Alain Corbin, *The Lure of the Sea: The Discovery of the Seaside, 1750–1840* (Harmondsworth, 1994), ch. 1.
9. John K. Walton, *The English Seaside Resort: A Social History, 1750–1914* (Leicester, 1983), pp. 10–12.
10. Richard Russell, *A Dissertation of the Use of Sea-Water* . . . (4th edn, London, 1760), p. vi.

11. See, for example, George Hartwig, *A Practical Treatise on Sea-Bathing and Sea-Air* (London, 1853) and E. J. Frampton, *Where Shall I Send my Patient? A Guide for Medical Practitioners and Book of Reference to the Health Resorts and Institutions for Patients of Great Britain* (Bournemouth, 1903).

12. Anon., *A Tour in Wales, and Through Several Counties of England, including both the Universities, Performed in the Summer of 1805* (London, 1806), p. 61. Also see John Travis, 'Continuity and change in English sea-bathing, 1730–1900: a case of swimming with the tide', in Stephen Fisher (ed.), *Recreation and the Sea* (Exeter, 1997), pp. 8–35: 11, and John K. Walton, *Blackpool* (Edinburgh, 1998), pp. 21–2.

13. Walton, *English Seaside Resort*, pp. 11–13.

14. John F. Travis, *The Rise of the Devon Seaside Resorts, 1750–1900* (Exeter, 1993); Harold Perkin, 'The social tone of Victorian seaside resorts in the north-west', *Northern History*, 11/1 (1976), 180–94; Durie, *Scotland for the Holidays*, ch. 3.

15. Walton, *English Seaside Resort*, pp. 60, 65; Nigel Yates, 'The Welsh seaside resorts: growth, decline, and survival', University of Wales, Lampeter, Occasional Papers, 1 (2006).

16. Peter Borsay, 'From port to resort: Tenby and narratives of transition, 1760–1914', in Peter Borsay and John K. Walton (eds), *Resorts and Ports: European Seaside Towns since 1700* (Bristol, 2011), pp. 86–111: 87–8.

17. *Star*, 29 June 1797.

18. Yates, 'Welsh seaside resorts', 7–8.

19. John Evans, *Letters Written during a Tour through South Wales in the Year 1803, and at Other Times . . . (London, 1804), p. 244.*

20. *Walton,* English Seaside Resort, p. 53.

21. *Cambrian*, 7 August 1824.

22. Anon., *Tour in Wales*, pp. 56–7.

23. Yates, 'Welsh seaside resorts', 5.

24. Walton, *English Seaside*, p. 53.

25. Yates, 'Welsh seaside resorts', 10–16; *North Wales Chronicle*, 26 June 1832. Also, see Allan Fletcher, 'The role of landowners, entrepreneurs and railways in the urban development of the north Wales coast during the nineteenth century', *Welsh History Review*, 16/4 (1993), 514–41: 518–26.

26. *North Wales Chronicle*, 18 July 1848.

27. Walton, *English Seaside Resort*, p. 65.

28. Yates, 'Welsh seaside resorts', 1.

29. Peter Borsay, 'Welsh seaside resorts: historiography, sources and themes', *Welsh History Review*, 24/2 (2008), 92–119: 100.

30. A similar experience was available in Scotland, too. See Durie, *Scotland for the Holidays*, p. 69.

31. Peter Borsay, 'A room with a view': visualizing the seaside, *c.* 1750–1914', *Transactions of the Royal Historical Society*, 23 (2013), 175–201: 196.

32. Henry Skrine, *Two Successive Tours throughout the Whole of Wales. . .* (London, 1798), p. 212.

33. Anon., 'Where to spend the holidays', *Hearth and Home*, 316 (3 June 1897),180.

34. Medicus, 'Advice to the delicate on the summer holiday', *Girl's Own Paper* (summer, 1884), 12.

35. *Cardiff Times*, 28 August 1869.

36. *Railway Herald* cited in *Cardiff Times*, 26 August 1893.

37. *Glamorgan Gazette*, 31 August 1906.

38. *Cardiff and Merthyr Guardian*, 27 March 1869.

39. David Llewellyn Jones and Robert Smith, 'Tourism and the Welsh language in the nineteenth century', in Geraint H. Jenkins (ed.), *The Welsh Language and its Social Domains, 1801–1911* (Cardiff, 2000), pp. 151–75: 152.

40. Richard Fenton, *Tours in Wales (1804–1813)* (London, 1917), p. 150.

41. Jones and Smith, 'Tourism and the Welsh language', p. 155.

42. Fenton, *Tours in Wales*, p. 96.

43. Zaring, 'The Romantic face of Wales', 407; one visitor, on first encountering Cader Idris, exclaimed that he had 'never saw an object more awfully sublime'. See, Anon., *A Collection of Tours in Wales, or a Display of the Beauties of Wales . . .* (London, 1799), p. 192.

44. Samuel Lewis, *A Topographical Dictionary of Wales . . .* vol. 1 (London, 1833 edn), n.p.

45. William Bingley, *North Wales: Including its Scenery, Antiquities, Customs, and Some Sketches of its Natural History*, vol. 2 (London, 1804), p. 24.

46. *Glamorgan, Monmouth and Brecon Gazette*, 6 September 1834.

47. Lewis, *Topographical Dictionary*, vol. 1.

48. *Glamorgan, Monmouth and Brecon Gazette*, 6 September 1834.

49. Anon., *The Tourist in Wales: A Series of Views, Picturesque Scenery, Towns, Castles, &c. with Historical and Topographical Notes* (London, 1851), p. 37.

50. Stephen V. Ward, *Selling Places: The Marketing and Promotion of Towns and Cities, 1850–2000* (London, 1998), pp. 29–31.

51. Anon., *An Account of the Principal Pleasure Tours in England and Wales* (London, 1822), p. 219; David Hughson, *Cambria Depicta: A Tour through North Wales* (London, 1816), p. 98.

52. *North Wales Gazette*, 2 June 1808.

53. *Cambrian*, 26 March 1808; *North Wales Gazette*, 16 June 1808.

54. Borsay, 'From port to resort', p. 90.

55. Richard Warner, *Second Walk through Wales* (London, 1800), p. 364; *Cambrian*, 16 June 1804.

56. Robert Anthony, '"A very thriving place": the peopling of Swansea in the eighteenth century', *Urban History*, 32/1 (2005), 68–87: 85; Louise Miskell, 'A town divided? Sea-bathing, dock-building, and oyster-fishing in nineteenth-century Swansea', in Peter Borsay and John K. Walton (eds), *Resorts and Ports: European Seaside Towns since 1700* (Bristol, 2011), pp. 113–25.

57. *Aberystwyth Observer*, 12 October 1867.

58. *Cambrian News*, 9 June 1882.

59. Walton, *English Seaside*, pp. 60, 65.

60. Jones and Smith, 'Tourism and the Welsh language', p. 153; L. J. Williams, 'The move from the land', in Trevor Herbert and Gareth Elwyn Jones (eds), *Wales 1880–1914* (Cardiff, 1988), pp. 11–47.

61. *Cambrian*, 24 February 1816.

62. Richard Fenton, *A Historical Tour through Pembrokeshire* (London, 1811), p. 158.

63. *Carmarthen Journal*, 5 September 1828.

64. *Glamorgan, Monmouth and Brecon Gazette*, 16 July 1836; *Cambrian*, 24 July 1824; *Cambrian*, 27 September 1823.

65. *Cambrian*, 4 September 1819 and 5 April 1823: *Cardiff and Merthyr Guardian*, 21 May 1859.

66. *Glamorgan, Monmouth and Brecon Gazette*, 17 May 1834.

67. *South Wales Star*, 24 July 1891.

68. See, for example, Henry Wigstead, *Remarks on a Tour to North and South Wales, in the Year 1797* (London, 1799).

69. Samuel Lewis, *A Topographical Dictionary of Wales . . .* vol. 1 (London, 1828), n.p.

70. *Cambrian*, 7 April 1821.

71. The phrase was oft-used to describe villages in the Vale of Glamorgan, as the most cursory search of the National Library of Wales's Welsh newspapers online database will confirm.

72. Griffiths, 'Landlords and tenants', p. 195.

73. *Cardiff Times*, 7 September 1866; *Western Mail*, 27 September 1878; *Cardiff and Merthyr Guardian*, 28 December 1861.

74. Thomas Hearne (ed.), *Itinerary of John Leland the Antiquary*, vol. 4, pt 1 (Oxford, 1769 edn), p. 44.

75. John Storrie, *Notes on Excavations made During the Summers of 1894–6 at Barry Island and Ely Racecourse* (Cardiff, 1896).

76. Gerald of Wales, *The Journey through Wales / The Description of Wales* (Harmondsworth, 1978), p. 125; for a guide discussing the rock 'to which if the ear is applied a noise is heard like that of smiths at work', see Thomas Walford, *The Scientific Tourist Through England, Wales & Scotland: By Which the Traveller is Directed to the Principal Objects of Antiquity, Art, Science & the Picturesque . . .* vol. 2 (London, 1818), n.p. Also see, *South Wales Echo*, 20 March 1896.

77. Evans had clearly read his Leland, too, for he used some of the same language to describe the Island as the Tudor antiquary. Both writers, for instance, adjudged the channel separating the Island from the mainland to be about the width of the Thames at London bridge.

78. Evans, *Letters*, pp. 105–6.

79. Evans, *Letters*, p. 106.

80. Skrine, *Two Successive Tours*, pp. 63–4.

81. Evans, *Letters*, p. 106.
82. *Bristol Mercury*, 25 April 1840.
83. *Cardiff and Merthyr Guardian*, 30 May 1846.
84. *Cardiff and Merthyr Guardian*, 7 August 1858.
85. *Cardiff Times*, 12 August 1864.
86. *Cardiff Times*, 27 July 1866.
87. *Cardiff Times*, 17 August 1866.
88. *Cardiff Times*, 24 April 1875.
89. *Caledonian Mercury*, 7 July 1825.
90. Census Returns.
91. *Cardiff Times*, 27 April 1866.
92. *Glamorgan, Monmouthshire and Brecon Gazette*, 15 July 1837.
93. John Armstrong and David M. Williams, 'The steamboat and popular tourism', *Journal of Transport History*, 26/1 (2005), 61–77: 69–70; Nigel Coombes, *Passenger Steamers of the Bristol Channel: A Pictorial Record* (Truro, 1990), p. 7.
94. *Cambrian*, 7 August 1824.
95. *Pembrokeshire Herald*, 15 August 1845.
96. *Cardiff Times*, 29 August 1862.
97. *Cambrian*, 20 July 1811.
98. *Cardiff Times*, 27 April 1866; *Western Mail*, 8 July 1881.
99. *Bristol Mercury*, 25 April 1840.
100. *Cardiff Times*, 6 September 1861.
101. Griffiths, 'Landlords and tenants', p. 195.
102. *Monmouthshire Merlin*, 16 July 1836.

CHAPTER 2

1. *Western Mail*, 17 July 1876.
2. Barry Library, Iorwerth M. Prothero, 'Barry and its Dock, Volume 1: The Schemes that Failed' (1993), 137.
3. Prothero, 'Barry and its Dock', 137.
4. *Western Mail*, 21 August 1874; *South Wales Daily News*, 5 June 1875.
5. *Western Mail*, 17 July 1876.
6. *Cardiff Times*, 24 July 1875.
7. *Western Mail*, 18 July 1877.
8. Tye R. Blackshaw, 'Seddon, John Pollard (1827–1906), architect', *Oxford Dictionary of National Biography*, *http://www.oxforddnb.com/view/10.1093/ref:odnb/9780198614128.001.0001/odnb-9780198614128-e-39357* (accessed 20 January 2018).
9. Iorwerth W. Prothero, 'The port and railways of Barry', in Donald Moore (ed.), *Barry: The Centenary Book* (2nd edn, Barry, 1985), pp. 209–69, 216.

10. Prothero, 'Barry and its Dock', 123.

11. *Cardiff and Merthyr Guardian*, 12 July 1873.

12. *British Architect*, 1/ 11 (13 March 1874), 167.

13. Prothero, 'The port and railways', p. 218.

14. Prothero, 'Barry and its Dock', 144.

15. Prothero, 'The port and railways', pp. 216–19.

16. *South Wales Daily News*, 9 July 1873.

17. Prothero, 'The port and railways', p. 216.

18. Prothero, 'The port and railways', p. 217.

19. *Western Mail*, 25 July 1874.

20. *South Wales Daily News*, 5 June 1875.

21. *Cardiff Times*, 27 April 1866.

22. *Cardiff and Merthyr Guardian*, 3 September 1870.

23. *Cardiff Times*, 26 August 1871.

24. *Cardiff and Merthyr Guardian*, 7 May 1870. Barry Island took its place in the guide alongside other places of interest such as Llandaff, Penarth and Castell Coch.

25. W. E. Minchinton 'Introduction: Industrial South Wales, 1750–1914', in W. E. Minchinton (ed.), *Industrial South Wales 1750–1914: Essays in Welsh Economic History* (London, 1969), pp. ix–xxxi: xvi; *Cardiff and Merthyr Guardian*, 24 October 1868.

26. *Glamorgan, Monmouth and Brecon Gazette*, 24 April 1841.

27. D. S. M. Barrie, *A Regional History of the Railways of Great Britain: Volume 12, South Wales* (Newton Abbot, 1980), ch. 4, 5, 6 and 7.

28. Douglas A. Reid, 'The "iron roads" and "the happiness of the working classes": the early development and social significance of the railway excursion', *Journal of Transport History*, 17/1 (1996), 57–73: 58; Jack Simmons, 'Excursion train', in Jack Simmons and Gordon Biddle (eds), *The Oxford Companion to British Railway History: From 1603 to the 1990s* (Oxford, 1997), pp. 149–52.

29. *Monmouthshire Merlin*, 3 August 1844.

30. *Merthyr Telegraph*, 14 September 1861.

31. *Monmouthshire Merlin*, 17 August 1850; *Monmouthshire Merlin*, 28 September 1850; *Cardiff and Merthyr Guardian*, 30 August 1851; *Cardiff Times*, 2 June 1865.

32. *Western Mail*, 1 September 1869.

33. *Cardiff and Merthyr Guardian*, 6 June 1868.

34. *Cardiff and Merthyr Guardian*, 22 May 1869.

35. *Bristol Mercury*, 4 June 1870.

36. *Pembrokeshire Herald*, 15 August 1845.

37. Nigel Coombes, *Passenger Steamers of the Bristol Channel: A Pictorial Record* (Truro, 1990), pp. 4–5.

38. *Monmouthshire Merlin*, 21 July 1876.

39. *Cardiff Times*, 6 June 1868; *Cambrian*, 22 July 1881; Louise Miskell, 'A town divided? Sea-bathing, dock-building, and oyster-fishing in

nineteenth-century Swansea', in Peter Borsay and John K. Walton (eds), *Resorts and Ports: European Seaside Towns since 1700* (Bristol, 2011), pp. 113–25: 118–19.

40. See M. J. Daunton, *Coal Metropolis: Cardiff, 1870–1914* (Leicester, 1977), p. 10.

41. *Cardiff and Merthyr Guardian*, 6 June 1868.

42. *Cardiff Times*, 27 April 1866.

43. *Cardiff Times*, 27 May 1864.

44. *South Wales Echo*, 2 July 1881; *Evening Express*, 10 July 1899.

45. *Cardiff Times*, 27 April 1866.

46. *Cardiff Times*, 27 April 1866.

47. *South Wales Daily News*, 23 October 1889.

48. Anon., 'Barry field meeting', *Cardiff Naturalists' Society: First Annual Report, 1867–8* (2nd edn, London, 1868), pp. 74–6.

49. *Cardiff Times*, 30 August 1873.

50. *Western Mail*, 10 August 1877.

51. *South Wales Daily News*, 31 August 1878.

52. *South Wales Daily News*, 13 April 1877.

53. *Monmouthshire Merlin*, 21 July 1876.

54. *Cardiff Times*, 26 August 1871.

55. *South Wales Daily News*, 6 June 1876.

56. *South Wales Daily News*, 6 June 1876.

57. *South Wales Daily News*, 18 June 1877.

58. *Cardiff Times*, 1 March 1861; *Cardiff Times*, 3 October 1862.

59. *Western Mail*, 28 July 1874; *South Wales Daily News*, 11 October 1877.

60. *Western Mail*, 17 July 1876.

61. *Cardiff and Merthyr Guardian*, 23 June 1854; Anon., 'Barry field meeting', pp. 74–6.

62. *South Wales Daily News*, 10 October 1876.

63. *Western Mail*, 18 July 1877.

64. John Beckerson and John K. Walton, 'Selling air: marketing the intangible at British resorts', in John K. Walton (ed.), *Histories of Tourism: Representation, Identity and Conflict* (Clevedon, 2005), pp. 55–68.

65. Anon., 'Barry field meeting', p. 75.

66. *Monmouthshire Merlin*, 23 July 1870; *Monmouthshire Merlin*, 21 July 1876.

67. *Monmouthshire Merlin*, 22 August 1863.

68. *South Wales Daily News*, 18 June 1877.

69. *Monmouthshire Merlin*, 23 July 1870.

70. *South Wales Daily News*, 8 March 1877.

71. *South Wales Daily News*, 29 August 1878.

72. *Western Mail*, 16 January 1877.

73. *Western Mail*, 11 October 1877.

74. *Western Mail*, 11 October 1877.

CHAPTER 3

1. Barry Library, Iorwerth W. Prothero, 'Barry and its Dock, Volume 1: The Schemes that Failed' (1993), 145; Iorwerth W. Prothero, 'The port and railways of Barry', in Donald Moore (ed.), *Barry: The Centenary Book* (2nd edn, Barry, 1985), pp. 209–69: 219.

2. *Cardiff and Merthyr Guardian*, 16 June 1865.

3. *Monmouthshire Merlin*, 2 December 1865.

4. *South Wales Daily News*, 25 January 1896.

5. *Cardiff Times*, 27 April 1866.

6. *South Wales Daily News*, 1 December 1875. For more on the calls for increased dock facilities in south Wales in the 1870s, see *South Wales Daily News*, 19 September 1873 and, especially, the article 'The Pontypridd, Caerphilly, and Newport Railway', *Monmouthshire Merlin*, 22 March 1878. Also see John Davies, *Cardiff and the Marquesses of Bute* (Cardiff, 1981), pp. 255–6.

7. Glamorgan Archives, DPL/834/163, Letter from Robert Forrest to John Tomson, 19 November 1876. For more on Robert Forrest, see William Linnard, '"Lord" Forrest of St Fagans: estate agent extraordinary', *Morgannwg*, 33 (1989), 55–68.

8. *Western Mail*, 4 December 1877; *Monmouthshire Merlin*, 7 December 1877; Glamorgan Archives, BB/C/52, Indenture made between the earl of Plymouth and the Barry Urban District Council, 31 July 1909.

9. *Cardiff Times*, 8 June 1879.

10. *Cardiff Times*, 8 June 1879; *South Wales Daily News*, 17 May 1879.

11. *Cambrian*, 23 May 1879.

12. The National Archives, MT 10/346, Letter from Robert Forrest to Assistant Secretary, Harbour Dept, Board of Trade, 27 October 1881; *Cambrian*, 18 November 1881.

13. *Weekly Mail*, 23 August 1879.

14. A search of the *Welsh Newspapers Online* database reveals no references to visitors on Barry Island in 1880, 1881, 1883 and 1884, and only one reference to visitors in the summer of 1882 (*Cardiff Times*, 2 September 1882; *Pontypridd Chronicle*, 26 August 1882).

15. *South Wales Daily News*, 8 April 1893.

16. *Barry Dock News*, 27 December 1889.

17. *Cardiff Times*, 21 August 1863.

18. *Cardiff Times*, 24 August 1867.

19. John K. Walton, *The British Seaside: Holidays and Resorts in the Twentieth Century* (Manchester, 2000), p. 126.

20. *Cardiff Times*, 6 December 1861.

21. *Webster and Company's Commercial and Postal Directory of the City of Bristol and the County of Glamorgan* (London, 1865), pp. 537–8; *Slater's . . . Directory. . . of North and South Wales* (Manchester, 1868), p. 189; *Worrall's Directory of South Wales* (Oldham, 1875), p. 306.

22. *Cardiff Times*, 7 July 1865.
23. Roy Thorne, *Penarth: A History* (Risca, 1976), p. 13.
24. *Cardiff and Merthyr Guardian*, 13 November 1869; M. J. Daunton, 'Suburban development in Cardiff: Grangetown and the Windsor estate 1857–1875', *Morgannwg*, 16 (1972), 53–66.
25. *Slater's*, p. 189; *Western Mail*, 12 November 1869.
26. *Cardiff Times*, 9 June 1865.
27. *Cardiff and Merthyr Guardian*, 16 June 1865.
28. *South Wales Daily News*, 12 October 1883 and 23 August 1894.
29. *South Wales Daily News*, 12 October 1883.
30. *Weekly Mail*, 13 September 1902.
31. *Western Mail*, 28 August 1878.
32. *Western Mail*, 8 April 1881.
33. *South Wales Daily News*, 27 June 1884.
34. *Cardiff Times*, 4 March 1882
35. Census Reports.
36. *Cardiff Times*, 9 May 1891; *Evening Express*, 8 April 1897.
37. *South Wales Daily News*, 27 June 1884.
38. See David Cannadine, *Lords and Landlords, the Aristocracy and the Town, 1774–1967* (Leicester, 1980).
39. Plymouth, 1st earl of (Robert George Windsor-Clive, 27 August 1857–6 March 1923), *Who's Who & Who Was Who* (1 December 2007), *https://www.ukwhoswho.com/view/10.1093/ww/9780199540891.001.0001/ww-9780199540884-e-201693* (accessed 19 May 2019).
40. Christine Stevens, 'Personal links between landlord and tenant on a Welsh estate: an absentee landlord's influence on the social life of an estate village in the nineteenth century', *Folk Life*, 50/1 (2012), 7–26. For the 'good earl' reference, see his obituary in *The Times*, 8 March 1923.
41. *Baner*, 2 November 1887, cited in David W. Howell, *Land and People in Nineteenth-century Wales* (London, 1977), p. 86. Also see Matthew Cragoe, '"A contemptible mimic of the Irish": the land question in Victorian Wales', in Matthew Cragoe and Paul Readman (eds), *The Land Question in Britain, 1750–1950* (Basingstoke, 2010), pp. 92–108.
42. Adfyfr, *Landlordism in Wales* (Cardiff, 1887), pp. 19–22.
43. Thomas E. Ellis, *Speeches and Addresses* (Wrexham, 1912), pp. 257–8.

CHAPTER 4

1. Peter Borsay and John K. Walton, 'Introduction: the resort-port relationship', in Peter Borsay and John K. Walton (eds), *Resorts and Ports: European Seaside Towns since 1700* (Bristol, 2011), pp. 1–17;

John K. Walton, 'Port and resort: symbiosis and conflict in "Old Whitby", England, since 1880', in Borsay and Walton (eds), *Resorts and Ports*, pp. 126–46: 132–5; Peter Borsay, 'From port to resort: Tenby and narratives of transition, 1760–1914', in Borsay and Walton (eds), *Resorts and Ports*, pp. 86–112: 104–6; Bernard Deacon, 'Imagining the fishing: artists and fishermen in late nineteenth-century Cornwall', *Rural History*, 12/2 (2001), 159–78.

2.   E. D. Lewis, *The Rhondda Valleys* (Cardiff, 1959), pp. 120–2; Barry Library, Iorwerth W. Prothero, 'Barry and its Dock, Volume 1: The Schemes that Failed' (1993), 238.

3.   Lewis, *Rhondda Valleys,* p. 230.

4.   For other works that explore the interesting relationship between port and resort functions, see the various essays in Walton and Borsay's edited collection. Louise Miskell's essay on Swansea is particularly interesting as another example drawn from the coast of industrial south Wales. For an incisive study of another, Porthcawl, see Ian Pincombe, 'From pit to paradise: Porthcawl's changing identity, from the eighteenth to the twentieth century', *Welsh History Review*, 25/4 (2011), 520–50.

5.   Neil Evans, 'The Welsh Victorian city: the middle class and civic and national consciousness in Cardiff, 1850–1914', *Welsh History Review*, 12/3 (1985), 350–87: 368.

6.   *Weekly Mail*, 22 November 1884; *Barry Dock News*, 5 July 1889; *South Wales Daily News*, 1 January 1896.

7.   *South Wales Echo*, 25 February 1885.

8.   *South Wales Echo*, 21 March 1885.

9.   *South Wales Daily News*, 6 May 1887.

10.   *Barry Dock News*, 27 June 1890.

11.   *Weekly Mail*, 23 April 1887.

12.   *Weekly Mail*, 23 April 1887; Census Reports.

13.   *Barry Dock News*, 29 May 1891; *South Wales Daily News*, 1 January 1896; *Barry Dock News*, 26 April 1901.

14.   *Barry Dock News*, 14 August 1891; emphasis in the original; *Western Mail*, 6 February 1889.

15.   *Barry Herald*, 12 June 1890.

16.   *Barry Dock News*, 19 January 1894.

17.   *South Wales Echo*, 1 July 1887 and 13 July 1887.

18.   *South Wales Echo*, 28 July 1885; *Western Mail*, 11 June 1889.

19.   *South Wales Daily News*, 6 May 1887. See *Western Mail*, 6 February 1889, for a report that emphasizes the rough qualities of the navvies at Barry.

20.   *Cardiff Times*, 2 July 1887.

21.   Clive Leivers, 'The modern Ishmaels? Navvy communities in the High Peak', *Family and Community History*, 9/2 (2006), 141–55.

22.   *Weekly Mail*, 20 December 1884.

23. *Cardiff Times*, 2 December 1882; *Western Mail*, 15 December 1885.
24. *Weekly Mail*, 12 February 1887.
25. *South Wales Echo*, 6 April 1886.
26. *South Wales Echo*, 30 April 1885; D. S. Barrie, *The Barry Railway* (Lingfield, 1962), p. 164.
27. *Barry and Cadoxton Journal*, 10 November 1888.
28. *South Wales Daily News*, 21 December 1888.
29. *South Wales Daily News*, 21 December 1888.
30. *South Wales Daily News*, 24 December 1888.
31. Barrie, *Barry Railway*, pp. 168–9; *Barry Dock News*, 22 November 1889.
32. *South Wales Echo*, 4 September 1885.
33. T. M. Hodges, 'The peopling of the hinterland and the port of Cardiff', *Economic History Review*, 17/1 (1947), 62–72: 67–8; Lewis, *Rhondda Valleys*, p. 230.
34. A. Otgaar, 'Towards a common agenda for the development of industrial tourism', *Tourism Management Perspectives*, 4 (2012), 86–91: 87.
35. *Barry Dock News*, 30 August 1889; W. E. Minchinton, 'Introduction: industrial South Wales, 1750–1914', in W. E. Minchinton (ed.), *Industrial South Wales 1750–1914: Essays in Welsh Economic History* (London, 1969), pp. ix–xxxi: xxi.
36. *Cardiff Times*, 21 July 1888.
37. *Weekly Mail*, 12 February 1887.
38. *Barry and Cadoxton Journal*, 26 May 1888.
39. *Weekly Mail*, 7 August 1886.
40. *Barry and Cadoxton Journal*, 26 May 1888; *South Wales Daily News*, 6 August 1889; *Barry Dock News*, 4 October 1889.
41. *Barry and Cadoxton Journal*, 26 April 1889.
42. *Barry and Cadoxton Journal*, 14 June 1889.
43. *Barry Dock News*, 15 November 1889.
44. *Weekly Mail*, 7 August 1886.
45. *South Wales Daily News*, 9 June 1888; *South Wales Echo*, 20 September 1888; *Barry and Cadoxton Journal*, 22 September 1888.
46. *Western Mail*, 11 July 1884.
47. *South Wales Echo*, 21 March 1885.
48. *South Wales Echo*, 12 March 1885 and 21 March 1885.
49. *Evening Express*, 1 June 1896.
50. *Barry and Cadoxton Journal*, 26 May 1888; *Western Mail*, 22 May 1888.
51. *Barry and Cadoxton Journal*, 26 May 1888.
52. *Cardiff Times*, 10 July 1886; *South Wales Echo*, 5 July 1886.
53. *Barry Dock News*, 13 December 1889,
54. *Barry Dock News*, 4 October 1889.
55. *Barry Dock News*, 18 July 1890.

CHAPTER 5

1. Before 31 December 1894, the successful candidates were returned to Barry and Cadoxton Local Board. After that date, they took their place alongside fellow members of the Barry Urban District Council (*Barry Dock News*, 14 December 1894).
2. *Barry and Cadoxton Journal*, 15 December 1888.
3. *South Wales Star*, 26 May 1891. Emphasis in the original.
4. *South Wales Daily News*, 18 May 1892; *Barry Dock News*, 1 September 1893.
5. *Barry Dock News*, 14 August 1891. Emphasis in the original.
6. *Barry Dock News*, 20 April 1894 for a discussion about 'Ambitious Barry'.
7. *Barry Herald*, 25 November 1898 for an article entitled 'The city of Barry in 1920' for a light-hearted vision of Barry's great future as an urban centre.
8. *Western Mail*, 4 September 1893.
9. *Barry Dock News*, 12 August 1898.
10. *Barry Dock News*, 19 August 1892.
11. *Western Mail*, 11 February 1899; *Barry Dock News*, 23 January 1891; *Merthyr Express*, 13 August 1910. For other examples of press speculation about new industries coming to Barry, see *South Wales Daily News*, 27 February 1896 and *Cardiff Times*, 21 January 1899.
12. *Barry Dock News*, 26 August 1910.
13. *Barry and Cadoxton Journal*, 18 July 1890.
14. *Barry Dock News*, 27 May 1892.
15. *Barry Dock News*, 9 June 1893.
16. *Barry Dock News*, 24 July 1903.
17. *Barry Herald*, 4 September 1908.
18. *Barry Dock News*, 30 March 1894.
19. *Barry Herald*, 12 June 1896.
20. *South Wales Star*, 3 June 1892.
21. *Barry Herald*, 12 June 1896.
22. *Barry Dock News*, 4 February 1898.
23. *Barry Herald*, 6 May 1910.
24. *Barry Dock News*, 1 April 1892; *South Wales Star*, 7 April 1893.
25. *Barry Dock News*, 27 September 1907.
26. *Barry Dock News*, 11 August 1893; *Barry Dock News*, 27 July 1894; *Barry Herald*, 5 June 1896; *Barry Dock News*, 4 February 1898; *Barry Herald*, 17 May 1901.
27. *South Wales Star*, 7 April 1893.
28. *Barry Dock News*, 22 June 1894.
29. *Barry Herald*, 2 July 1897.
30. *Barry Herald*, 2 July 1897 and 21 October 1898.
31. *Barry Herald*, 21 October 1910.
32. *Barry Herald*, 25 November 1898.

33. *Barry Herald*, 22 June 1906.
34. *Barry Dock News*, 19 April 1907, 7 June 1907 and 12 July 1907.
35. *Barry Herald*, 8 October 1909 and 6 May 1910.
36. *Barry Dock News*, 8 July 1904.
37. *Barry Herald*, 17 June 1904.
38. *Cardiff Times*, 7 July 1888; *South Wales Star*, 19 February 1892.
39. *Barry Herald*, 28 August 1896.
40. *Barry Herald*, 23 November 1900.
41. *Barry Herald*, 13 June 1902.
42. *Barry Dock News*, 10 October 1902.
43. *Barry Herald*, 5 June 1903.
44. *Pontypridd Chronicle*, 20 March 1896.
45. *Barry Dock News*, 7 August 1896.
46. *Barry Dock News*, 29 June 1894.
47. *Barry Dock News*, 31 July 1896.
48. *Barry Dock News*, 7 August 1896; *South Wales Echo*, 8 August 1896.
49. D. S. Barrie, *The Barry Railway* (Lingfield, 1962), pp. 175–6.
50. *Barry Dock News*, 19 July 1889.
51. *Barry Dock News*, 2 May 1890.
52. *Evening Express*, 30 May 1893.
53. *Barry Dock News*, 30 March 1894; *Barry Dock News*, 2 June 1893; *Evening Express*, 30 May 1893; *South Wales Daily News*, 10 August 1894; Vale of Glamorgan Council, *Vale of Glamorgan County Treasures: Barry* (Barry, 2007), p. 9.
54. *Barry Dock News*, 2 June 1893.
55. The sense that the 'white house' at Friars Point was out of bounds prevailed at least until the middle years of the twentieth century. In the 1940s and 1950s, youngsters from Barry thought of it as a place that they would do well to avoid: they were not welcome. Interview with Denis McCarthy, 7 June 2014.
56. John K. Walton, *The English Seaside Resort: A Social History, 1750–1914* (Leicester, 1983), pp. 108–9; Nigel J. Morgan and Annette Pritchard, *Power and Politics at the Seaside: The Development of Devon's Resorts in the Twentieth Century* (Exeter, 1999), pp. 45–50; Sue Farrant, 'London by the Sea: resort development on the south coast of England 1880–1939', *Journal of Contemporary History*, 22/1 (1987), 137–62: 148.
57. *Evening Express*, 3 August 1894.
58. *Barry Dock News*, 13 August 1897.
59. *Barry Dock News*, 7 June 1895; *Barry Herald*, 11 February 1910.
60. *Barry Dock News*, 20 July 1894.
61. *South Wales Daily News*, 10 August 1894; *Barry Dock News*, 30 August 1895; *Barry Herald*, 13 August 1909.
62. *Barry Dock News*, 17 August 1894.
63. *Barry Dock News*, 30 March 1894; *South Wales Star*, 30 March 1894; *Western Mail*, 4 August 1894.

64. *South Wales Echo*, 10 August 1894; *Evening Express*, 4 August 1894.

65. *Barry Herald*, 20 November 1896.

66. *Barry Herald*, 21 May 1897.

67. *Barry Dock News*, 30 March 1894; *South Wales Star*, 30 March 1894.

68. *South Wales Echo*, 23 March 1897.

69. H. E. Meller, *Leisure and the Changing City, 1870–1914* (London, 1976), pp. 96–8.

70. Richard Roberts, 'The Corporation as impresario: the municipal provision of entertainment in Victorian and Edwardian Bournemouth', in John K. Walton and James Walvin (eds), *Leisure in Britain, 1780–1939* (Manchester, 1983), pp. 136–57: 154–5.

CHAPTER 6

1. *Barry Dock News*, 20 March 1908; *Barry Dock News*, 15 May 1908; *Evening Express*, 29 September 1910.

2. *Weekly Mail*, 15 August 1903; *Barry Herald*, 6 November 1903; *Barry Herald*, 12 February 1904.

3. *Evening Express*, 4 September 1907.

4. *Barry Dock News*, 20 March 1908; *Barry Herald*, 10 December 1909; *Barry Herald*, 16 February 1912.

5. *Weekly Mail*, 12 May 1906.

6. *Barry Dock News*, 12 April 1907.

7. *Barry Dock News*, 28 June 1907.

8. *Barry Dock News*, 6 July 1900.

9. *Barry Dock News*, 25 August 1905; *Weekly Mail*, 26 August 1905.

10. *Barry Herald*, 5 March 1909.

11. *Barry Herald*, 8 March 1912.

12. *Barry Herald*, 16 August 1912.

13. *Barry Herald*, 9 August 1912.

14. Richard W. Thomas, 'The building of Barry', in Donald Moore (ed.), *Barry: The Centenary Book* (2nd edn, Barry, 1985), pp. 333–65: 340–50.

15. *Barry Dock News*, 9 June 1893; *Barry Dock News*, 24 July 1903.

16. C. Michael Hall, *Tourism Planning: Policies, Processes, and Relationships* (2nd edn, London, 2008), p. 55.

17. For the comparison with Scarborough, see *Barry Herald*, 27 September 1907. For the 'Queen of Welsh watering places' reference, see *Barry Dock News*, 1 September 1893 (although Aberystwyth and Llandudno, to name but two, laid claim to that title too). For Barry as the 'Blackpool of Wales', see *Evening Express*, 20 December 1906 and for references to it as the 'Brighton of South Wales', see *Barry Dock News*, 24 July 1903 and *Barry Herald*, 13 August 1909.

18. *South Wales Star*, 15 July 1892.

19. *Barry Dock News*, 24 November 1911.

20. *Barry Herald*, 18 May 1900.
21. *Barry Dock News*, 1 March 1907.
22. *Barry Dock News*, 25 May 1900.
23. *Barry Dock News*, 15 September 1911.
24. *Barry Dock News*, 22 March 1907.
25. *Barry Herald*, 11 August 1905.
26. *Barry Herald*, 11 September 1908.
27. *Barry Dock News*, 6 September 1907.
28. *Barry Herald*, 25 May 1906.
29. *Barry Dock News*, 27 September 1907.
30. *Barry Herald*, 27 September 1907.
31. *Barry Herald*, 8 May 1896.
32. *Barry Dock News*, 11 October 1907.
33. *Barry Dock News*, 24 January 1913.
34. *Barry Dock News*, 20 July 1894.
35. *Barry Dock News*, 17 May 1901.
36. *Cardiff Times*, 7 September 1907.
37. *Barry Herald*, 18 May 1906; *Barry Dock News*, 17 May 1907; *Barry Dock News*, 17 April 1907;
38. *Barry Dock News*, 12 August 1907, *Weekly Mail*, 24 August 1907 and *Evening Express*, 16 August 1907.
39. *Barry Dock News*, 29 September 1905.
40. *Weekly Mail*, 8 July 1905. 1901 Census.
41. The National Archives, MT 10/1288, Railway Poster illustrating the Sands of Whitmore Bay, *c.*1910.
42. *Barry Dock News*, 13 October 1911.
43. *Barry Dock News*, 3 August 1894.
44. *Barry Dock News*, 18 March 1910. Also see *Barry Dock News*, 24 January 1913 for a report lamenting the excursionists' high levels of self-sufficiency.
45. *Barry Herald*, 20 May 1910.
46. Peter Borsay, 'A room with a view: visualising the seaside, *c.*1750–1914', *Transactions of the Royal Historical Society*, 23 (2013), 175–201: 187–8.
47. *Barry Herald*, 20 April 1900.
48. *Barry Herald*, 3 March 1914.
49. *Barry Herald*, 8 May 1896. Emphasis in the original.
50. For the 'Biarritz of Wales', see *Barry Herald*, 25 August 1905 and *Barry Dock News*, 12 April 1907.
51. *South Wales Star*, 16 December 1892; Brian C. Luxton, 'Ambition, vice and virtue: social life, 1884–1914', in Moore (ed.), *Barry*, p. 271; D. S. Barrie, *The Barry Railway* (Lingfield, 1962), p. 153; *Weekly Mail*, 3 February 1894.
52. Gary L. Browning, 'Civilization and nature in Boris Pil'njak's Machines and Wolves', *Slavic and East European Journal*, 20/2 (1976), 155–66: 162.

53. *Barry Herald*, 20 April 1900.
54. *Barry Dock News*, 13 April 1894; *South Wales Star*, 6 April 1894 and 22 June 1894.
55. *Barry Herald*, 15 July 1898 and 29 July 1898. Also see *Barry Dock News*, 5 October 1900 and 11 July 1902.
56. *Barry Dock News*, 13 September 1907.
57. *Barry Dock News*, 5 June 1914. For an earlier statement of this argument, see *Barry Herald*, 21 October 1898.
58. *Barry Herald*, 1 October 1909.
59. *Barry Dock News*, 13 September 1907.
60. *Barry Dock News*, 10 January 1913.
61. *Barry Herald*, 1 October 1909.
62. *Barry Herald*, 23 November 1900.
63. *South Wales Echo*, 29 April 1885.
64. *Cardiff Times*, 6 January 1895; *Western Mail*, 21 December 1888.
65. *South Wales Star*, 27 October 1893; *Barry Dock News*, 3 May 1895; *Evening Express*, 12 September 1904.
66. *Cardiff Times*, 5 April 1902.
67. *Barry Herald*, 3 December 1912.
68. *Barry Herald*, 16 September 1904 and *Barry Dock News*, 16 September 1904.
69. *Barry Herald*, 16 September 1904.
70. *Barry Herald*, 17 October 1902; *Barry Dock News*, 23 May 1903; *Rhondda Leader*, 18 August 1906.
71. *Barry Dock News*, 8 September 1905.
72. *Barry Dock News*, 19 June 1903.
73. Glamorgan Archives, BB/C/52. Supplemental Agreement between the Earl of Plymouth and the Barry Urban District Council, 19 December 1908.
74. Glamorgan Archives, D/D Pl 834/135, Letter from Robert Forrest to J. Tomson, 22 August 1876. Emphasis in the original.
75. *Barry Herald*, 14 August 1903; *Weekly Mail*, 15 August 1903.
76. *Barry Herald*, 1 July 1904.
77. *Barry Dock News*, 5 August 1904.
78. *Barry Herald*, 1 July 1904.
79. *Barry Herald*, 15 July 1904.
80. *Cardiff Times*, 16 July 1904.
81. Matthew Cragoe, '"A contemptible mimic of the Irish": the land question in Victorian Wales', in Matthew Cragoe and Paul Readman (eds), *The Land Question in Britain, 1750–1950* (Basingstoke, 2010), pp. 92–108.
82. *Barry Herald*, 3 February 1905; *Barry Dock News*, 3 February 1905; *Evening Express*, 1 February 1905.
83. *Barry Dock News*, 17 August 1894.
84. John K. Walton, *The British Seaside: Holidays and Resorts in the Twentieth Century* (Manchester, 2000), p. 126.

85. *Barry Herald*, 26 August 1904.

86. *Barry Herald*, 30 June 1905.

87. *Barry Dock News*, 15 September 1905; *Barry Herald*, 15 September 1905.

88. *Barry Dock News*, 30 June 1905.

89. *Barry Herald*, 2 September 1904.

90. *Barry Dock News*, 15 September 1905.

91. *Barry Dock News*, 13 August 1909.

92. Glamorgan Archives, BB/C/52. Supplemental Agreement between the Earl of Plymouth and the Barry Urban District Council, 19 December 1908.

93. *Barry Dock News*, 22 March 1907.

94. Glamorgan Archives, BB/C/52. Supplemental Agreement between the Earl of Plymouth and the Barry Urban District Council, 19 December 1908; *Cardiff Times*, 13 July 1907.

95. TNA, BD 28/713: Letter from S. A. Luen to James Griffiths, Secretary of State for Wales, 29 October 1964.

CHAPTER 7

1.   Peter Stead, 'The town that had come of age: Barry, 1918–1938', in Donald Moore (ed.), *Barry: The Centenary Book* (2nd edn, Barry, 1985), pp. 367–428: 380.

2.   For the label 'Trippers' Mecca', see *Barry Dock News*, 5 June 1925.

3.   *Barry Dock News*, 14 October 1892.

4.   *South Wales Echo*, 3 August 1897.

5.   *Barry Dock News*, 4 August 1910.

6.   *Cardiff Times*, 6 July 1907.

7.   *Cardiff Times*, 11 August 1894; *Barry Dock News*, 10 August 1894.

8.   *Barry Dock News*, 7 April 1893.

9.   *Barry Herald*, 14 August 1896.

10. *Barry Herald*, 11 August 1899.

11. *Barry Dock News*, 9 August 1907; *Barry Dock News*, 8 August 1913.

12. *Barry Herald*, 11 August 1905.

13. *Barry Dock News*, 16 September 1892; *Evening Express*, 10 August 1909.

14. *South Wales Echo*, 8 August 1896; *Barry Dock News*, 13 October 1911.

15. Robert Poole, 'Oldham wakes', in John K. Walton and James Walvin (eds), *Leisure in Britain, 1780–1939* (Manchester, 1983), pp. 71–98; 87–9; John K. Walton, 'The demand for working-class seaside holidays in Victorian England', *Economic History Review*, new series, 34/2 (1981), 249–65.

16. H. Cunningham, 'Leisure and culture', in F. M. L. Thompson (ed.), *The Cambridge Social History of Britain, 1750–1950: Vol. 2, People and Their Environment* (Cambridge, 1990), pp. 279–339: 313.

17. W. R. Lambert, 'Drink and work discipline in industrial south Wales, *c.*1800–1870', *Welsh History Review*, 7/3 (1975), 289–306; Sidney Pollard, 'Discipline in the industrial revolution', *Economic History Review*, new series, 16/2 (1963), 254–71: 256.

18. Hugh Cunningham, *Leisure in the Industrial Revolution, c. 1780–1880* (London, 1980), p. 65.

19. Catriona M. Parratt, *'More than Mere Amusement': Working-Class Women's Leisure in England, 1750–1914* (Boston, 2001), p. 93.

20. Not everyone was convinced that the bank holidays were a success, some arguing that they merely provided workers with an opportunity to get drunk. See St. John E. C. Hankin, 'The sins of St Lubbock', *The Nineteenth Century: A Monthly Review*, 41/231 (March 1897), 467–73.

21. *Cardiff Times*, 8 August 1885; *Aberdare Times*, 6 August 1887 and 11 August 1888.

22. *Cardiff Times*, 3 June 1882.

23. *Cardiff Times*, 7 August 1886.

24. *Pall Mall Gazette*, 2 August 1897.

25. *Western Mail*, 7 August 1888; Jack Jones, *Black Parade* (London, 1935), p. 81.

26. Miners' Eight Hour Day Committee, *Final Report of the Departmental Committee . . . to Inquire into the Probable Economic Effect of a Limit of Eight Hours to the Working Day of Coal Miner*s, Part II, Cd. 3506 (1907), p. 8.

27. *Llais Llafur*, 23 September 1916.

28. For more on British workers' 'quest for leisure', see Douglas A. Reid, 'Playing and praying', in Martin Daunton (ed.), *The Cambridge Urban History of Britain. Volume 3, 1840–1950* (Cambridge, 2000), pp. 745–807: 746–57.

29. See, for example, *Barry Dock News*, 9 September 1892; *Barry Herald*, 10 July 1896; *South Wales Daily News*, 6 July 1897.

30. *Barry Herald*, 14 August 1896. For more on Mabon's Day, see Andy Croll, 'Mabon's Day: the rise and fall of a Lib-Lab holiday in the south Wales coalfield, 1888–1898', *Labour History Review*, 72/1 (2007), 49–68.

31. *Barry Dock News*, 8 April 1892.

32. *Barry Herald*, 20 July 1900.

33. *South Wales Echo*, 3 August 1897.

34. *Barry Dock News*, 14 July 1899.

35. *Cambrian*, 16 August 1895.

36. *Penarth Chronicle*, 9 August 1890.

37. *Denbighshire Free Press*, 9 October 1897.

38. *South Wales Star*, 9 February 1894; *Barry Dock News*, 6 February 1891; *Barry Dock News*, 6 March 1891; *Barry Dock News*, 2 February 1894.

39. *Barry Dock News*, 7 April 1893.

40. *Barry Dock News*, 22 November 1889.

41. *South Wales Daily News*, 24 December 1888.

42. *Penarth Chronicle*, 9 August 1890.
43. D. S. Barrie, *The Barry Railway* (Lingfield, 1962), p. 166; Iorwerth W. Prothero, 'The port and railways of Barry', in Donald Moore (ed.), *Barry: The Centenary Book* (2nd edn, Barry, 1985), pp. 209–69: 260.
44. *Barry Dock News*, 27 May 1892.
45. *Barry Dock News*, 28 June 1895.
46. *Barry Dock News*, 14 October 1892.
47. *Barry Dock News*, 23 May 1890.
48. *Barry Dock News*, 14 October 1892.
49. *Barry Dock News*, 23 February 1894, 11 January 1895 and 18 October 1895.
50. *South Wales Echo*, 17 March 1896.
51. *Pontypridd Chronicle*, 20 March 1896.
52. *Barry Dock News*, 20 March 1896.
53. Barrie, *The Barry Railway*, p. 153.
54. *Barry Dock News*, 14 July 1893.
55. John K. Walton, *Blackpool* (Edinburgh, 1998), p. 56. Also see John K. Walton, 'Railways and resort development in Victorian England: the case of Silloth', *Northern History*, 15/1 (1979), 191–209.
56. Barrie, *The Barry Railway*, p. 160.
57. *Barry Dock News*, 24 November 1893.
58. *Barry Dock News*, 31 July 1896.
59. *Rhondda Leader*, 23 May 1903, 9 July 1910 and 27 July 1912.
60. *Barry Dock News*, 17 August 1894.
61. *Barry Herald*, 28 February 1902.
62. *Barry Herald*, 21 August 1903.
63. *Barry Herald*, 29 July 1904 and 18 September 1903.
64. *Barry Dock News*, 22 July 1904.
65. *Barry Herald*, 18 September 1903.
66. *South Wales Echo*, 3 August 1897. Emphasis in the original.
67. *Barry Dock News*, 21 July 1911.
68. *Barry Herald*, 2 September 1904.
69. *Barry Herald*, 29 July 1898.
70. *Barry Herald*, 1 July 1904.
71. *Barry Dock News*, 29 July 1904 and 19 July 1907.
72. *Barry Dock News*, 29 July 1904; *Barry Dock News*, 18 August 1905; *Barry Herald*, 2 August 1907.
73. *Barry Herald*, 21 June 1907; *Barry Dock News*, 19 July 1907; *Barry Herald*, 21 February 1908; Justice of the Peace, 28 March 1908, pp. 142–4.
74. See, for instance, *Barry Dock News*, 25 August 1911 and *Barry Herald*, 14 June 1912.
75. *Barry Herald*, 11 August 1899.
76. *Rhondda Leader*, 7 July 1900.
77. *Barry Dock News*, 30 June 1905.

78. *Barry Dock News*, 17 August 1906.

79. *Barry Dock News*, 1 June 1906.

80. *Barry Dock News*, 14 August 1896.

81. *South Wales Echo*, 3 August 1897.

82. *Barry Herald*, 20 July 1900.

83. *Barry Herald*, 30 July 1897.

84. *South Wales Daily News*, 30 August 1897; *Barry Herald*, 30 July 1897.

85. *Barry Herald*, 20 July 1900.

86. *Barry Dock News*, 20 July 1900.

87. *Barry Dock News*, 7 July 1900.

88. Asa Briggs, *Mass Entertainment: The Origins of a Modern Industry* (Adelaide, 1960).

89. See, for example, Eric Hobsbawm, *Worlds of Labour: Further Studies in the History of Labour* (London, 1984), ch. 11. Also, Neville Kirk, *Change, Continuity and Class: Labour in British Society, 1850–1920* (Manchester, 1998), chap. 9.

90. John K. Walton, *The English Seaside Resort: A Social History, 1750–1914* (Leicester, 1983), p. 157.

91. Darren Webb, 'Bakhtin at the seaside: utopia, modernity and the carnivalesque', *Theory, Culture and Society*, 22/3 (2005), 121–38: 128.

92. Walton, *Blackpool*, pp. 90–1. For Coney Island as another example of the seaside as an outcrop of modernity, see John F. Kasson, *Amusing the Million: Coney Island at the Turn of the Century* (New York, 1978).

93. Keith G. Debbage and Dimitri Ioannides, 'The cultural turn? Towards a more critical economic geography of tourism', in Alan A. Lew, C. Michael Hall and Allan M. Williams (eds), *A Companion to Tourism* (Oxford, 2004), pp. 99–109: 100.

94. *Barry Dock News*, 13 September 1907.

95. *Barry Herald*, 24 July 1896; *South Wales Echo*, 21 November 1900; *Evening Express*, 7 June 1910.

96. *South Wales Echo*, 26 November 1895; *Barry Dock News*, 5 August 1910.

97. *Barry Herald*, 11 June 1897.

98. *Barry and Cadoxton Journal*, 28 July 1888.

99. *Barry Dock News*, 25 March 1904.

100. Gary S. Cross and John K. Walton, *The Playful Crowd: Pleasure Places in the Twentieth Century* (New York, 2005), p. 18; *Glamorgan Free Press*, 17 July 1897.

101. Erin McLaughlin-Jenkins, 'Walking the low road: the pursuit of scientific knowledge in late Victorian working-class communities', *Public Understanding of Science*, 12/2 (2003), 147–66. For the interest of south Wales miners in geology, see Catherine E. Preston, 'Geology, visualisation and the 1893 Hauliers' Strike: an interdisciplinary exploration' (unpublished PhD thesis, Cardiff University, 2010), 32–3.

102. John Storrie, *Notes on Excavations made During the Summers of 1894–6 at Barry Island and Ely Racecourse* (Cardiff, 1896), pp. 52–4.

103. Walter Haydn Davies, *The Right Place, The Right Time: Memories of Boyhood Days in a Welsh Mining Community* (Swansea, 1975), p. 159.

104. *Cardiff and Merthyr Guardian*, 24 October 1868; *Barry Dock News*, 1 July 1904.

105. *Barry Herald*, 6 August 1910; *South Wales Echo*, 3 August 1897.

106. *Cardiff Times*, 6 August 1910.

107. *Evening Express*, 27 June 1910.

108. *Barry Herald*, 6 August 1909.

109. *Barry Herald*, 12 June 1908.

110. *Barry Herald*, 10 April 1896.

111. *South Wales Daily News*, 18 November 1893.

112. *Barry Dock News*, 18 August 1893.

113. *South Wales Daily News*, 18 November 1893.

114. *South Wales Echo*, 12 August 1893.

115. Reports of the cruel treatment of donkeys appeared regularly in the Barry newspapers. See, for example, *Barry Dock News*, 10 May 1907, 4 August 1911 and 22 August 1913.

116. *Barry Dock News*, 26 May 1899.

117. Davies, *Right Place*, p. 162.

118. For a discussion of the relaxation of normal rules at Coney Island, see Kasson, *Amusing the Million*, pp. 44–50.

119. *Rhondda Leader*, 28 July 1900.

120. *Aberdare Leader*, 16 July 1904.

121. Barry A. Thomas, *Barry Island and Cold Knap* (Machynlleth, 2010), p. 25.

122. *Barry Herald*, 14 August 1896.

123. Walton, *English Seaside Resort*, p. 41.

124. John Beckerson and John K. Walton, 'Selling air: marketing the intangible at British resorts', in John K. Walton (ed.), *Histories of Tourism: Representation, Identity and Conflict* (Clevedon, 2005), pp. 55–68.

125. *Evening Express*, 27 June 1901.

126. Medicus, 'Health and enjoyment by the seaside', *Lily Leaves . . . the Extra Summer Part of the Girl's Own Paper* (1886), 25–7: 26.

127. *Barry Dock News*, 16 September 1892.

128. *Barry Dock News*, 15 September 1893.

129. *Evening Express*, 12 August 1904.

130. *Barry Dock News*, 15 September 1893.

131. *Barry Herald*, 18 August 1905.

132. *Barry Herald*, 5 August 1910; *Barry Dock News*, 28 August 1908; *Weekly Mail*, 12 August 1905.

133. *Barry Dock News*, 6 August 1897.

134. *Barry Dock News*, 1 July 1904.

135. *Barry Herald*, 18 August 1905; *Evening Express*, 15 August 1905.

136. The *Cambria Daily Leader* (2 June 1915) reported that the headless and naked body of a young man who had drowned a month earlier at Whitmore Bay was washed ashore 'in an advanced state of decomposition'.

137. *Barry Dock News*, 29 July 1904.
138. See *Evening Express*, 23 August 1899 for an account of such intimidatory behaviour at Porthcawl.
139. *Barry Dock News*, 7 September 1900.
140. *Barry Dock News*, 24 August 1906.
141. *Barry Dock News*, 16 September 1904.
142. *South Wales Star*, 2 September 1892.
143. *Barry Dock News*, 18 July 1890.
144. *Barry Dock News*, 17 June 1892.
145. *Barry Dock News*, 17 June 1892.
146. *Barry Dock News*, 2 September 1892.
147. *Barry Dock News*, 26 August 1892.
148. *South Wales Star*, 1 September 1893.
149. *South Wales Star*, 24 April 1891; *Barry Dock News*, 4 September 1891; *South Wales Star*, 9 October 1891; *South Wales Star*, 26 February 1892.
150. *South Wales Star*, 5 August 1892 and 12 August 1892.
151. *Barry Dock News*, 6 April 1894, 8 June 1894 and 24 April 1896.
152. *Barry Dock News*, 14 July 1911; *Barry Herald*, 7 June 1912.
153. *Barry Herald*, 19 August 1904.
154. *Barry Dock News*, 5 June 1914.
155. *Rhondda Leader*, 23 June 1900.

CHAPTER 8

1. *Barry Dock News*, 7 August 1914.
2. *Barry Dock News*, 14 August 1914.
3. *Monmouth Guardian*, 26 March 1915.
4. *The Times*, 2 April 1915.
5. *Abergavenny Chronicle*, 2 April 1915.
6. *Glamorgan Gazette*, 14 May 1915.
7. *The Times*, 1 January 1917.
8. John K. Walton, 'Leisure towns in wartime: the impact of the First World War in Blackpool and San Sebastián', *Journal of Contemporary History*, 31/4 (1996), 603–18: 605.
9. *The Times*, 3 April 1915.
10. *Barry Dock News*, 26 March 1915 and 2 April 1915.
11. *Barry Herald*, 14 May 1915.
12. *Barry Dock News*, 9 April 1915.
13. *Barry Herald*, 28 May 1915. The miners restricted – but did not abandon – their Easter and Whitsun holidays in 1915 in the interests of the war effort. See Anthony Mór-O'Brien, 'Patriotism on trial: the strike of the south Wales miners, July 1915', *Welsh History Review*, 12/1 (1984), 76–104: 88.
14. *Barry Dock News*, 6 August 1915.
15. *Brecon and Radnor Express*, 27 May 1915.

16. *Barry Herald*, 16 June 1916.
17. *Glamorgan Gazette*, 16 June 1916.
18. *Barry Dock News*, 1 September 1916.
19. *Barry Dock News*, 10 August 1917.
20. *Barry Dock News*, 11 August 1916. Also see Walton, 'Leisure towns', 613.
21. Catriona Pennell, *A Kingdom United: Popular Responses to the Outbreak of the First World War in Britain and Ireland* (Oxford, 2012), pp. 153–4.
22. *Barry Dock News*, 9 July 1915.
23. *Barry Herald*, 9 June 1916.
24. *South Wales Weekly Post*, 26 May 1917; *Cambria Daily Leader*, 17 May 1917. But not all of them did: some chapel leaders objected to the proposition that innocent children should suffer whilst brewers were allowed to carry on consuming foodstuffs to produce their 'Demon Drink' (*Barry Dock News*, 18 May 1917; *Barry Dock News*, 1 June 1917).
25. *Barry Herald*, 3 March 1916.
26. *Barry Herald*, 18 May 1917.
27. *Barry Dock News*, 30 July 1915.
28. *Barry Dock News*, 21 May 1915.
29. *Barry Herald*, 2 May 1915.
30. *Barry Dock News*, 19 May 1916.
31. *Barry Dock News*, 6 August 1915.
32. *Barry Dock News*, 21 May 1915.
33. *Barry Herald*, 28 May 1915, 6 August 1915 and 28 April 1916.
34. *Barry Dock News*, 30 June 1916.
35. *Glamorgan Gazette*, 14 May 1915.
36. *Cambrian News*, 3 September 1915.
37. *Barry Dock News*, 27 February 1920.
38. *Cambria Daily Leader*, 21 May 1919; *Aberdare Leader*, 20 September 1919.
39. *Barry Dock News*, 13 June 1919.
40. *Rhondda Leader*, 9 August 1919.
41. *Barry Dock News*, 29 May 1925.
42. *Barry Dock News*, 28 May 1920; *Barry and District News*, 6 June 1926; *Barry Herald*, 5 October 1934.
43. *Barry Herald*, 10 August 1923.
44. *Barry Herald*, 24 August 1934.
45. *Barry and District News*, 11 August 1933.
46. Kenneth O. Morgan, *Rebirth of a Nation: A History of Modern Wales* (Oxford, 1981), p. 210.
47. Andy Croll, 'Poverty, mass unemployment and welfare', in Chris Williams and Andy Croll (eds), *The Gwent County History: Volume 5, The Twentieth Century* (Cardiff, 2013), pp. 207–27.
48. E. D. Lewis, *The Rhondda Valleys* (Cardiff, 1959), p. 254.
49. Mari A. Williams, 'In the wars, 1914–45', in Gareth Elwyn Jones and Dai Smith (eds), *The People of Wales: A Millennium History* (Llandysul, 1999), pp. 179–206. For the impact of poverty on the health of women in the

coalfield, see Deidre Beddoe, *Out of the Shadows: A History of Women in Twentieth-century Wales* (Cardiff, 2000); for the impact on rugby, see Gareth Williams, 'From grand slam to great slump: economy, society and rugby football in Wales during the depression', *Welsh History Review*, 11/3 (1982), 338–57.

50.   Andrew Davies, *Leisure, Gender and Poverty: Working-Class Culture in Salford and Manchester, 1900–1939* (Buckingham, 1992).

51.   See Daryl Leeworthy's *Fields of Play: The Sporting Heritage of Wales* (Llandysul, 2012) for an excellent discussion of an important type of leisure space, the sporting arena.

52.   Philip Massey, *Portrait of a Mining Town* (London, 1937), pp. 48–53.

53.   For examples of northern workers unable to enjoy the delights of Blackpool because of poverty, see Davies, *Leisure, Gender and Poverty*, pp. 41–2.

54.   *Barry and District News*, 28 May 1926.

55.   *Barry Dock News*, 10 June 1921.

56.   *Barry Dock News*, 27 July 1923.

57.   Massey, *Portrait*, pp. 48–53, 75–6.

58.   Alastair Durie, 'No holiday this year? The depression of the 1930s and tourism in Scotland', *Journal of Tourism History*, 2/2 (2010), 67–82. Also see, John K. Walton, *The British Seaside: Holidays and Resorts in the Twentieth Century* (Manchester, 2000), p. 57 for a discussion of the persistence of the day-tripping habit in the late 1930s Lancashire cotton district, where 90 per cent of the population were taking day trips.

59.   Mike Huggins and John K Walton, 'The Teesside seaside between the wars: Redcar and its neighbours, 1919–1939', *Papers in North-eastern History* (University of Teesside 2003): *http://insight.cumbria.ac.uk/id/eprint/2633/* (accessed 22 June 2019).

60.   *Barry and District News*, 20 January 1928.

61.   Peter Stead, 'The town that had come of age: Barry, 1918–1938', in Donald Moore (ed.), *Barry: The Centenary Book* (2nd edn, Barry, 1985), pp. 367–428: 377.

62.   Iorwerth W. Prothero, 'The port and railways of Barry', in Moore (ed.), *Barry*, pp. 209–70: 260.

63.   *Barry Dock News*, 22 October 1920 and 29 October 1920.

64.   *Barry Dock News*, 21 January 1921.

65.   *Barry Dock News*, 21 November 1924.

66.   *Barry and District News*, 25 June 1926.

67.   *Barry Dock News*, 5 November 1920.

68.   *Barry Dock News*, 22 October 1920.

69.   *Barry Dock News*, 2 December 1921. For the work of the Unemployment Grants Committee, see *Provision of Work for Relief of Unemployment. Memorandum*, Cmd. 2196 (1924), p. 4 and W. R. Garside, *British Unemployment 1919–1939: A Study in Public Policy* (Cambridge, 1990), p. 303.

70. *Barry Dock News*, 30 December 1921.

71. *Barry Dock News*, 20 January 1922 and 3 February 1922.

72. *Barry Herald*, 12 January 1923.

73. *Barry Herald*, 11 May 1923.

74. *Barry Dock News*, 29 February 1924.

75. *Barry Dock News*, 3 February 1922; *Barry Dock News*, 22 June 1923; *Barry Dock News*, 2 November 1923; *Barry Dock News*, 3 April 1925; *Barry Herald*, 29 May 1925.

76. *Barry Dock News*, 24 February 1922.

77. *Barry Dock News*, 16 January 1920.

78. *Barry Dock News*, 29 May 1925.

79. *Barry and District News*, 7 May 1926; Janet Smith, *Liquid Assets: The Lidos and Open-Air Swimming Pools of Britain* (London, 2005), pp. 68–9; Leeworthy, *Fields of Play*, pp. 44–52.

80. *Barry Herald*, 9 February 1923.

81. *Barry Dock News*, 29 May 1925.

82. *Barry Herald*, 25 January 1924.

83. Margaret Campbell, 'What tuberculosis did for modernism: the influence of a curative environment on modernist design and architecture', *Medical History*, 49 (2005), 463–88: 464–5.

84. *Barry Herald*, 17 June 1927.

85. *Barry and District News*, 18 May 1928.

86. *Barry Herald*, 24 June 1932.

87. *Barry Dock News*, 14 October 1921.

88. *Barry Herald*, 26 July 1929.

89. *Barry Herald*, 26 July 1929.

90. Rob Shields, 'The "system of pleasure": liminality and the carnivalesque at Brighton', *Theory, Culture and Society*, 7/1 (1990), 39–72; Robert Preston-Whyte, 'The beach as liminal space', in Alan A. Lew, C. Michael Hall and Allan M. Williams (eds), *A Companion to Tourism* (Oxford, 2004).

91. *Barry Herald*, 12 August 1927.

92. *Barry Herald*, 19 July 1929.

93. Norbert Elias, *The Civilizing Process: Sociogenetic and Psychogenetic Investigations* (Oxford, 1994 edn), p. 119; Cas Wouters, *Informalization: Manners and Emotions since 1890* (London, 2007), p. 138; Ryan Powell, 'Spaces of informalisation: playscapes, power and the governance of behaviour', *Space and Polity*, 14/2 (2010), 189–206: 197–200; Angela J. Latham, *Posing a Threat: Flappers, Chorus Girls, and Other Brazen Performers of the American 1920s* (Middletown, Connecticut, 2000), ch. 3.

94. *Barry Dock News*, 26 June 1925; Darren Webb, 'Bakhtin at the seaside: utopia, modernity and the carnivalesque', *Theory, Culture and Society*, 22/3 (2005), 121–38.

95. *Barry Herald*, 18 January 1929.

96. *Barry Herald*, 22 April 1932; *Barry Herald*, 29 April 1932.

97. *Barry Dock News*, 25 July 1924.
98. *Daily Telegraph*, 24 September 1941.
99. *The Times*, 24 September 1941.
100. Richard Haines, 'Social tone, resort image and urban space: Welsh seaside resorts during the interwar period' (unpublished MA thesis, Cardiff University, 2008), 31–2; *Llandudno Advertiser*, 18 January 1901; *Cambrian News*, 30 November 1906 and 20 March 1908.
101. He first applied to Barry council in 1908 but does not seem to have been granted permission on that occasion (*Barry Dock News*, 28 February 1908).
102. *Barry Herald*, 3 December 1909.
103. *Barry and District News*, 30 April 1926.
104. *Barry Herald*, 12 July 1929.
105. *Barry Dock News*, 16 January 1925.
106. *Barry Herald*, 5 July 1929.
107. Vanessa Toulmin, 'Collins, Patrick (1859–1943), showman and politician', *Oxford Dictionary of National Biography* (2008), *http://www.oxforddnb.com/view/10.1093/ref:odnb/9780198614128.001.0001/odnb-9780198614128-e-73080* (accessed 7 April 2019).
108. *Cardiff Times*, 7 August 1909; *Barry Herald*, 27 August 1909.
109. *Rhondda Leader*, 27 July 1912.
110. Barry A. Thomas, *Barry Island and Cold Knap* (Machynlleth, 2010), p. 70.
111. *Barry Herald*, 25 May 1923. Newspaper reports of accidents at the pleasure ground suggest adults were the primary customers. See, for example, the *Barry Dock News*, 5 June 1925: a Rhondda man got hit on the head by a swing; a Barry woman got flung out of a flying boat; and a collier from Abertridwr fell off the Figure Eight ride. In 1946, it was announced that efforts were being made to cater more for children now than in the past (*Barry Herald*, 19 April 1946). The absence of children at Coney Island's pleasure parks was also noticed at this time. See Gary S. Cross and John K. Walton, *The Playful Crowd: Pleasure Places in the Twentieth Century* (New York, 2005), p. 71.
112. *Barry Herald*, 9 June 1922 and 26 August 1927.
113. *Barry Herald*, 14 March 1930.
114. *Barry Herald*, 13 June 1930 and 14 March 1930.
115. *Barry and District News*, 16 June 1933; *Barry Herald*, 14 September 1934.
116. *Barry Herald*, 20 August 1919.
117. *Barry Herald*, 18 July 1919; *Barry Dock News*, 29 January 1921.
118. *Barry Dock News*, 30 July 1920; *Barry Dock News*, 30 January 1920; *Barry Herald*, 1 March 1929; *Barry Herald*, 2 May 1919; *Barry Herald*, 4 July 1919; *Barry Dock News*, 1 July 1921; *Barry Herald*, 15 August 1919.
119. *Barry and District News*, 28 May 1926.
120. *Barry and District News*, 29 June 1928.
121. *Barry Herald*, 4 May 1934.
122. *Barry Herald*, 31 August 1934 and 14 September 1934.
123. *Barry Herald*, 31 August 1934; *Barry Herald*, 14 September 1934.

124. *Barry Herald*, 5 October 1934.
125. *Barry and District News*, 3 March 1944.
126. *Barry Herald*, 31 August 1934; *Barry Herald*, 14 September 1934.
127. *Barry Herald*, 2 April 1937.
128. *Barry Dock News*, 5 June 1925.
129. *Barry Dock News*, 13 October 1911; *Barry Herald*, 24 August 1934; *Barry Herald*, 26 August 1927.
130. See, for example, the *Barry Herald*, 18 May 1934 for a report of Barry Island 'aching with emptiness' because of a spell of cold weather – and seaside caterers expressing their concern.
131. Interview with Edward Evans, 13 August 2013.
132. *Barry Dock News*, 25 September 1925.
133. *Barry Herald*, 19 January 1934.
134. *Barry Dock News*, 13 May 1921, 10 June 1921 and 29 July 1921.
135. Bernard Harris, *The Origins of the British Welfare State: Social Welfare in England and Wales, 1800–1945* (Basingstoke, 2004), p. 203.
136. Interview with Edward Evans.
137. *Barry Dock News*, 15 July 1921.
138. *Barry Dock News*, 1 July 1921.
139. Fred Gray, '1930s architecture and the cult of the sun', in Lara Feigel and Alexandra Harris (eds), *Modernism on Sea: Art and Culture at the British Seaside* (Oxford, 2009), pp. 159–78; Nigel Barker, Allan Brodie, Nick Dermott, Lucy Jessop and Gary Winter, *Margate's Seaside Heritage* (Swindon, 2007), p. 45.
140. *Barry Dock News*, 2 October 1925 and 9 October 1925.
141. *Barry and District News*, 23 July 1926.
142. *Barry Herald*, 9 August 1929.
143. *Barry Dock News*, 25 September 1925.
144. *Barry and District News*, 27 July 1928; *Barry Herald*, 12 July 1929.
145. *Barry Dock News*, 29 May 1925; *Barry Herald*, 11 January 1946.
146. *Barry Dock News*, 19 June 1925. Amongst other things, Dan Evans was a strong supporter of the Liberal Party, a teetotaller and father of the leading Welsh nationalist of his generation, Gwynfor Evans. For more, see Rhys Evans, *Gwynfor: Portrait of a Patriot* (Talybont, 2008), pp. 19, 23. I am grateful to Bill Jones for this reference.
147. *Barry Dock News*, 5 June 1925; *Barry Dock News*, 2 October 1925.
148. *Barry Dock News*, 2 October 1925.
149. *Barry and District News*, 23 July 1926.
150. *Barry and District News*, 27 July 1928.
151. *Barry Herald*, 24 August 1934; *Barry Herald*, 26 August 1927.
152. *Barry Dock News*, 2 October 1925.
153. Glamorgan Archives, BB/C/8/320, Letter from P. Cooke, Cheltenham, to Barry Town Councillors, Received 27 June 1956.
154. *Barry and District News*, 16 July 1926.
155. *Barry and District News*, 24 September 1926.

156. *Barry Herald*, 19 January 1934.
157. *Barry Dock News*, 17 August 1923; *Barry Dock News*, 30 September 1921; *Barry Dock News*, 29 August 1924.
158. *Barry and District News*, 13 August 1926.
159. *Barry and District News*, 17 October 1957.
160. *Barry Herald*, 10 August 1923.
161. *Barry Herald*, 24 May 1929.
162. *Barry and District News*, 8 September 1944.
163. *Barry Herald*, 24 May 1929.
164. *Barry and District News*, 13 April 1928.
165. *Barry and District News*, 5 August 1938.
166. *Barry Dock News*, 4 April 1924 and 12 June 1925; *Barry and District News*, 28 May 1926 and 20 April 1928; *Barry Herald*, 12 February 1926.
167. *Barry Herald*, 9 June 1922 and 20 May 1921. For positive descriptions of Blackpool's holiday crowds as non-threatening and playful, see Cross and Walton, *The Playful Crowd*, pp. 106–113.
168. *Barry and District News*, 17 August 1928.
169. *Barry Herald*, 5 August 1927.
170. *Barry and District News*, 12 July 1935.
171. *Barry and District News*, 10 August 1928.
172. *Barry and District News*, 12 July 1935.
173. Interview with Edward Evans.
174. *Barry Herald*, 3 August 1934.
175. *Barry Herald*, 18 February 1927.
176. *Barry Herald*, 11 August 1922; *Barry Herald*, 18 August 1922.
177. *Barry Dock News*, 5 September 1924.
178. *Barry Dock News*, 15 August 1924.
179. *Barry Herald*, 17 August 1934.
180. *Barry Herald*, 3 August 1934.
181. *Barry and District News*, 20 April 1928.
182. *Barry Herald*, 18 August 1922.
183. *Barry Dock News*, 15 August 1924.
184. *Barry Herald*, 15 July 1932.
185. *Barry Dock News*, 15 August 1924.
186. *Barry Herald*, 25 August 1922; *Barry Dock News*, 15 August 1924.
187. *Barry and District News*, 25 May 1928.
188. *Barry and District News*, 25 May 1928.
189. *Barry and District News*, 23 August 1935.
190. *Barry and District News*, 30 August 1935.
191. *Barry Herald*, 3 August 1915.
192. *Barry Dock News*, 2 January 1925.
193. *Barry and District News*, 28 April 1933.
194. *Barry Herald*, 27 April 1934.
195. *Barry Herald*, 12 July 1929.
196. *Barry and District News*, 8 March 1935.

197. *Barry Herald*, 12 October 1934.
198. *Barry and District News*, 20 September 1935.
199. *Barry Herald*, 27 April 1934.
200. *Barry Herald*, 27 April 1934.
201. *Barry Herald*, 27 July 1927.
202. Chapelton v Barry UDC [1940] 1 KB 532, [1940] 1 All ER 356.
203. *Barry and District News*, 29 September 1955.
204. *Barry and District News*, 28 January 1938.
205. *Barry and District News*, 29 April 1938 and 1 July 1938.
206. *Barry Herald*, 28 June 1940.
207. *Barry and District News*, 25 April 1941; *Barry Herald*, 8 May 1942; *Barry Herald*, 29 May 1942; *Barry Herald*, 4 August 1944.
208. Chris Sladen, 'Holidays at home in the Second World War', *Journal of Contemporary History*, 37/1 (2002), 67–89.
209. *Barry Herald*, 17 May 1940.
210. *Barry and District News*, 26 April 1940.
211. *Barry and District News*, 9 August 1940.
212. *Barry and District News*, 6 June 1941 and 8 August 1941.
213. *Barry Herald*, 8 August 1941.
214. *Barry Herald*, 11 August 1944.
215. *Barry and District News*, 22 March 1940; *Barry Herald*, 22 March 1940.
216. *Barry Herald*, 24 May 1940.
217. Stephen G. Jones, 'The leisure industry in Britain, 1918–39', *Service Industries Journal*, 5/1 (1985), 90–106: 103.
218. *Barry Herald*, 19 November 1943.
219. *The Times*, 18 September 1929; *Barry Herald*, 19 July 1929, 16 August 1929, 2 August 1929, 9 August 1929, 13 September 1929 and 20 September 1929. The impact of their feats of endurance on these hunger entertainers could be profound. Ricardo Sacco – real name Richard Jones – died just weeks after his fast at the age of 48 (*London Gazette*, 22 April 1930; *The Times*, 5 November 1929).
220. *Barry and District News*, 10 August 1928.

CONCLUSION

1. Idris Davies, 'The Angry Summer', in Islwyn Jenkins (ed.), *The Complete Poems of Idris Davies* (Llandysul, 1972), p. 103.
2. *Barry and Cadoxton Journal*, 15 December 1888; *Cardiff Times*, 15 September 1906.
3. Brian C. Luxton, 'Ambition, vice and virtue: social life, 1884–1914', in Donald Moore (ed.), *Barry: The Centenary Book* (2nd edn, Barry, 1985), p. 310.
4. *Barry Dock News*, 14 July 1899 and *South Wales Echo*, 3 August 1897.

5. Glamorgan Archives, D/D Pl 834/135, Letter from Robert Forrest to J. Tomson, 22 August 1876.

6. Christina Beatty, Steve Fothergill, Tony Gore and Ian Wilson, *The Seaside Tourist Industry in England and Wales: Employment, Economic Output, Location and Trends* (Sheffield, 2010), pp. 44–6.

7. Jack Simmons, *The Railway in the Town and Country, 1830–1914* (Newton Abbot, 1986), p. 244.

8. M. J. Daunton, *Coal Metropolis: Cardiff, 1870–1914* (Leicester, 1977), p. 147.

9. Richard Butler, 'The tourism area life cycle in the twenty-first century', in Alan A. Lew, C. Michael Hall and Allan M. Williams (eds), *A Companion to Tourism* (Oxford, 2004), pp. 159–69: 163.

10. R. W. Butler, 'The concept of a tourist area cycle of evolution: implications for management of resources', *Canadian Geographer*, 24/1 (1980), 5–12: 7–9.

11. John K. Walton, *The British Seaside: Holidays and Resorts in the Twentieth Century* (Manchester, 2000), pp. 21–2.

12. *Barry Herald*, 24 July 1896.

BIBLIOGRAPHY

PRIMARY SOURCES

1. Manuscript collections

Glamorgan Archives
BB/C/8/320, Letter from P. Cooke, Cheltenham, to Barry Town Councillors,
    Received 27 June 1956.
D/D Pl 834/135, Letter from Robert Forrest to John Tomson, 22 August 1876.
DPL/834/163, Letter from Robert Forrest to John Tomson, 19 November 1876.
BB/C/52, Supplemental Agreement between the Earl of Plymouth and the
    Barry Urban District Council, 19 December 1908.

The National Archives
MT 10/1288, Railway poster illustrating the Sands of Whitmore Bay, *c*.1910.
BD28/713, G. A. Jellicoe, 'A landscape design for the foreshore of Barry, South
    Wales', 1 September 1956.
BD28/713, Letter from S. A. Luen to James Griffiths, Secretary of State for Wales,
    29 October 1964.
BD28/713, Application for Permission to Develop Land by Butlin's Ltd to
    Glamorgan County Council, submitted 16 November 1962.
BD28/713, Letter from Raymond Gower to Keith Joseph, Minister of Housing
    and Local Government, 2 April 1963.

2. Newspapers and journals

Aberdare Leader
Aberdare Times
Abergavenny Chronicle

Aberystwyth Observer
Barry and Cadoxton Journal
Barry and District News
Barry Dock News
Barry Herald
Brecon and Radnor Express
Bristol Mercury
British Architect
Caledonian Mercury
Cambria Daily Leader
Cambrian
Cambrian News
Cardiff and Merthyr Guardian
Cardiff Times
Carmarthen Journal
Daily Telegraph
Denbighshire Free Press
Evening Express
Glamorgan, Monmouth and Brecon Gazette
Glamorgan Gazette
Justice of the Peace
Llais Llafur
Llandudno Advertiser
London Gazette
Merthyr Express
Merthyr Telegraph
Monmouth Guardian
Monmouthshire Merlin
North Wales Chronicle
North Wales Gazette
Pall Mall Gazette
Pembrokeshire Herald
Penarth Chronicle
Pontypridd Chronicle
Rhondda Leader
South Wales Daily News
South Wales Echo
South Wales Star
South Wales Weekly Post
Star
The Times
Weekly Mail
Western Mail

3. Official publications

Provision of Work for Relief of Unemployment. Memorandum, Cmd. 2196 (1924).
Miners' Eight Hour Day Committee, *Final Report of the Departmental Committee
. . . to Inquire into the Probable Economic Effect of a Limit of Eight Hours to
the Working Day of Coal Miners*, Part II, Cd. 3506, (1907).
Chapelton v Barry UDC [1940] 1 KB 532, [1940] 1 All ER 356.

4. Works of reference

Slater's . . . Directory . . . of North and South Wales (Manchester, 1868).
*Webster and Company's Commercial and Postal Directory of the City of Bristol
and the County of Glamorgan* (London, 1865).
Worrall's Directory of South Wales (Oldham, 1875).

5. Oral history interviews

Interview with Edward Evans, 13 August 2013.
Interview with Denis McCarthy, 7 June 2014.

6. Published works

Adfyfr, *Landlordism in Wales* (Cardiff, 1887).
Anon., *A Collection of Tours in Wales, or a Display of the Beauties of Wales . . .*
(London, 1799).
Anon., *A Tour in Wales, and Through Several Counties of England, including
both the Universities, Performed in the Summer of 1805* (London, 1806).
Anon., *An Account of the Principal Pleasure Tours in England and Wales*
(London, 1822).
Anon., *The Tourist in Wales: A Series of Views, Picturesque Scenery, Towns,
Castles, &c. with Historical and Topographical Notes* (London, 1851).
Anon., 'Where to spend the holidays', *Hearth and Home*, 316 (3 June 1897), 180.
Barry Borough Council Development Committee, *Barry* (Barry, 1940).
Bingley, William, *North Wales: Including its Scenery, Antiquities, Customs, and
Some Sketches of its Natural History*, vol. 2 (London, 1804).
Davies, Idris, 'The Angry Summer', in Islwyn Jenkins (ed.), *The Complete Poems
of Idris Davies* (Llandysul, 1972).
Davies, Walter Haydn, *The Right Place, The Right Time: Memories of Boyhood
Days in a Welsh Mining Community* (Swansea, 1975).
Ellis, Thomas E., *Speeches and Addresses* (Wrexham, 1912).
Evans, John, *Letters Written during a Tour through South Wales in the Year
1803, and at Other Times . . .* (London, 1804).
Fenton, Richard, *A Historical Tour through Pembrokeshire* (London, 1811).
Fenton, Richard, *Tours in Wales (1804–1813)* (London, 1917).
Frampton, E. J., *Where Shall I Send my Patient? A Guide for Medical
Practitioners and Book of Reference to the Health Resorts and Institutions
for Patients of Great Britain* (Bournemouth, 1903).

Gerald of Wales, *The Journey through Wales / The Description of Wales* (Harmondsworth, 1978).

Hankin, St. John E. C., 'The sins of St Lubbock', *The Nineteenth Century: A Monthly Review*, 41/231 (March 1897), 467–73.

Hartwig, George, *A Practical Treatise on Sea-Bathing and Sea-Air* (London, 1853).

Hearne, Thomas (ed.), *Itinerary of John Leland the Antiquary*, vol. 4, pt 1 (Oxford, 1769 edn).

Hughson, David, *Cambria Depicta: A Tour through North Wales* (London, 1816).

Jones, Jack, *Black Parade* (London, 1935).

Lewis, Samuel, *A Topographical Dictionary of Wales . . .* vol. 1 (London, 1828).

Lewis, Samuel, *A Topographical Dictionary of Wales . . .* vol. 1 (London, 1833 edn).

Massey, Philip, *Portrait of a Mining Town* (London, 1937).

Medicus, 'Advice to the delicate on the summer holiday', *Girl's Own Paper* (summer, 1884).

Medicus, 'Health and enjoyment by the seaside', *Lily Leaves . . . the Extra Summer Part of the Girl's Own Paper* (1886), 25–7.

Russell, Richard, *A Dissertation of the Use of Sea-Water . . .* (4th edn, London, 1760).

Skrine, Henry, *Two Successive Tours throughout the Whole of Wales . . .* (London, 1798).

Storrie, John, *Notes on Excavations made During the Summers of 1894–6 at Barry Island and Ely Racecourse* (Cardiff, 1896).

Walford, Thomas, *The Scientific Tourist Through England, Wales & Scotland: By Which the Traveller is Directed to the Principal Objects of Antiquity, Art, Science & the Picturesque . . .* vol. 2 (London, 1818).

Warner, Richard, *Second Walk through Wales* (London, 1800).

Wigstead, Henry, *Remarks on a Tour to North and South Wales, in the Year 1797* (London, 1799).

Wyndham, Henry Penruddocke, *A Gentleman's Tour through Monmouthshire and Wales, in the Months of June and July, 1774* (London, 1775).

SECONDARY SOURCES

1. Unpublished manuscript

Barry Library, Prothero, Iorwerth W., 'Barry and its Dock, Volume 1: The Schemes that Failed' (1993).

2. Published works

Akhtar, Miriam and Humphries, Steve, *Some Liked it Hot: The British on Holiday at Home and Abroad* (London, 2000).

Anthony, Robert, '"A very thriving place": the peopling of Swansea in the eighteenth century', *Urban History*, 32/1 (2005), 68–87.

Armstrong, John, and Williams, David M., 'The steamboat and popular tourism', *Journal of Transport History*, 26/1 (2005), 61–77.

Barker, Nigel, Brodie, Allan, Dermott, Nick, Jessop, Lucy and Winter, Gary, *Margate's Seaside Heritage* (Swindon, 2007).

Barrie, D. S., *The Barry Railway* (Lingfield, 1962).

Barrie, D. S. M., *A Regional History of the Railways of Great Britain: Volume 12, South Wales* (Newton Abbot, 1980).

Beatty, Christina, Fothergill, Steve, Gore, Tony and Wilson, Ian, *The Seaside Tourist Industry in England and Wales: Employment, Economic Output, Location and Trends* (Sheffield, 2010).

Beckerson, John and Walton, John K., 'Selling air: marketing the intangible at British resorts', in John K. Walton (ed.), *Histories of Tourism: Representation, Identity and Conflict* (Clevedon, 2005), pp. 55–68.

Beddoe, Deidre, *Out of the Shadows: A History of Women in Twentieth-century Wales* (Cardiff, 2000).

Blackshaw, Tye R., 'Seddon, John Pollard (1827–1906), architect', *Oxford Dictionary of National Biography, http://www.oxforddnb. com/view/10.1093/ref:odnb/9780198614128.001.0001/odnb-9780198614128-e-39357* (accessed 20 January 2018).

Borsay, Peter, 'Welsh seaside resorts: historiography, sources and themes', *Welsh History Review*, 24/2 (2008), 92–119.

Borsay, Peter, 'From port to resort: Tenby and narratives of transition, 1760–1914', in Peter Borsay and John K. Walton (eds), *Resorts and Ports: European Seaside Towns since 1700* (Bristol, 2011), pp. 86–111.

Borsay, Peter and Walton, John K., 'Introduction: the resort-port relationship', in Peter Borsay and John K. Walton (eds), *Resorts and Ports: European Seaside Towns since 1700* (Bristol, 2011), pp. 1–17.

Borsay, Peter, 'A room with a view: visualizing the seaside, *c*.1750–1914', *Transactions of the Royal Historical Society*, 23 (2013), 175–201.

Briggs, Asa, *Mass Entertainment: The Origins of a Modern Industry* (Adelaide, 1960).

Browning, Gary L., 'Civilization and nature in Boris Pil'njak's Machines and Wolves', *Slavic and East European Journal*, 20/2 (1976), 155–66.

Butler, R. W., 'The concept of a tourist area cycle of evolution: implications for management of resources', *Canadian Geographer*, 24/1 (1980), 5–12.

Butler, Richard, 'The tourism area life cycle in the twenty-first century', in Alan A. Lew, C. Michael Hall and Allan M. Williams (eds), *A Companion to Tourism* (Oxford, 2004), pp. 159–69.

Butler, Richard W., 'Sustainable tourism: a state-of-the-art review', *Tourism Geographies*, 1/1 (1999), 7–25.

Campbell, Margaret, 'What tuberculosis did for modernism: the influence of a curative environment on modernist design and architecture', *Medical History*, 49 (2005), 463–88.

Cannadine, David, *Lords and Landlords, the Aristocracy and the Town, 1774–1967* (Leicester, 1980).

Constantine, Mary-Ann, 'Beauty spot, blind spot: Romantic Wales', *Literature Compass*, 5/3 (2008), 577–90.

Coombes, Nigel, *Passenger Steamers of the Bristol Channel: A Pictorial Record* (Truro, 1990).

Corbin, Alain, *The Lure of the Sea: The Discovery of the Seaside, 1750–1840* (Harmondsworth, 1994).

Cragoe, Matthew, '"A contemptible mimic of the Irish": the land question in Victorian Wales', in Matthew Cragoe and Paul Readman (eds), *The Land Question in Britain, 1750–1950* (Basingstoke, 2010), pp. 92–108.

Croll, Andy, 'Mabon's Day: the rise and fall of a Lib-Lab holiday in the south Wales coalfield, 1888–1898', *Labour History Review*, 72/1 (2007), 49–68.

Croll, Andy, 'Poverty, mass unemployment and welfare', in Chris Williams and Andy Croll (eds), *The Gwent County History: Volume 5, The Twentieth Century* (Cardiff, 2013), pp. 207–27.

Cross, Gary S. and Walton, John K., *The Playful Crowd: Pleasure Places in the Twentieth Century* (New York, 2005).

Cunningham, H., 'Leisure and culture', in F. M. L. Thompson (ed.), *The Cambridge Social History of Britain, 1750–1950: Vol. 2, People and Their Environment* (Cambridge, 1990), pp. 279–339.

Cunningham, Hugh, *Leisure in the Industrial Revolution, c. 1780–1880* (London, 1980).

Daunton, M. J., 'Suburban development in Cardiff: Grangetown and the Windsor estate 1857–1875', *Morgannwg*, 16 (1972), 53–66.

Daunton, M. J., *Coal Metropolis: Cardiff, 1870–1914* (Leicester, 1977).

Davies, Andrew, *Leisure, Gender and Poverty: Working-Class Culture in Salford and Manchester, 1900–1939* (Buckingham, 1992).

Davies, Hywel M., 'Wales in English travel writing 1791–8: the Welsh critique of Theophilus Jones', *Welsh History Review*, 23/3 (2007), 65–93.

Davies, John, *Cardiff and the Marquesses of Bute* (Cardiff, 1981).

Davies, John, *A History of Wales* (Harmondsworth, 1993).

Deacon, Bernard, 'Imagining the fishing: artists and fishermen in late nineteenth-century Cornwall', *Rural History*, 12/2 (2001), 159–78.

Debbage, Keith G. and Ioannides, Dimitri, 'The cultural turn? Towards a more critical economic geography of tourism', in Alan A. Lew, C. Michael Hall and Allan M. Williams (eds), *A Companion to Tourism* (Oxford, 2004), pp. 99–109.

Dunthorne, Hugh, 'Early Romantic travellers in Wales and the Netherlands during the late eighteenth century', *Dutch Crossing*, 24/2 (2000), 208–21.

Durie, Alastair, 'No holiday this year? The depression of the 1930s and tourism in Scotland', *Journal of Tourism History*, 2/2 (2010), 67–82.

Durie, Alastair J., *Scotland for the Holidays: Tourism in Scotland c. 1780–1939* (East Linton, 2003).

Elias, Norbert, *The Civilizing Process: Sociogenetic and Psychogenetic Investigations* (Oxford, 1994 edn).

Evans, Neil, 'The Welsh Victorian city: the middle class and civic and national consciousness in Cardiff, 1850–1914', *Welsh History Review*, 12/3 (1985), 350–87.

Evans, Rhys, *Gwynfor: Portrait of a Patriot* (Talybont, 2008).

Farrant, Sue, 'London by the Sea: resort development on the south coast of England 1880–1939', *Journal of Contemporary History*, 22/1 (1987), 137–62.

Fletcher, Allan, 'The role of landowners, entrepreneurs and railways in the urban development of the north Wales coast during the nineteenth century', *Welsh History Review*, 16/4 (1993), 514–41.

Garside, W. R., *British Unemployment 1919–1939: A Study in Public Policy* (Cambridge, 1990).

Gold, John R. and Gold, Margaret M., *Imagining Scotland: Tradition, Representation and Promotion in Scottish Tourism Since 1750* (Aldershot, 1995).

Gray, Fred, *Designing the Seaside: Architecture, Society and Nature* (London, 2006).

Gray, Fred, '1930s architecture and the cult of the sun', in Lara Feigel and Alexandra Harris (eds), *Modernism on Sea: Art and Culture at the British Seaside* (Oxford, 2009), pp. 159–78.

Griffiths, Matthew, 'Landlords and tenants, 1700–1880', in Donald Moore (ed.), *Barry: The Centenary Book* (2nd edn, Barry, 1985), pp. 165–207.

Hall, C. Michael, *Tourism Planning: Policies, Processes, and Relationships* (2nd edn, London, 2008).

Harris, Bernard, *The Origins of the British Welfare State: Social Welfare in England and Wales, 1800–1945* (Basingstoke, 2004).

Hassan, John, *The Seaside, Health and the Environment in England and Wales since 1800* (Aldershot, 2003).

Hayman, Richard, '"All impetuous rage": The cult of waterfalls in eighteenth-century Wales', *Landscapes*, 15/1 (2014), 23–43.

Hobsbawm, Eric, *Worlds of Labour: Further Studies in the History of Labour* (London, 1984).

Hodges, T. M., 'The peopling of the hinterland and the port of Cardiff', *Economic History Review*, 17/1 (1947), 62–72.

Howell, David W., *Land and People in Nineteenth-century Wales* (London, 1977).

Huggins, Mike and Walton, John K, 'The Teesside seaside between the wars: Redcar and its neighbours, 1919–1939', Papers in North-eastern History (University of Teesside 2003), *http://insight.cumbria.ac.uk/id/eprint/2633/* (accessed 22 June 2019).

Jones, David Llewellyn and Smith, Robert, 'Tourism and the Welsh language in the nineteenth century', in Geraint H. Jenkins (ed.), *The Welsh Language and its Social Domains, 1801–1911* (Cardiff, 2000), pp. 151–75.

Jones, Geoff, *Cardiff Airport at Rhoose: 70 Years of Aviation History* (Stroud, 2011).

Jones, Kathryn N., Tully, Carol, and Williams, Heather, 'Introduction: travel writing and Wales', *Studies in Travel Writing*, 18/2 (2014), 101–6.

Jones, Stephen G., 'The leisure industry in Britain, 1918–39', *Service Industries Journal*, 5/1 (1985).

Kasson, John F., *Amusing the Million: Coney Island at the Turn of the Century* (New York, 1978).

Kirk, Neville, *Change, Continuity and Class: Labour in British Society, 1850–1920* (Manchester, 1998).

Kristian, Jens and Steen Jacobsen, 'Roaming Romantics: solitude-seeking and self-centredness in scenic sightseeing', *Scandinavian Journal of Hospitality and Tourism*, 4/1 (2004), 5–23.

Lambert, Mark and Jonathan Lambert, *Secret Barry Island* (Stroud, 2017).

Lambert, W. R., 'Drink and work discipline in industrial south Wales, *c*.1800–1870', *Welsh History Review*, 7/3 (1975), 289–306.

Latham, Angela J., *Posing a Threat: Flappers, Chorus Girls, and Other Brazen Performers of the American 1920s* (Middletown, Connecticut, 2000).

Leeworthy, Daryl, *Fields of Play: The Sporting Heritage of Wales* (Llandysul, 2012).

Leivers, Clive, 'The modern Ishmaels? Navvy communities in the High Peak', *Family and Community History*, 9/2 (2006), 141–55.

Lěncek, Lena and Bosker, Gideon, *The Beach: The History of Paradise on Earth* (London, 1998).

Lewis, E. D., *The Rhondda Valleys* (Cardiff, 1959).

Linnard, William, '"Lord" Forrest of St Fagans: estate agent extraordinary', *Morgannwg*, 33 (1989), 55–68.

Luxton, Brian C., 'Ambition, vice and virtue: social life, 1884–1914', in Donald Moore (ed.), *Barry: The Centenary Book* (2nd edn, Barry, 1985), pp. 271–331.

McLaughlin-Jenkins, Erin, 'Walking the low road: the pursuit of scientific knowledge in late Victorian working-class communities', *Public Understanding of Science*, 12/2 (2003), 147–66.

Meller, H. E., *Leisure and the Changing City, 1870–1914* (London, 1976).

Minchinton, W. E., 'Introduction: Industrial South Wales, 1750–1914', in W. E. Minchinton (ed.), *Industrial South Wales 1750–1914: Essays in Welsh Economic History* (London, 1969), pp. ix–xxxi.

Miskell, Louise, 'A town divided? Sea-bathing, dock-building, and oyster-fishing in nineteenth-century Swansea', in Peter Borsay and John K. Walton (eds), *Resorts and Ports: European Seaside Towns since 1700* (Bristol, 2011), pp. 113–25.

Moir, Esther, *The Discovery of Britain: The English Tourists, 1540–1840* (London, 1964), pp. 123–38.

Mór-O'Brien, Anthony, 'Patriotism on trial: the strike of the south Wales miners, July 1915', *Welsh History Review*, 12/1 (1984), 76–104.

Morgan, Kenneth O., *Rebirth of a Nation: A History of Modern Wales* (Oxford, 1981).

Morgan, Nigel J. and Pritchard, Annette, *Power and Politics at the Seaside: The Development of Devon's Resorts in the Twentieth Century* (Exeter, 1999)

Morgan, Prys, 'Wild Wales: civilizing the Welsh from the sixteenth to the nineteenth centuries', in Peter Burke, Brian Harrison and Paul Slack (eds), *Civil Histories: Essays Presented to Sir Keith Thomas* (Oxford, 2000), pp. 265–84.

Mullins, Patrick, 'Tourism urbanization', *International Journal of Urban and Regional Research*, 15/3 (1991), 326–42.

Mullins, Patrick, 'Cities for pleasure: the emergence of tourism urbanization in Australia', *Built Environment*, 18/3 (1992), 187–98.

Otgaar, A., 'Towards a common agenda for the development of industrial tourism', *Tourism Management Perspectives*, 4 (2012), 86–91.

Parratt, Catriona M., *'More than Mere Amusement': Working-Class Women's Leisure in England, 1750–1914* (Boston, 2001).

Pennell, Catriona, *A Kingdom United: Popular Responses to the Outbreak of the First World War in Britain and Ireland* (Oxford, 2012).

Perkin, Harold, 'The social tone of Victorian seaside resorts in the north-west', *Northern History*, 11/1 (1976), 180–94.

Pincombe, Ian, 'From pit to paradise: Porthcawl's changing identity, from the eighteenth to the twentieth century', *Welsh History Review*, 25/4 (2011), 520–50.

Pollard, Sidney, 'Discipline in the industrial revolution', *Economic History Review*, new series, 16/2 (1963), 254–71.

Poole, Robert, 'Oldham wakes', in John K. Walton and James Walvin (eds), *Leisure in Britain, 1780–1939* (Manchester, 1983), pp. 71–98.

Powell, Ryan, 'Spaces of informalisation: playscapes, power and the governance of behaviour', *Space and Polity*, 14/2 (2010), 189–206: 197–200.

Preston-Whyte, Robert, 'The beach as liminal space', in Alan A. Lew, C. Michael Hall and Allan M. Williams (eds), *A Companion to Tourism* (Oxford, 2004).

Prothero, Iorwerth W., 'The port and railways of Barry' in Donald Moore (ed.), *Barry: The Centenary Book* (Barry, 2nd edn, 1985), pp. 209–269.

Reid, Douglas A., 'The "iron roads" and "the happiness of the working classes": the early development and social significance of the railway excursion', *Journal of Transport History*, 17/1 (1996), 57–73: 58.

Reid, Douglas A., 'Playing and praying', in Martin Daunton (ed.), *The Cambridge Urban History of Britain. Volume 3, 1840–1950* (Cambridge, 2000), pp. 745–807.

Roberts, Richard, 'The Corporation as impresario: the municipal provision of entertainment in Victorian and Edwardian Bournemouth', in John K. Walton and James Walvin (eds), *Leisure in Britain, 1780–1939* (Manchester, 1983), pp. 136–57.

Shields, Rob, 'The "system of pleasure": liminality and the carnivalesque at Brighton', *Theory, Culture and Society*, 7/1 (1990), 39–72.

Simmons, Jack, *The Railway in the Town and Country, 1830–1914* (Newton Abbot, 1986).

Simmons, Jack, 'Excursion train', in Jack Simmons and Gordon Biddle (eds), *The Oxford Companion to British Railway History: From 1603 to the 1990s* (Oxford, 1997), pp. 149–52.

Sladen, Chris, 'Holidays at home in the Second World War', *Journal of Contemporary History*, 37/1 (2002), 67–89.

Smith, Dai, 'Barry: a town out of time', *Morgannwg*, 29 (1985), 80–5.

Smith, Dai, *Aneurin Bevan and the World of South Wales* (Cardiff, 1993).

Smith, Janet, *Liquid Assets: The Lidos and Open-Air Swimming Pools of Britain* (London, 2005).

Stead, Peter, 'The town that had come of age: Barry, 1918–1938', in Donald Moore (ed.), *Barry: The Centenary Book* (2nd edn, Barry, 1985), pp. 367–428.

Stevens, Christine, 'Personal links between landlord and tenant on a Welsh estate: an absentee landlord's influence on the social life of an estate village in the nineteenth century', *Folk Life*, 50/1 (2012), 7–26.

Thomas, Barry A., *Barry Island and Cold Knap* (Machynlleth, 2010).

Thomas, Gwyn, *A Welsh Eye* (London, 1964).

Thomas, Richard W., 'The building of Barry', in Donald Moore (ed.), *Barry: The Centenary Book* (2nd edn, Barry, 1985).

Thorne, Roy, *Penarth: A History* (Risca, 1976).

Toulmin, Vanessa, 'Collins, Patrick (1859–1943), showman and politician', *Oxford Dictionary of National Biography* (2008), http://www.oxforddnb. com/view/10.1093/ref:odnb/9780198614128.001.0001/odnb-9780198614128-e-73080 (accessed 7 April 2019).

Travis, John, 'Continuity and change in English sea-bathing, 1730–1900: a case of swimming with the tide', in Stephen Fisher (ed.), *Recreation and the Sea* (Exeter, 1997), pp. 8–35.

Travis, John F., *The Rise of the Devon Seaside Resorts, 1750–1900* (Exeter, 1993).

Urry, John, *The Tourist Gaze: Leisure and Travel in Contemporary Societies* (London, 1990).

Vale of Glamorgan Council, *Vale of Glamorgan County Treasures: Barry* (Barry, 2007).

Waller, P. J., *Town, City and Nation: England, 1850–1914* (Oxford, 1983).

Walton, John K., 'Railways and resort development in Victorian England: the case of Silloth', *Northern History*, 15/1 (1979), 191–209.

Walton, John K., 'The demand for working-class seaside holidays in Victorian England', *Economic History Review*, new series, 34/2 (1981), 249–65.

Walton, John K., *The English Seaside Resort: A Social History, 1750–1914* (Leicester, 1983).

Walton, John K., 'Leisure towns in wartime: the impact of the First World War in Blackpool and San Sebastián', *Journal of Contemporary History*, 31/4 (1996), 603–18.

Walton, John K., 'The seaside resorts of western Europe, 1750–1939', in Stephen Fisher (ed.), *Recreation and the Sea* (Exeter, 1997), pp. 36–56.

Walton, John K., *Blackpool* (Edinburgh, 1998).

Walton, John K., *The British Seaside: Holidays and Resorts in the Twentieth Century* (Manchester, 2000).

Walton, John K., 'The origins of the modern package tour? British motor–coach tours in Europe, 1930–70', *Journal of Transport History*, 32/2 (2011), 145–63.

Walton, John K., 'Port and resort: symbiosis and conflict in "Old Whitby", England, since 1880', in Peter Borsay and John K. Walton (eds), *Resorts and Ports: European Seaside Towns since 1700* (Bristol, 2011), pp. 126–46.

Walton, John K., 'British tourists and the beaches of Europe, from the eighteenth century to the 1960s', in Martin Farr and Xavier Guégan (eds), *The British Abroad Since the Eighteenth Century, Volume 1: Travellers and Tourists* (Basingstoke, 2014), pp. 19–37.

Ward, Stephen V., *Selling Places: The Marketing and Promotion of Towns and Cities, 1850–2000* (London, 1998).

Webb, Darren, 'Bakhtin at the seaside: utopia, modernity and the carnivalesque', *Theory, Culture and Society*, 22/3 (2005), 121–38.

Williams, Gareth, 'From grand slam to great slump: economy, society and rugby football in Wales during the depression', *Welsh History Review*, 11/3 (1982), 338–57.

Williams, L. J., 'The move from the land', in Trevor Herbert and Gareth Elwyn Jones (eds), *Wales 1880–1914* (Cardiff, 1988), pp. 11–47.

Williams, Mari A., 'In the wars, 1914–45', in Gareth Elwyn Jones and Dai Smith (eds), *The People of Wales: A Millennium History* (Llandysul, 1999), pp. 179–206.

Wouters, Cas, *Informalization: Manners and Emotions since 1890* (London, 2007).

Yates, Nigel, 'The Welsh seaside resorts: growth, decline, and survival', University of Wales, Lampeter, Occasional Papers, 1 (2006).

Zaring, Jane, 'The Romantic face of Wales', *Annals of the Association of American Geographers*, 67/3 (1977), 397–418.

3. Works of reference

Plymouth, 1st earl of (Robert George Windsor-Clive, 27 August 1857–6 March 1923), *Who's Who & Who Was Who* (1 December 2007), *https://www.ukwhoswho.com/view/10.1093/ww/9780199540891.001.0001/ww-9780199540884-e-201693* (accessed 19 May 2019).

4. Unpublished theses

Bradley, David, 'The development of Barry, Penarth and Porthcawl as seaside resorts, 1881–1939' (unpublished MA thesis, University of Wales, College of Cardiff, 1990).

Haines, Richard, 'Social tone, resort image and urban space: Welsh seaside resorts during the interwar period' (unpublished MA thesis, Cardiff University, 2008).

Preston, Catherine E., 'Geology, visualisation and the 1893 Hauliers' Strike: an interdisciplinary exploration' (unpublished PhD thesis, Cardiff University, 2010).

INDEX